Dennis Jones is an extraordinary individual. He is a brilliant and insightful businessman and entrepreneur. Amazingly, he is also a missionary statesman with a clear view of the challenges and problems facing church congregations at home and abroad.

Dennis has become a voice of inspiration, enlightenment, and encouragement to individuals, business leaders, and local churches who find themselves facing adversity in these trying and uncertain times. What Dennis shares in this book, he has lived. But Dennis is quick to note that only by the grace of God has he taken the hits and continued the race.

As you read this amazing recounting of Dennis' life and the insights that the Lord has imparted to him, let your heart be encouraged, knowing that it's never too late to do the right thing and, by doing so, you've begun the journey to climbing out of adversity.

—Pat Robertson, Founder/Chairman of the Board
The Christian Broadcasting Network, Inc.

A captivating testimony that will encourage anyone and offer a provocative challenge to every Christian and church leader. Life changing is an overused term in Christian circles, but Dennis shares real life examples of God's power to transform one's life from the depths of despair. This book reveals the grace of God in a deep and edifying way that will cause you never to look at the redeeming work of Jesus in the same way. Jones' impassioned charge to the church and our nation will surely challenge your heart and mind.

—Bobby Hill, EdD, Director
The Center for Christian Thought and Action,
Regent University
International Director, Vanguard Ministries

You did not pick up this book by accident. God means for you to read and digest the biblical principles contained in it. Dennis Jones is my long-standing dear friend and brother—I always say, "You can choose your friends, but you can't choose your brothers."—and I have chosen Dennis to be one of my closest friends. Dennis starts off his book with the theme of "An Accidental Rebel." He certainly is open regarding his "rebel" life, and this helped his book become a powerful testimony. At the time of his born-again experience, it was no accident that God called Dennis to help "usher in the return of the Lord." Later, he was miraculously baptized in the Holy Spirit, and yes it's true, during a sales meeting! These miracles follow Dennis' life throughout this book, in business, ministry, and missions work around the world. I've had the joy of Dennis traveling with me on multiple mission trips and seeing the power and fruit of his ministry. Stay with Dennis all the way through this book. The final six chapters are tremendous prophetic warnings and encouragement to be biblically correct instead of politically correct. This final chapter on "Finishing Well" is superb and every reader will want to meditate on what God has given us through Dennis.

—Dr. Howard Foltz, President
Accelerating International Mission Strategies
Professor Emeritus, Regent University

We live in the information age with millions of books available for our reading. With so many books to choose from, why purchase this book? This book contains life lessons from a remarkable man of God. Dennis didn't write a book to make money, he wrote a book to transform lives. The Holy Spirit is active in the life of Dennis Jones. His life journey will inspire you and challenge you to embrace a divine destiny! My life has been forever changed because of Dennis Jones and his radical obedience to Jesus!

—William Breon, Senior Pastor
Immanuel Church, Wilmington, Delaware

In your hands you are holding more than just a book. You are holding an incredible gift—one man's life story that provides a remarkable glimpse inside Dennis R. Jones' journey for the truth; a journey in which he discovers the power of love, faith, and forgiveness.

It has been said that experience is when you learn from your mistakes but wisdom is when you learn from the mistakes of others, and through Dennis' experiences, readers can be one step closer to discovering their own personal wisdom. While Dennis certainly took the hard road, his incredible trials, countless mistakes and inspiring successes, remind readers that the life we are born into certainly doesn't have to be the life we lead, that we don't have to be the victim of our pasts and that no matter how good life is, or how much success we have, none of it matters unless God is in it.

Dennis' incredible transformation from a lost child to a blessed child of God will fill your heart with hope and your soul with God's love. Thank you Dennis for sharing your story—good, bad, ugly, and everything in between—and for reminding us that by being who God wants us to be on the inside will eventually start to show on the outside too.

—GREG PROVENZANO, PRESIDENT AND CO-FOUNDER
ACN

CLIMBING
OUT OF
ADVERSITY

**A STORY OF LIFE'S LESSONS
TO ENCOURAGE THE HEART
AWAKEN THE CHURCH AND
CHALLENGE THE NATION**

God bless you

Dennis R Jones

Proverbs 3:5+6

CLIMBING OUT OF ADVERSITY

A STORY OF LIFE'S LESSONS TO ENCOURAGE THE HEART AWAKEN THE CHURCH AND CHALLENGE THE NATION

DENNIS R. JONES

CLIMBING OUT OF ADVERSITY by Dennis Jones
Published by Excel Books
A Charisma Media Company
600 Rinehart Road
Lake Mary, Florida 32746
www.charismamedia.com

Unless otherwise noted, all Scripture quotations are from the New King James Version of the Bible. Copyright © 1979, 1980, 1982 by Thomas Nelson, Inc., publishers. Used by permission.

Scripture quotations marked KJV are from the King James Version of the Bible.

Cover design by Design Director: Bill Johnson

Visit the author's website: www.DennisRJones.com

Library of Congress Control Number: 2011920463
International Standard Book Number: 978-1-61638-455-5
E-book: 978-1-61638-465-4

First Edition

11 12 13 14 15 — 9 8 7 6 5 4 3 2 1
Printed in the United States of America

DEDICATION

I dedicate this book to the two most influential people in my life: my mother and my wife, Cookie. They are the two people, who not only believed in me, supported me, and trusted me, but they never gave up on me even when everyone else did. When others said I would never amount to anything, they helped me to believe that, with God's help, there wasn't anything I could not accomplish, if I really wanted to. They looked beyond the circumstances I was in and saw the potential in me that no one else could see, and they offered encouragement in many cases when I thought opportunity had passed me by.

I also want to thank my good friends Howard Foltz and John Deal who imparted truths into my life for which I will be forever grateful. As I began to live out these truths, along with the principles the Lord has revealed to me, the things I learned began to grow, expand, and mature as I applied them to my life's circumstances, and then I began to share them with others.

Thirdly, this book and all I ever hope to accomplish is dedicated to the One to whom I owe all that I am or ever will be: my Lord and Savior, my Redeemer, the lover of my soul, and my dearest friend, Jesus Christ. He is the friend who saw in me what I could never have seen in myself. He redeemed me from the destructive course my life was on for many years as a young man. He renewed me and gave me a life worth living, and today He is teaching me that He will not only bless the labor of my hands in the business world but will be with me and work through me to touch the lives of others around the world.

CONTENTS

INTRODUCTION

THERE ARE THOSE who read about the experiences of others, and then there are those who experience what others only read about. Many friends and business acquaintances over the years have encouraged me to tell my story because of the things I've seen and done—both the struggles and the adventures that have made this such an exceptional life. The Lord has given me that kind of life.

From the beginning it was a hard life. But even before I was aware of the Lord's presence and compassion, He was there protecting and preserving me, bringing me along, step by step. Every day I am amazed that I survived to speak about it. But this is my story.

Along the way I discovered that life is about respect, honor, courage, and integrity. It's possible to take the easy road and avoid life's challenges. It is possible to look the other way when others are in trouble. But that is not the life I have lived. I grew up in tough times in a tough place. Courage was not optional—it was essential to my survival—and I learned that no one respects the man or woman who does not live by and display those qualities.

So in a sense, this is a book about seeking to obtain honor, integrity, courage, and those rarest pearls of great price, peace and fulfillment in life. But this is also a book about learning and implementing the principles necessary to succeed in life. It's about some of the lessons I have learned in the process of starting, growing, and managing several successful businesses, along with a discussion of what I believe to be the meaning of true success.

I should add, however, that I could not share the lessons and principles I have learned without first acknowledging where they come from and the reality and intimacy of my personal relationship with Jesus Christ. Without Him my life would not only have been a total failure but I'm convinced I would not be alive today to share this story with you.

Let me also say what this book is not about. It is not about religion, or about being a perfect man or someone who has "arrived"—not even close. I have made more mistakes and committed more sins over my life than I want to remember. This is a book about a man who has experienced most of what life has to offer—the good, the very good, and the very bad. Through it all, I have experienced the indescribable mercy and forgiveness of a loving heavenly Father, and I have been allowed to enter into a small part of the treasures of His wisdom. From this and this alone comes the principles of living a successful life that I want to share.

Even if someone reading this book does not have a relationship with God but is just seeking peace in his or her life and insight into the universal laws of successful living, I trust that many of the principles and experiences I will be discussing in these pages will answer some of the questions you may be asking. I hope it may also inspire you to live a life of honor, courage, and integrity, always seeking the truth. When you find what you're looking for by living life to the fullest, without compromising your integrity, you will be that much closer to the one and only truth that makes us free.

Chapter One

AN ACCIDENTAL REBEL

L IFE IS FULL of twists and turns. No one has ever made this point better than the Old Testament patriarch, Job, when he said, "Man who is born of woman is of few days and full of trouble" (Job 14:1). Every life will have its ups and downs, and at times it may seem there are more downs than ups. But how we respond to the circumstances we encounter along the way will determine the amount of success or failure we experience in every area of life. This is one of the most important lessons I have learned in my life.

As I begin this book, I find myself at a place far exceeding anything I ever dreamed of, even though I have had some pretty lofty dreams. I have been a millionaire many times over, and have had the privilege of giving millions of dollars away. I have experienced the adventure of pioneering industry movements and launching new businesses from the time I was seventeen years of age. But there were also lots of hard knocks and missed opportunities along the way.

My mother and father weren't orphans, but they were raised that way. My mother was born in a first generation Italian-American family. Her father and mother didn't speak a word of English. Her father died not long after she was born; and with fourteen children to raise, her mother soon found she couldn't support all of them. So she placed my mother, along with a younger brother and an older sister, in a Catholic orphanage.

On a couple of occasions, my mother told us about some of the hardships she had suffered at the orphanage, and the cruel punishments that she and the other children were subjected to. It was hard to believe that such things were possible. But despite the hardships, she lived there until she was sixteen, when she was finally released to go back home to her mother, so she could find work to help support the family. Life during the Great Depression was very hard, and it was heartbreaking to hear about some of the things my mother was forced to endure.

My father's situation was no better. He was born on the family farm in Fredericksburg, Virginia, but his mother died when he was a young boy. After his father remarried, he and his new stepmother did not get along, so my dad was sent out to work on neighboring farms. He was forced to live with some of those families for years, and he was treated very badly—more like a slave than a neighbor boy, in some cases. He slept in barns and suffered physical and emotional abuse for many years.

Because his life was so hard, my father ran away from home several times. Most of the time he was dragged back to the farm and punished even more severely. But the last time he ran away he ended up in Newport News, where he falsified his age to get a job in the shipyard. He was a hardworking man and never missed a day on the job. A few years later he met my mother. After a brief courtship they were married and began their new lives together—two lonely, insecure people who had already suffered so much. And that was the environment into which my two brothers, Marvin and Freddie, and I were born.

One of my first memories as a child was my aunt asking my brothers and me what we wanted to be when we grew up. My older brother said he wanted to work in the shipyard like our daddy, and my younger brother said the same thing. But when my aunt asked me what I wanted to be, I said I wanted to be a preacher. And I added that I also wanted to be a millionaire.

Of course, I had no idea that those two things do not generally go together, but that did not matter. I was a kid and I had a bold imagination. But I had also watched my dad come home from work every day with burns on his shirt and scars on his body from working with a welding torch and red-hot steel, and I knew that wasn't something I wanted to do. But some of my family laughed at me. In fact, everyone but my mother laughed at me. Some of my relatives even got angry with me for saying I wanted to do something else. They said, "What makes you so special, Dennis? Do you think you are better than us?"

My mother understood what I meant. She always understood what I was thinking, and I remember her saying, "It's OK, Denny. I believe that's exactly what you will do." When she spoke those words, something was imparted deep within my soul. If my mother believed in me, I must be OK. And I knew the things I hoped to achieve might really be possible. I also knew that my mother wanted something more for me than spending the rest of my life in the shipyard. My father did the best he could, but he ended up working at the same job for forty-seven years and retired with a pension of a little more than seven hundred dollars a month. Even as a young boy of five or six years of age, I knew there had to be something better.

For most of his life my father thought that only rich people could own their own homes. So my first real goal was to buy my parents their first home. Their dreams weren't very large. My mother wanted a brick home and my father just wanted a garage. They never expected to get them. But because I chose to go a different direction, I was eventually able to buy them the first house they ever owned. It was one of the greatest privileges of my life.

I remember seeing two people on our little black-and-white television who had a big impact on my life in those days. The first was Billy Graham. He was such a powerful speaker, and I knew he was speaking the truth. I thought how great it would be to stand before a large audience someday and speak like that, telling people about the love of God and how to be saved. I didn't realize how rare it is for God to raise up a man like Billy Graham. But I knew that was something I wanted to do.

I especially remember how people's lives were changed when he preached. This was in the early 1950s, and Billy Graham was the most powerful preacher any of us had ever seen. When he reached the end of his message and gave the invitation, calling on people to come forward to receive Jesus, the aisles were immediately packed with men and women whose lives were changed forever. Many of them were weeping as they came, and even on television you could feel the emotion. It was electric, and that's what I wanted to do. I wanted to be able to see people's lives changed like that.

The second thing I remember seeing on that old TV was a program that came on every Monday night, called *The Millionaire*. Maybe you've seen it, too. Most of the time it would be the story of a man or woman who was going through hard times, and just when things seemed hopeless, a dapper gentleman in a bowler hat would show up and knock on the door. He identified himself as Michael Anthony, the personal representative of the multimillionaire John Beresford Tipton. After explaining that the individual had been chosen to receive a special gift, Michael Anthony would present them with a check for one million dollars, tax-free.

From that moment, everything changed for the new millionaire. Some of the people who received the money were blessed by it, while others made tragic mistakes. That was the real point of the show: to see how people respond to such a magnificent gift. A million dollars was worth a great deal more in the 1950s than it is today, and that made a real impression on me. The program had so many important moral lessons, but I knew one thing: I wanted that to be me. Of course, I would have liked to be the recipient of a million-dollar check. Who wouldn't? But I also wondered what it would be like to be as rich as Mr. Tipton, who could give away that much money every week and change people's lives in such a dramatic way.

Well, that was just a dream. But I know now that dreams can be real. The circumstances of life will try to steal our dreams away, but we never have to accept defeat. We're never without options, and even the most far-fetched dreams can become reality if we go about it in the right way.

I never did very well in school. Looking back, I realize I could have done much better if I had tried. Today when I'm sharing my story I joke that even though I only have a limited formal education, I have invested millions of dollars in what I call the continual entrepreneurial school of life experience. That is actually how I list my educational background on my résumé, because I have literally invested millions of dollars getting the experience that God has used to move my life forward and accomplish the things in and through me that He has.

Nevertheless, on my first day of school I was brought to the principal's office, where they called my parents and told them to come and take me home until I learned how to behave myself. I started school when I was seven years old, and before class started on the first day, I was sitting at my desk reading one of my *Dennis the Menace* comic books. The boy sitting next to me saw what I was doing and asked, "Can I read one of those?"

I said, "Sure," and handed him one. But before long he started passing my comic book around to the other kids, and when I asked for it back, they would not give it to me. So I told this kid to give it back, and he said no. Finally, when I got a chance, I tried to grab it but he wouldn't let go, so I hit him. When I did, my desk fell over and it cut the tip of my finger off—which is a permanent reminder of that first day of school. When the teacher came back into the room and saw what had happened, she didn't ask for an explanation. She decided I was the culprit and dragged me down to the office, finger bleeding and all, and the principal kicked me out of school. So from the first hour of the first day of the first grade, I knew I was going to have a problem with education.

From that point on I was marked as a troublemaker. Every teacher in the school knew my name. They thought I was trouble, and I began to live up to their expectations. I ran away from home many times during those years. I was in the fourth grade the first time. I could get into trouble without much help, but I was also accused of many things I didn't do. I was teased and goaded all the time. They expected me to be a troublemaker, even though I really didn't want to be.

If it was rough for me in elementary school, things only got worse in junior high school. It seemed like every time I went to the boys' restroom between classes I would get in trouble. The bathrooms were then—as I suspect they still are—the place where some of the kids would go to smoke cigarettes. But it didn't matter whether I was smoking or not, the assistant principal would walk in, and without even looking to see who it was, he would say, "Dennis Jones, come to the office." I was the easy scapegoat for every disturbance. If something happened and I was anywhere nearby, I would be hauled down to the office and suspended.

Oddly enough, some of the teachers liked me a lot, and one older teacher really took me under her wing. She really seemed to care about me, and I have some fond memories of that teacher. But I was tall and independent, and the older boys were always challenging me. So there were many days when I would be outside after school in a fight with some of those guys. I never lost a fight. If I was going to be in a fight and there was no way out, then I made sure I always got in the first punch.

I grew up rough. My dad was the same way, a tough guy, and we really did not get along very well. But the straw that broke the camel's back for me came when I was in the eighth grade. The assistant principal hauled me down to his office one day and accused me of smoking. I told him I had not been smoking, but he refused to believe me. When I protested, he shoved me, and that did it. As soon as he pushed me, I socked him in the jaw and knocked him out cold. At that point I knew it was all over, so I just walked out of the office, left school, and went home. That was the end of my formal education.

Thirty years later, when my wife and I were in business in Virginia Beach, Cookie was helping a customer and his wife who had been teachers at that school. As they were leaving our clinic, he noticed a sign that said the owner's name was Dennis Jones. So he asked, "Is Dennis Jones from Newport News?"

Cookie said, "Yes, he grew up there."

Then the guy asked, "Did he go to Warwick High School by any chance?"

Cookie said, "Yes, but he was always in trouble and they finally kicked him out in the eighth grade."

At that point, the middle-aged couple just smiled and shook their heads. Then, after a short pause, the man said, "The last time any of us saw Dennis Jones, we were all in class and we heard this loud roar out in the hall. So all the teachers opened their doors to see what was going on, and there was Dennis Jones on a Harley-Davidson motorcycle doing a wheelie down the hallway. He went all the way to one end of the hall, then turned around and roared all the way back to the other end. Then he used the front wheel of his motorcycle to bust the doors open, and suddenly he was gone. That was the last time we saw Dennis Jones."

Cookie asked me later if that was a true story and I had to tell her, "Yes. Sorry to say, that's what happened all right." The fact is, as shocking as it was for the whole school to see me roaring down the hall on a Harley, most of them loved it—even the teachers.

My mother had warned me many times to avoid bad company, but I'm sorry to say I didn't always listen to her advice. My next-door neighbor was a boy about my own age who had already been in reformatory school, and we started hanging out together. My mother would say, "Dennis, if you hang around with the wrong sorts of people it won't be long before you'll be as bad as they are." Well, she was right about that, and it wasn't long before I was just as bad as he was.

We would slip out of the house at night and hotwire cars. We would always bring them back—we told ourselves we weren't actually stealing them, we were just borrowing them—but we would take those cars out to a country road and race them. Sometimes we would steal a car and drive out to a place called Snake Hollow and see how fast we could go around the curves. A couple of times we wrecked them, and we didn't bring those back. But we returned most of them only a little worse for wear.

That's the life I was in. But one night when I was just fourteen years of age, this neighbor kid went out by himself and robbed a service station, using a knife. Afterward, he came to my house and knocked on my window, and said, "Hey, Dennis. Come on. I've got a car. Let's go."

I said OK, got dressed, slipped out of the window, and we took off. After a while he said, "Let's just run away." Again, I went along with him and said OK. My dad and I weren't getting along very well at the time, so that seemed like a good enough reason to take off.

By the time we got to Charlottesville, Virginia, about 150 miles from Newport News, the guy told me what he had done, and suddenly I realized we couldn't go back home. We decided we would have to make a run for it, so we dropped that car in Charlottesville, hot-wired another one on the campus of the University of Virginia, and drove on to West Virginia. We didn't know it at the time, but at that point we were involved in interstate auto theft, which is a federal offense. After we got into West Virginia, we decided to ditch the car and hitchhike, and after an hour or so thumbing on the roadside we were picked up by a guy who took us all the way into Kentucky. He dropped us off right in front of the Keeneland Race Track in Lexington.

As soon as we realized where we were, I walked up to one of the horse barns and talked to some of the guys standing around there. I asked one of the old-timers if we could get a job there, and he said, "Sure, young fella. Just go up to the boss man and tell him you're a professional hot-walker and groomer." So that's what we did.

Somebody pointed out the foreman to me, and I went over to him and asked if we could get a job. He said, "Well, that depends. What can you do?" I didn't have any idea what it meant, but I took the old-timer's advice and said, "I'm a professional hot-walker and groomer."

The foreman could probably tell that we were as green as they come, but he walked me over to a long row of stalls and handed me a shovel and basket.

Then he pointed to a long row of stalls where there was all this horse poop, and he said, "Here you go, son. Go ahead and groom those stalls."

So that's what I did. We ended up staying there about three weeks. But it wasn't long before the other kid started getting homesick. One morning he told me he'd had enough, so he left and headed back to Newport News. When he got home and told his mother where he had been, she called my parents, and a couple of days later my mom and dad drove up to Lexington to get me. They rounded me up at the horse barn and brought me back home.

But that wasn't the end of it. The next time this other kid did something bad—which was only a couple of weeks later—he was picked up by the police, and he told them that I had been with him. That wasn't true this time. I didn't have anything to do with that crime, whatever it was, and even though I had never been in trouble or had a run in with the law, the judge decided he was going to pile it on. Because my parents could not come up with bail, I ended up spending ninety-seven days in the Newport News city jail waiting for my trial.

That was one of the hardest things I've ever been through in my life. My mother was a good Christian lady, and even though I was a terrible disappointment to her, she never stopped loving me. And, most important, she never stopped praying for me. They would let the prisoners go down to the day room for a short time each day, and I will never forget looking out the window and seeing my mother standing there on the curb, on the other side of Twenty-fifth Street, just staring up at those bars until she could catch a glimpse of me and know that I was OK.

She would come down every day and bring me cookies or cigarettes or whatever I needed. It didn't matter whether it was raining or snowing, freezing cold or whatever, she would be there. It was painful to see her there because I knew her heart was broken for me, and it was only because of me that she was put into that position. One of the worst things that ever happened in my life was looking out the window one day and seeing a policeman cross the street and grab my mother. All she was doing was watching, waiting to see me, to make sure I was all right, but they were going to arrest her for communicating with a prisoner. As soon as he saw what was happening, my father ran over there. When the policeman grabbed my mother, my father hit him. So then they arrested my father and put him in jail for assaulting an officer of the law.

Fortunately, when they took him to court the next day, the judge threw the case out. He understood what happened. But knowing that I had put my mother and father in that situation was gut-wrenching for me. I wanted to die, but I couldn't do a thing to help, and at that point I realized what my disobedience and rebellion were really doing. My mother was a small, frail woman, just 105 pounds, and she was physically weak and ill most of the time, for thirty-five years. She never tasted alcohol in her life, never smoked a cigarette, and never drove a car. She took care of our home, and she had a very close relationship with the Lord. Without exaggeration, she would spend from seven to twelve hours every day in the scriptures and in prayer. That was her life.

She loved watching Billy Graham on television, but if my father happened to walk through the room while it was on, he would say, "Get that crap off the television. I don't want to listen to that." My mother would just turn it off. My father was so insecure that he wouldn't let her drive the car or even go out of the house alone. He worked on the second shift at the shipyard, from 4:00 p.m. to midnight, and she stayed right there. She learned to be content. She loved her husband and children, and knew little else. But she had a ministry of cards. If she knew anyone who was sick or shut in or going through tough times, she would send him or her a card. There were days when she would send as many as thirty or forty cards, and each one included a kind word and a Bible verse to cheer them up.

It was a very hard thing for me to see my mother being mistreated, knowing that it was all because of me. I knew I needed to turn my life around, but when the neighbor kid and I finally got to court for our trial, the judge sentenced both of us to nine years in prison. I hadn't even been in on that crime, but that didn't matter. He sentenced me to nine years as well. That was a shock for all of us. But I'll never forget what the judge said to me. He said,

"You boys are no longer going to be able to commit crimes and get away with it. I'm going to make an example of you right now."

One of the officers had assured my parents that, more than likely, the worst I would get would be six months in reform school. I was only fourteen, after all. But the judge said, "Young man, you've committed a man's crime, and you're going to pull a man's time." So he gave me nine years in prison without a recommendation of parole.

So after spending ninety-seven days in the cellblock at Newport News, they sent me to the state farm. I was the youngest person there. But even then, when I didn't even know Him, the Lord was with me. I came into contact with every kind of criminal you can imagine—thieves, robbers, murderers, rapists, and everything else. We were separated into cells, but we could talk to each other and you needed to be quick on your feet to keep out of trouble. Fortunately, some of the older prisoners at the city jail had warned me about what to expect when I got to prison. If they hadn't, things could have been a lot worse for me.

One of the older convicts told me, "If any of those prisoners offers you anything, don't take it, no matter what; candy, cigarettes, whatever. Don't take it. If you do, they'll come back one day and it will be payday." In fact, I saw that happen with other young guys while I was there, and I saw what the inmates did to them. Even though my ninety-seven days in the jail at Newport News were the hardest days in my life up to that time, they helped prepare me, and what I learned about survival in that place helped me get through the bad days that were coming.

⁓

Most of us who were around in 1963 can remember where we were when we first heard the news that President Kennedy had been shot. I was out on work detail at the prison that day, plowing the fields. Someone yelled out that the president had been shot, and at first nobody believed it. That wasn't possible. But as we learned more, we realized it was true, and it was a shock, even in that place.

While I was in prison, I learned how to slaughter hogs and make chitlins. I had to do just about everything the older prisoners had to do, but one day the warden called me down to his office and told me he had decided I was doing OK, and he wanted me to be the office boy. So for the next several weeks my job was to take care of the office, clean up, make the beds, and all sorts of odd jobs to help the warden. At the time I would have said I was just lucky. But I realize now that, even then, God had favor on me.

But, sadly, it wasn't to last. I had only been doing that job a short time when I was pulled into a major conflict with another prisoner, and I was thrown into solitary confinement. Fourteen years old, and they put me in the hole. The guards stripped me down to my underwear, and threw me in a cell eight-feet-long by five-feet-wide, with no bed. There was a sink, a toilet, and a blanket, and that was it.

They gave me bread and water every day, but the state required that I get food every third day, so they brought me beans and macaroni. I was there for thirty long, miserable days. To help preserve a little of my humanity, some of the inmates I had become friends with would sneak little treats into my cell. The cell where I was confined happened to be right next to the cellblock, and there was a small hole in the wall where the heating pipe was attached. Occasionally the guys would poke a cigarette and matches through the hole so I could at least have a smoke now and then.

But while I was there, locked in that cold, damp place, I came down with pneumonia. My parents came to visit me, but the warden told them I was too sick to have visitors. You can imagine how they must have felt when they eventually found out what I'd been going through. But the guards ended up taking me to the hospital where I was treated for double pneumonia.

Later it crossed my mind that my story was like the story of Joseph in the Old Testament. Joseph was thrown in jail but managed to get a good job in Potiphar's house. Then, just when things were looking up, he was thrown back in jail again for a crime he didn't commit. After I got out of the hospital and was returned to my old cellblock, I got a call, and the guards told me, "OK, Dennis. It's time for you to leave. You're getting out of here tomorrow."

That was the best news I had heard in a long time. But before I could celebrate, they told me, "Go get your mattress and blanket, and bring them on up to the front."

That surprised me. So I said, "I thought you said I was going to get out tomorrow."

"Just do as I say," the guard yelled at me. "Go get your stuff and bring it up here."

By that point I had already spent over a year in prison, but when I got up to the front, there were two police officers standing there waiting for me. They arrested me, read me my rights, and took me back to the Newport News city jail. Then after taking care of the paperwork and picking up a new set of charges, they drove me back to Charlottesville where I was going to be tried for interstate auto theft. Rather than trying me all at one time for my various crimes, they were going to do it one crime at a time. And just when I was so happy, thinking I was going home, it started all over again.

I spent that first night in the jail in Charlottesville, and the next day I was taken to stand trial at the courthouse. As serious as my situation was, I couldn't help laughing when we got there. The courtroom looked like something out of the television program, *Mayberry RFD*, with Barney Fife and Andy Griffith and the gang. The judge was sitting there in his chair, with an open window behind him. Whenever a train would come by, the judge would tell everybody to just sit still and wait until it passed. So we sat there and watched the trains go by, and when the room was quiet again he would say, "OK, continue."

But I have to give that judge due credit. He was incomparably wiser and more humane than the judge at my first trial. After he heard the charges against me, the judge looked over my record, then he looked at me and said, "Come up here, son." So I got up from my chair and walked over to the bench, which was really just a desk. When he looked up, he leaned back in his chair and said, "Young man, I've been looking at your record here. Is this your first offense?"

I was frightened because I didn't know what was going to happen to me. I had already been through more than I wanted to remember, but I summoned my courage and answered, "Yes, your honor."

"You've never been in trouble before?"

I said, "No, Sir."

Then, slamming his hands down on the desk, he said, "What's the matter with that guy? That last judge gave you nine years? What was he thinking?" After a short pause he looked back at me and said, "Are your mother and father in the courtroom, son?"

I said, "Yes, sir," and pointed to my parents in the back of the room. He called out, "Mr. and Mrs. Jones, please come to the front."

When they approached the desk, the judge said, "Mr. and Mrs. Jones, take your son home. These charges are outrageous. I'm dismissing his case." At that point he instructed the bailiff to release me, and he dismissed my case. So, suddenly, much to my surprise and great joy, I was free to go. And that act of kindness proved to be a major turning point in my life.

When we got back home, I apologized to my mother and father and assured them I was going to leave the past behind. I was ready for a new beginning. I even tried to go back to high school, but the principal wouldn't let me enroll. He said, "We don't want you here. We don't need any ex-cons in our school." Actually, that was fine with me. I had never liked school anyway. But it also meant that I would have to find a job right away.

To get started, I decided I would take any odd jobs I could find, and a few days later I happened to be cutting my neighbor's hedges. I was just trying to make a couple of bucks, but when I finished I went to the door to get my money, and the neighbor lady said to me, "Dennis, you really did a beautiful job with those hedges. You know, I think you have an eye for that sort of thing. Maybe you should think about becoming a barber." And as soon as she said the words something clicked. It felt right.

When I got home I told my mother what the neighbor had said, and she thought it sounded like a good idea. So the next day I went down to the barber school and signed up for classes. To pay the tuition, I got a job at a small fast-food restaurant that doesn't exist anymore. I went to barber school from 8:00 a.m. until 5:30 at night. Then, from 6:30 p.m. until 2:00 a.m., I worked at Burger Chef. That's how I worked my way through barber school.

After the first week I bought my first car—fifty dollars for a 1952 Buick. I had to get to school and work somehow. Nine months later when I finished barber school, things began to happen. There was a new shopping center just opening up in town. I suppose it wasn't all that much by today's standards, but this was 1965, and the new center was going to be "the place to be" in Newport News.

I wanted to work with the best, and this was where the Vis-à-Vis Barber Shop was located. It was an elegant eight-chair shop run by a guy named Bob Smith, who happened to be one of the best-known guys in our area. So I went in and introduced myself. I told Mr. Smith that I was looking for a job. He was nice enough, but he told me he had all the barbers he needed, and there was already a long list of barbers waiting for the next available opening.

But Bob's father, who was in his seventies at the time, saw me. He said, "Come over here, son." So I went over to him. He asked where I'd gone to barber school and I told him. Then, after we chatted for a few minutes, he said, "Bob, give this boy a job."

Bob repeated what he'd already told me, that there weren't any open chairs. But after he thought about it for a minute, he said, "Actually, vacation time is coming up in a couple of days, and each of these barbers will be taking one week each. I'll tell you what I can do. If you can cut hair, I'll give you eight weeks—one week at each chair." That was all I needed to hear. The next day I showed up for work, and suddenly I was working at the best barber shop in town. By the time the eight weeks was up, one of the other barbers had decided to move on. Bob said I had been doing a good job, so he gave me my own chair and took me on full-time.

Bob was an honorable man, a good Christian, and he was a friend and mentor to me for many years. He gave me my chance, and it turned out that I was very good at it. Everybody in Newport News at that time knew Bob Smith. They even convinced him to run for city council on one occasion. He agreed to run, but he dropped out of the race before the election. When we asked him why he pulled out so soon, he said, "I didn't think I could honor the Lord the way I wanted to and also do all the things that the city government would be asking me to do." I wasn't a Christian, myself, but I thought that was an honorable decision.

Bob was like a second father to me, and a good man. But now and then he had to put up with some of my bad behaviors. On one memorable occasion, the same assistant principal who had thrown me out of school came into the shop for a haircut; and, wouldn't you know, he ended up in my chair. I could see that he recognized me but he couldn't quite remember who I was. I didn't say anything right away, but I went ahead and gave him a standard haircut.

In those days we would put hot lather around the customer's neck and ears after we finished the haircut and shave along the hair line with a straight razor. As I was sharpening my razor on the razor strap, I knew I had to say something. So I looked at the guy and said, "You don't remember me, do you?"

He said, "You look very familiar. But I don't recall your name."

I said, "I'm Dennis Jones," and I just kept sharpening the razor.

Suddenly he got very tense. So I asked him, "Do you remember the time you threw me out of school for smoking?"

By this time his eyes were getting bigger and bigger, and he said, "Yeah, I guess I do."

When he said that, I took his ear, pulled it down, and I just nicked it with the razor. He jumped about a foot, and I said, "Oh, gosh. Look what I've done!" But then I took the styptic powder, which stops the bleeding but really stings, and I dabbed it on the cut.

I offered a halfhearted apology, but he jumped up from the chair, pulled the cloth from around his neck and threw it on the floor. As he headed for the door, he yelled back, "Bob, I don't want that boy cutting my hair anymore!" I hate to say it, but vengeance is sweet when you don't know the Lord. I realize that was a rotten thing for me to do, but it felt pretty good at the time. After the customer was gone, Bob gave me a very disapproving look, and then we all had a good laugh about it.

Chapter Two

RADICAL TRANSFORMATION

A FTER I'D BEEN working at the barbershop for a couple of years, I was beginning to feel there was more I could be doing. At the time there wasn't anyone in our area doing what we know today as hairstyling. There were barbershops for men and beauty shops for women, but there were no styling salons in the area. I decided that's what I wanted to do, so I started doing hairstyling in the barbershop.

From the first day, business was very good. I was charging double what I'd charged for a regular haircut, and I had more customers than I could handle. When I heard that a major hairstyling competition was coming to Virginia, I entered the contest and won first place. Then a few months later I went to a national hairstyling competition and won that one as well.

This was in the late sixties and hair was a bigger issue than it had ever been. The Beatles had come to America and created a huge sensation with what the media called their "mop tops." All of a sudden men's hair was getting longer, and the more extreme the styles the better they liked it. After all, this was the era of the Broadway show, "Hair." The hippies were doing their thing on the West Coast, and all that focus on hair and hairstyling was just putting money in my bank account.

All the styling I was doing at that time was for men, but it wouldn't be long before I was doing it for both men and women. The big styling shows were a major attraction, so I became a regular at those events. In 1967 I won national and international hairstyling competitions. I worked the platforms in New York, Atlanta, Miami, and many other places, doing men and women's hair and putting on a show.

It was really a big deal at the time, and we would do all sorts of crazy stunts to draw a crowd. On several occasions I would hang an attractive young woman upside down by her feet, so that her hair was hanging straight down. Then I would cut her hair with a knife. At another show I broke a glass bottle and cut the model's hair with the broken glass. It was supposed to be spectacular, and I always drew big crowds. I created all kinds of hairstyles, and that's how I made a name for myself in the world of styling.

Over the next couple of years I continued to expand my horizons, and I started thinking about how I could register trademarks and patents for all the new products and technologies I was coming up with. In the meantime, my own hair was getting longer and longer, so that by the early seventies it was down to my waist. Remember, this was the era of Woodstock and all that crazy stuff. I was having the time of my life—or so it seemed at the time—and my goal was to be as extreme and original as I could be. The faster and harder and deeper I went, the more outrageous I became, and the more success I was having.

But despite all my success, I began to think I needed a bigger and bolder challenge. Newport News wasn't big enough for me; I thought that I needed to be in a bigger city. So I packed up all my trophies and tools, tossed everything into the back of my Ford Falcon, and I headed for Miami Beach. I had no idea where I was going, but when I pulled into a little diner just off the freeway on the outskirts of Miami at two o'clock in the morning, I was ready for anything.

I ordered a cup of coffee, and while I was sitting there, I struck up a conversation with a hot looking young woman sitting next to me. She looked like a hooker and it didn't take long to find out that's exactly what she was. She asked where I was staying, and I told her I had just pulled into town and didn't have anyplace to stay yet. So she said, "Well, come on, then. You can stay with me until you find a place."

So there I was. Twenty-one years old, out to seek my fortune, with no idea how or where I would end up. But two days later, that young woman introduced me to the guy who ran the styling salon at the Doral Hotel. He was reportedly the best women's hairstylist in Miami Beach. Once we got to know each other, he told me he was thinking about opening a new salon. So I told him what I had been doing, about my success on the platform and all that sort of thing, and he suggested we go in together to open a hairstyling studio. I didn't hesitate. That was just what I had in mind.

There wasn't anything like it at the time, and I liked the idea a lot. We opened the first hairstyling studio in the North Bay Shopping Center in Miami Beach. But it wasn't just a salon: in the vernacular of the day, it was a "happening." We were open twenty-one hours a day, from 9:00 a.m. until 6:00 the following morning. We closed from 6:00 a.m. to 9:00 a.m. so we could go home and bathe and change clothes. Other than that, we were open all day and all night.

But I quickly discovered there was a dark side to the life I had chosen. Within twenty-four hours of arriving in that city, I was introduced to every kind of drug you can imagine. First it was marijuana, then LSD, psychedelic mushrooms, and everything else that was going around in those days. This was the height of the so-called "cultural revolution," and I got into it heavy. I functioned like that, strung out most of the time, and I did all kinds of stuff that I won't mention here and would love to forget. But, worst of all, I was on drugs day and night.

I was only in Miami a year and a half, but anyone who looked at me objectively in those days could have seen that I was burning myself out. There were people coming into the salon at ten, eleven, twelve o'clock at night to have their hair done before going out to dinner. This was Miami in the late sixties.

It was a wild place, the drug culture was at its height, and it could also be very dangerous. There were even machine-gun murders in North Bay Village.

All of this was going on, but, by the grace of God, after I had been there a year and a half, I got a call from my friend and mentor, Bob Smith. It wasn't a long conversation, but it was all I needed to hear. He said, "Dennis, I really need you. Can you come back and help me?"

I knew I needed a change of scenery, and I knew I had gone about as far as I wanted to go in Miami. So I said yes, packed up my car, and drove straight back to Newport News. I agreed to help Bob with his business problems, but I knew right away that ordinary styling wasn't going to cut it for me any longer. I did help Bob get the business turned around. But when I told him about the kind of styling I had been doing the past couple of years, he agreed that I really needed to be on my own. So after a few months at Bob's shop, one of my clients offered to set me up in my own styling salon in a new building he was opening. I thought it was a wonderful opportunity, and I opened a new salon in Newport News called El Matador.

This was the first unisex hairstyling salon in the state, and it was an instant success. During our first year, more than a hundred barbershops shut their doors in the state of Virginia. Now that men were growing their hair longer, and more and more of them were growing beards as well, the traditional barbershops didn't know how to deal with the new fashions. Most of them decided they didn't want to go back to school to learn the new styles, so they just shut the doors and got out of the business.

My studio was a beneficiary of this new trend, and we did incredible business at that time. Unfortunately, I was still into the drug scene. People would come to my house on weekends and trip out on acid for three days straight. There were times when as many as a half dozen hookers would be hanging out at the salon, looking to attract customers. I never got involved with them and never took a penny from any of them, but many of the doctors, lawyers, and prominent businessmen in the area were regular customers. We had judges, government officials, and corporate executives coming in for a shampoo, cut, and style, and it was good for business to be able to introduce them to one of the girls.

The salon did more than $160,000 in business the first year, which was a lot of money in 1970. Coming from my background, I thought that was some serious money. When I first started out, I was cutting hair for fifty cents, and it was still just over a dollar when I left to go to Miami. But now I was charging twelve to fifteen dollars or more for a haircut and style. I was still living the same way, and the drugs were still a big part of my life. But some dramatic changes were on the way.

One day a friend of mine invited me to drive up to the Shenandoah Valley with him, and this was when things really started to happen. We had known each other since the second grade. His mother was Italian, like mine, and we had gone to grade school and junior high together. He told me that he, his father, and his younger brother, Bobby, had been selling ski resort property up in the mountains, and he wanted me to come up and see what was happening. He showed me around, and at the end of the day he asked if I'd like to come up on weekends as part of the sales team. When I saw how he was living and the kind of money he was making, I didn't hesitate. I said yes, then I asked a couple of guys who worked with me at the hair salon to take charge of the business while I was away, and I found a place to stay up in the mountains.

Even though I was only working weekends at first, I was like a duck in water. It didn't take me long to learn the ropes. If I thought the business at El Matador was good, this was outrageous. Suddenly I was making more money than I had ever dreamed of. I was bringing home five to seven thousand dollars a month without breaking a sweat. After a few months I could see where this could take me, and I felt like I really needed a change, so I just signed El Matador over to the two guys who worked for me. I gave them the business and left town. At that point I packed up everything and relocated to the Shenandoah Valley.

I was selling land, and almost immediately I became one of the top salesman. I had developed a good relationship with my friend's father, who managed the property, and he offered me the job of sales manager at a new resort development called Leisure Point. And from there I was offered a position at the top ski resort in the valley, at Bryce Mountain. This was in the summer of 1973, and before long I was making from ten to fifteen thousand dollars a month, and I thought I was on top of the world.

I was rolling in dough, and at the top of my success I decided I could afford to take a little break. So I drove down to Newport News, and I ended up spending the weekend with a couple of girls in a hotel room down there. We were high the whole time, and at some point I heard a strange voice, laughing at me. Now, some people who did a lot of drugs in those days would freak out and hear voices or see things, but that had never happened to me. No matter how stoned I got, I always knew where I was, and I was aware of what was going on around me. But this was different. When I heard that voice, I spun around, and there was the devil himself, sitting on the edge of the bed, just laughing and mocking me. He sneered at me and said, "There's nothing left for you to do. I've got you now."

I knew this was a private vision, but I also knew it was very real, and it really scared me. So I immediately told the girls to get dressed and leave. As soon as they were gone, I showered, got dressed, checked out of the hotel, and headed straight back to the mountains.

There's a scenic overlook near the summit of Shenandoah Mountain called Reddish Knob. From the top of the mountain you get a 360-degree panorama of the valleys and surrounding hills. It's so high that, especially during the fall and winter, you'll actually be looking down on the clouds below you. It's so beautiful and peaceful up there that I would often drive up just to clear my mind. I remember walking out to the edge of that overlook on one occasion and saying, "Dennis Jones, you've made it. You are literally on top of the world. They all said you'd never amount to anything, but look at you now!"

I had been running so hard for such a long time, pushing every button and diving headfirst into every illicit pleasure this world has to offer. Having grown up with so little, I couldn't get enough. But in my mad dash to fame, fortune, and relentless sensual indulgence, I was getting closer and closer to the edge, in more ways than one. I knew I was at risk. I knew that bad things happen to people who live the way I was living. I had seen friends I grew up with overdose, and others died violently; but I had already gone so far, I didn't know how to stop.

One week later, the vision I saw in the hotel room that day was still haunting me in the back of my mind. I convinced myself it had to be the drugs talking, but it bothered me nonetheless. The demonic figure I had seen sitting on the edge of the bed that day, laughing, pointing at me, sneering with such bitter scorn, was as real as anything I had ever seen. It was frightening, and I couldn't shake that image.

When I went back to work, I decided I would stay away from the drugs for a while. It would be the first time in a long time, but suddenly I wanted to get clean. I knew there would be bad days, but I thought I could work through it. I thought about drugs all the time, but I wasn't using, and that was good. But one afternoon I drove out to that spot at Reddish Knob. I parked right at the edge of the overlook, and as I was looking out at all the beautiful colors on a fall afternoon, suddenly I felt a supernatural presence in the car with me.

I didn't see anything, but this felt different. It wasn't what I feared. I sense that this was something completely different. But as I was sitting there, everything suddenly went black—totally black. At that point I was really scared. I didn't know if I was hallucinating, having a flashback, or dying, but something was definitely going on.

As I was trying to figure out what was happening to me, I began seeing a vision of my mother, my father, and my brother, Marvin. I was surprised because my parents were so young. I didn't remember ever seeing them looking so young, but there they were, and my older brother was just a baby. One by one, scenes from their early life began passing before my eyes—things I had no way of knowing. First, my brother was born, and then I saw my mother giving birth to another son, but the child died at birth. Then I saw my father in his military uniform. He was so young, but they sent him off to fight in the

Korean War, and then he came back and went to work in the shipyard. After a while he lost his job and ended up under a doctor's care for war nerves. All these images just kept coming, on and on.

I had no knowledge of anything that had happened to my parents before I was born. We never talked about such things, and there was no way I could have known any of this. But as all these incredible scenes were flashing before my eyes like a movie, I saw myself being born. The day I was born my father rejected me. He was still under a doctor's care, and he was yelling that he didn't have the money to support another child. The last thing he wanted, he said, was another mouth to feed. But when he rejected me, my mother just drew me closer, and that only made my father resent me that much more.

Then I began seeing scenes from my own life, my problems in school, fights in the schoolyard, getting kicked out of high school, and going to jail. My entire life was being played out right before my eyes. And the amazing thing was that, after all this was over and the images faded away, my sight returned to normal, but all the resentment and hurt I had felt for so many years had vanished.

My anger because of the bad relationship with my father was gone. The bitterness toward my teachers, my fellow students, and the principal who had kicked me out of school—all gone. At last, I understood what had happened. I still didn't have any actual knowledge of the facts, but the images I had seen told me there was a lot more to the story than I had ever imagined, and my father and mother weren't to blame for the things that had happened to me.

But then, just as I was regaining my composure and feeling this intense sense of relief, I saw the Lord standing there in front of me. It was Jesus, and He looked similar to what I had imagined Him to look like all my life. He was radiant, dressed all in white, and surrounded by this incredible radiant light. He said, "Everything you've done in your life, Dennis, has led you to this moment." And as He looked me straight in the eyes, He said, "I love you." At that point I broke down in tears. I hadn't cried like that since I was a little boy. I had become so hardened over the years, and tears weren't part of my repertoire. But suddenly my heart was broken, and I cried out to the Lord, "Why me?"

Understand that, prior to this time, I had spent five years as a Zen Buddhist. I had studied astral projection, transcendental meditation, mental telepathy, and reincarnation. In one way or another, every one of them had given me short-term satisfaction, but I always knew there had to be something more. What I liked best was the idea of reincarnation, because if it was real, then I could come back again and again, which would be a sort of immortality.

For a time I had been a follower of Meher Baba, who claimed to be God in 1969, and then I became a follower of his successor. I had been going to meetings at a Buddhist ashram four or five times a week, striving for that mystical sense of enlightenment. But one night when I was sitting there in the lotus position, with my current girlfriend sitting beside me, something happened. The air was perfumed with the scent of sandalwood, sitar music was playing in the background, and the master was teaching us the principles of the eight-fold way. But at one point he said, "As Baba has said, 'It's destined unto man to live one million, five-hundred-thousand lifetimes, and then we all come into oneness.'" It was a fairly typical lesson, but for some reason that sentence stopped me right where I was.

Normally you don't speak or ask questions when the master is speaking, but I had never been very good at following rules. So I said, "Excuse me, Master. Are you saying that no matter how I live my life, and no matter how I do it, I'm going to end up in the same place as everybody else?"

The master looked at me and said, "Yes, that's true."

"So no matter what I do," I said, "I'm going to keep coming back, over and over, until I reach perfection?"

"Yes," he said, "that is also true."

"So if I took a .38 caliber revolver and blew the brains out of this girl sitting next to me, I would still end up in the same place as her?"

This time the master paused briefly. Then he looked at me soberly and answered, "That is true."

Hearing that, I jumped to my feet and said, "You've got to be kidding me. If that's true, this is the biggest pile of garbage I've ever heard in my life. What kind of god would put such a small premium on human life?" The master became agitated at that point. But as he started to speak, I yelled louder, "If what you say is true, I don't want any part of it." And with that I turned on my heel, yanked my girlfriend to her feet, and walked out. That was the end of my wandering in the world of Eastern mysticism and the occult. After all I had seen and done, I realized that none of those things would ever give me the peace I was seeking. But I was still looking for the truth.

When I was sitting in my car on the mountain that day, the Lord had revealed Himself to me. He didn't send a prophet or a guru. He came to me in a vision, and He said, "The silver and the gold are Mine." I didn't know it at the time, but that's in Scripture. He said, "The silver is Mine, and the gold is Mine," and "I own the cattle on a thousand hills" (Hag. 2:8 and Ps. 50:10, respectively). Then He said, "These things are Mine, but they have been stolen by the enemy and used for his purposes. But I am calling you and many like you to come and possess what is Mine and use it to usher in the coming of My Son" (author's paraphrase).

Those words have burned in my heart since that moment in 1973: "use it to usher in the coming of My Son." I believe that we will see the return of Jesus Christ in our lifetime. But even if that doesn't happen, we're going to be used by God to help usher in the return of the Messiah. That was the call that God put on my life that day. He put a lot of other things in my heart as well, and He just kept telling me that He loved me.

But again, I asked Him, "Lord, why me?" I asked so many questions that day and He just kept answering until I was so overcome with emotion that I couldn't speak. It was the most incredible experience of my life. It was a conversation with the Spirit of the living God. Every question I had was answered that day, and when He left me I was overwhelmed by the deepest sense of peace and joy I had ever known.

When I drove back down the mountain, nothing looked the same anymore. Nothing smelled the same or sounded the same. I had no idea what had just happened to me, but I was totally born-again. I was truly a new creation in Christ. When I got back to my office, I immediately started telling everybody I met that Jesus Christ is the Son of God. He really did rise from the dead! He is alive! That's all I knew, but I knew that, and I knew it for sure. Meanwhile, everybody around me was shaking their head and saying, "Oh, boy! Jones is really losing it." I heard that, but I wasn't dissuaded in the least. The first thing I did was to rush down to the nearest bookstore to buy myself a Bible. I immediately went back to my place at Leisure Point, and after gathering up all the drugs in the house and setting them on fire in a barrel outside, I started poring over and devouring every word in the Bible. There was still a lot of it I didn't understand, but the parts I did understand were dynamite.

Then, three days later as I was sitting there in my favorite chair reading the Word, a voice came into my head saying, "Do you honestly believe that what you experienced on that mountain is real? Don't be ridiculous. That was nothing but a drug flashback. You just had a vision and that's all it was."

But before I could even process the thought, the Lord spoke to me again and said, "Go home and speak to your mother."

It was about 6:30 p.m. by that time, so I called my mother and said, "Mom, I need to talk to you right away, and I'm coming home tonight." Without further ado, I jumped in my car and drove straight through from Harrisonburg, Virginia, all the way to Newport News in less than four hours.

I knew that if my mother confirmed the things I had seen on the mountaintop, then it had to be real. On the other hand, if she said none of it happened, or that only part of it was true, then I'd know it really was just a flashback. So I drove as fast as I could and pulled in at mom's house a little after ten o'clock that evening. She was waiting for me and my father hadn't gotten home from work yet. He was still working the night shift.

So I said, "Mama, I need to ask you some questions."

I could see by her expression that she was worried. She had no idea what I might be up to, but she did her best to remain calm, and said, "Sure, Denny. What is it?"

My parents had seen the best and worst sides of me, and I'm sure she expected the worst. For years I would come home like that and try my best to tell her about Buddha, but she would just look at me and say, "No, no, Denny. Jesus is the way. Ask Him to show you the truth and He will." On other occasions, I would try to tell her about astral travel or transcendental meditation or whatever I happened to be into at the time, and every time it was the same. She was so sweet, so patient with me. She would just say, "No, no, Denny. Jesus is the way."

Sometimes I would say, "Mama, how can you be so naive?" For a long time I didn't believe Jesus had ever lived. I thought the Bible was just a bunch of fairy tales. But this time I came home, and I told her what happened to me on the mountain, and I wanted to know if any of it was true.

I said, "Mama, here's what I saw. I saw my older brother, Marvin, when he was born. But then I saw that you gave birth to another son, and he died."

When she heard those words, she started crying. Over the next several minutes, I discovered that my mother, her sister, and my father were the only ones who knew about that. But it was true; I had an older brother who died in childbirth. They had kept it a secret all those years. She asked me, "How do you know this, Denny?"

I said, "All I know is this is what I saw, Mama. I just want to know if it's true. And I saw that when I was born, Daddy was under a doctor's care for war nerves, and he rejected me at birth because he was out of work and didn't want another mouth to feed."

Hearing that, she started crying again. She began defending my father. "He didn't mean it, Denny."

She tried to explain, but I interrupted her and said, "No, no, that doesn't matter, Mama. I just want to know if it's true. That's all that matters. Because if it's true, then I really met God. God came to me. But if it's not true, then I'll know that it wasn't real."

After a long pause, she looked up at me and said, "Yes, Denny, it's all true. Our second child died at birth, and when you were born your father was very upset." She went on to confirm everything I had seen in the vision that pertained to her and our family in those early days. They were all things no one in the family had ever spoken about, but I had seen them in vivid detail. And now I knew that what I had seen was true, and the implications for me would be overwhelming.

When I left the house that night, I knew that I'd had a conversation with God. The more I learned, the more I wanted to tell everyone I met about the Lord, and all this time the Lord was speaking Scripture into my heart. The apostle Paul says that the Lord occasionally reveals Himself to those who aren't even seeking Him. I may have needed Him desperately, but I wasn't seeking Him. It's true, I was seeking something, but it wasn't Jesus. But when I realized that everything in that vision was really true, I knew the Lord had visited me, and that changed the direction of my life forever.

One week later I was back on the job, leading the sales meeting in my office at Bryce Mountain when the presence of the Lord came all over me. It was so strong I thought I was having a heart attack. The Holy Spirit filled me so forcefully that I thought I was dying. I was talking and all of a sudden I started speaking words that sounded like nonsense. I tried to start over, but it wouldn't stop. I couldn't speak a word of English. All that would come out of my mouth was some language I didn't know. And all I could do at that point was to look at everyone with a confused look on my face, walk outside, get in my car, and drive back to the spot where I met God.

As soon as I got in my Suburban, I headed up the mountain and drove to the top of Reddish Knob, and my heart was so full of emotion that I was literally in pain. Tears were pouring down my face. But I got out of the car and walked over to the edge of the overlook and fell down on my face on the ground. It was a beautiful sunny afternoon, but as I lay there, I had the sensation that God had His finger right in the middle of my chest, pressing down. And He said, "Son, this is what it's like for the natural man to be in My presence."

I said, "Lord, it hurts. But it feels so good to be here." It was the most remarkable feeling: the pain of Him allowing me to be in His presence felt so good that it hurt. That's the only way I can explain it.

As soon as I was able to get up, I walked back to my car and drove straight home. I was starving for the Word of God. So I grabbed my Bible from the table where I had left it that morning and flipped it open. I was going to start reading at the first place I came to, and when I saw the place it fell opened to, I was amazed. It was Acts, chapter 1. That's where I began reading, and I devoured those passages. The first and second chapters of Acts reveal the coming of the Holy Spirit and the birth of the New Testament church, and I saw how the gifts of the Spirit had descended on the people of God, and I knew that, once again, God was speaking to my heart.

This is how it was for me, month after month. Anyone who has accepted Christ as an adult knows that you get this incredible free ride for the first five or six months. Everything you see or do seems to affirm the decision you've made. The Lord is holding your hand, guiding and directing you, touching you, as close as the air you breathe. All I wanted to do was tell people about Jesus.

I was going through this incredible awakening, but I still had to make a living, so I continued selling resort property during the day. But to say that my life was a contradiction in terms would be an understatement. Some of the guys I was working with at that time could tell stories that would make even the most unscrupulous used car salesman blush. They used every trick in the book. They would do just about anything to make a sale. But it wasn't long before I realized I couldn't continue working in that environment.

Then, as all this stuff was going on in my mind, I had the exact same dream three nights in a row. In fact, ever since that time, every major turning point in my life has come to me in a dream. I found that whenever God was getting ready to move me in a new direction, it would always begin with a dream. In this dream, however, I was back in Newport News working with Bob Smith. But it wasn't Bob's Smith's Barber Shop; it was called Bob Smith's Hairstyling Studio. In the dream, I was working in a little room. All the barber chairs were still there in the shop just like before, but there was a separate paneled room that wasn't there the last time I visited Bob's place. I also saw two of the barbers I had worked with, and two other guys I didn't know. And it was precisely the same dream, three nights in a row.

On the fourth day I had put in a long day at the resort and when I got home that night I got a phone call from Bob Smith. I hadn't spoken to Bob for five years or more. He said, "Dennis, I went to see my attorney today. Business has been really bad around here. I talked to him about going bankrupt. When I got back home, I was praying about all that, and the Lord put it on my heart to call you. I need you, Dennis. Will you come and help me?"

I said, "Bob, do you need a hair stylist?"

He said, "No, I need you."

It was a simple request. Bob was asking for help. So I thought, "What would Jesus say?" But I already knew the answer. So I went to the sales office the next morning and resigned from my position at Bryce Mountain. I loaded everything I owned in a U-Haul trailer the following weekend and headed south to Newport News. When I got there, I drove over to Bob's Barber Shop and there were the two guys I had never met, and there was the paneled room I had seen only in my dreams.

At that point I said, "Bob, I believe God has sent me here to get you back on a solid financial basis, and to retire you." Bob was already seventy-two years of age at that point, and it was time for him to retire. But I told him we'd have to change the name of the shop. It could no longer be Bob Smith's Barber Shop. It would have to be Bob Smith's Hairstyling Studio. So I asked him, "Would that be all right with you?" and he said yes.

A few weeks later, after we had made several important changes in the shop, a reporter came by to do a story for the newspaper. When the article appeared, the headline said, "Dennis Jones Is Back: But God Has Given Him a New Heart." It was amazing, but it was true. I had changed so much that anyone could see it, and that changed the way we did business as well.

When I had worked there before, I didn't have any tolerance for religion or religious people, and sometimes that made it hard on Bob. Whenever one of the local pastors would come in to get a haircut, Bob would normally ask the barbers to put down their tools for a minute, and he would say, "Pastor, would you pray for us?" But the minute I saw it coming, I'd blow a fuse. I would say, "I'm not putting up with that! Call me when you're finished," and I'd head out the door and smoke a cigarette. That's how I was. But now, as the newspaper correctly reported, God had given Dennis a new heart.

So I went back to work at Bob's, and God immediately starting blessing the business. I knew instinctively what to do to get new customers coming in, so I took over the marketing and we started running ads in the newspaper and on the local radio stations. Before long we had more business than we could handle. God was just blessing us in every way. Revenue shot up and we were able to get Bob caught up on all his past-due bills.

I ended up staying there from 1974 to 1977, and by the end of the first year all the bills were paid and we had made a substantial profit. To help grow the business, I also brought in a new line of shampoos and conditioners, along with all sorts of hair-care products, and it was a tremendous success. Everything we touched turned to gold.

After I had been back in Newport News for about seven months, I heard about a new church that was just getting started up in Williamsburg, so I decided to drive up and see for myself what was happening. One of the Presbyterian congregations was letting them use their building on Friday nights, so I went up there for one of those meetings. It was obvious that something was happening there. Attendance increased at every service, and before long they were able to add a Wednesday night Bible study. I went up for that as well. But while I was learning and growing in the Lord, deepening my spiritual roots, I sensed that things were changing in the business world, and I began bracing for whatever the Lord might be bringing for me next.

In a relatively short time Bob Smith's business grew from a simple barber shop to a very successful hairstyling salon, and I started working platform again, meaning that I was going to the various styling exhibitions and competitions all over the East Coast. The more God would raise me up, the more the business would prosper. As the volume of business increased, I decided this would be a good time to get into the hair replacement business. We could charge ten to twelve dollars for a haircut and style, but a good stylist could make four hundred dollars or more for a well-designed hairpiece. Most of the profit would go to Bob, which was what I had intended all along, but it was obvious that God was blessing me as well.

At the time I was giving most of my money away. Money had been my god in the old days, and I didn't want to go back there. I was afraid to start accumulating wealth, so I gave it away as fast as I could. As just one example, I was headed down to North Carolina on one occasion and I stopped at a small diner along the highway for lunch. When I sat down at the counter, I struck up a conversation with the waitress and she was so excited because she had just accepted the Lord at church the previous Sunday.

We talked for several minutes and she introduced me to her sister who worked there as well. One of them worked the morning shift, and the other one worked in the evening. They told me they didn't have a place to stay yet. In fact, they were sleeping in their car until they could come up with the five hundred dollars they needed to get a decent apartment. When I got ready to leave, I looked in my wallet and it turned out I had exactly $510. I was really touched by their story, so I handed her five hundred and said, "Here, take this. God has a way of taking care of His own, and I hope this will help you get the place you need."

That was a lot of money, but it was an even greater blessing for me to be able to help somebody that way. I was a single guy. I had more money than I needed and I didn't want to fall into the old money trap of my past, so that's how I was. I kept very little of what I earned. At the same time I was getting more and more involved in the church in Williamsburg, and I was growing every day and in every way.

God had me on a fast track, and I was experiencing all kinds of things.

People were being healed. The word of knowledge and the word of wisdom were flowing through me like water. From the first day I started going to that little church, I spent a lot of time getting to know the pastors and elders, and they were such a blessing to me. I became very active in the church, and I was getting one revelation from the Lord after another. It was a tremendous time of spiritual growth, but I still had a lot to learn.

Chapter Three

PARTNERS WITH PURPOSE

O NE OF THE most difficult lessons I've ever had to learn as a Christian began one day while I was doing hair replacement work at the shop. A young boy named Ronnie Angel came in with his mother. He was sixteen years old and he was suffering with leukemia. He had lost all his hair from the chemotherapy, and his mother wanted to get him a hairpiece. She made an appointment and when they came back the following day, I took them to that little paneled room at the back of the shop. After I made a plaster-of-Paris cast of his head and took some measurements, I asked him, "Ronnie, can I pray for you? If it's OK with you and your mother, I'd like to pray for you, and ask God to heal you."

I had no doubt that the Lord would heal this young boy. I had already witnessed so many miracles, and I was sure that God had brought Ronnie to me so I could pray for him to be healed. Both Ronnie and his mother were more than willing, and when I prayed we all felt the presence of God in that room in a way I have rarely felt it. There was no doubt in my mind that God could and would heal Ronnie that day.

After we finished praying, Ronnie and his mother thanked me and left the shop. Ten weeks later when the hairpiece came in, I called his mother and said, "Mrs. Angel, I'm just calling to set Ronnie up for his appointment, to give him his new hairpiece."

Then she said, so quietly and sweetly, "Dennis, the Lord took Ronnie home last night."

When I heard those words I was stunned. Devastated, in fact. But I wasn't just devastated, I was angry. I was angry with God, and I couldn't believe that He had ignored our prayer for Ronnie's healing. As soon as I told Mrs. Angel how sorry I was, I hung up the phone, and I began to weep. Then I yelled at God in my anger. "How could You do that?" I said. "Your Word says, 'If you ask anything in My name, I will do it.' Well, I did. I asked in Your name, and I believed You would spare Ronnie's life, but You didn't do it. Why wouldn't You do that? How do I know I can trust You? You said to pray, never doubting, and that's what I did. God, You are what I'm betting my life on, and You're not doing what You said You would do."

I must have stood there in emotional agony for an hour or more, just pouring my heart out and grieving over Ronnie. A short while later the phone rang and it was a friend from the church. There was supposed to be a service that evening and he was helping to put the program together. He asked, "Will you be there tonight, Dennis?"

Talk about bad timing. He had called right in the middle of my outrage and frustration. I couldn't control my emotions, so I snapped and said, "No, I'm done. I'm not going back." Then I said a hasty good-bye and hung up the phone.

I was defeated, hurt, and angry. I knew I wouldn't be able to do any more work that day, so I got in my car and headed toward home. I was on Interstate 64, approaching an area of Newport News called Yoder's Dairy, when I noticed a guy on the side of the road up ahead, hitchhiking. He had long hair and a beard, and he was wearing a robe and sandals, which wasn't all that unusual in those days. This was the mid-seventies and there were still plenty of hippies around. In fact, when I first starting working in the mountains, my own hair was down below my belt.

Giving a hippie a lift in 1974 wasn't all that strange. I thought about stopping, but as I got closer I wasn't so sure. I looked at the guy and decided to keep going, but the Holy Spirit spoke to me and said, "Stop and pick him up." I didn't stop. I just kept driving. Then the Spirit spoke again, a bit louder, "Stop and pick him up!" But, again, I just kept driving. This time the voice was much louder, "Stop!" By that time I was at least a half mile down the road, but I got the message and I stopped. I put the car in reverse and immediately began backing up on the interstate.

When I finally got back to where the guy was standing, he got in the passenger side, and without a moment's hesitation, he said, "The Lord has sent me here to tell you this." Over the next several minutes, he revisited everything the Lord had told me on the mountaintop at Reddish Knob over a year earlier. He reminded me of God's calling on my life, what the Lord wanted me to do, and where He had taken me over all those months. Then, when he finished going over all of that, he said, "You can let me out here."

When I looked at the road ahead I realized that the guardrail was very close to the highway—too close to let someone off without causing an accident. So I said, "Don't you want me to take you to the next exit?"

He said, "No, this is fine."

So I pulled over beside the guardrail, and beyond that there was nothing but an open field. He opened the door to get out, and I opened my door to go around the car, and when I got to the other side he was gone. I looked everywhere, back, front, even under the car, but he was gone. If I had ever doubted God's provision for me, that experience took care of my doubts once and for all. Suddenly I knew that the Lord had sent an angel to reassure me and get me back on track. It was such a powerful encounter, but it was also a very humbling experience; and that sort of thing has now happened to me twice.

Needless to say, I didn't bother going home. Instead, I headed straight to church in Williamsburg. The Lord wanted to teach me something, and He knew just how to do it. When I got there the service had already begun, so

I walked down about halfway and took a seat on the aisle. I had never seen the man who was speaking that night, but I learned that he was an evangelist and a powerful man of God. He was a big man, maybe 250 pounds, and he was well known for the ministry of signs and wonders. His name was Ray Jennings, and we have since become good friends.

As he was preaching that night, he walked up the aisle and stopped right where I was sitting. He said, "Many of you are praying for God to do signs and wonders, to work miracles through you. But I want to ask you this..." As he spoke those words he slapped his hand down on my right shoulder. He said, "What are you going to do if you're standing up there preaching the gospel, and you call for people to come forward and be healed, and a hundred people come forward? When you lay your hands on the first person, he drops dead. When you lay your hand on the second person, nothing happens. You lay your hands on the third one and, again, nothing happens. You lay your hand on the fourth one and he drops dead. You lay your hands on the fifth one and, again, nothing happens. At that point you realize you have ninety-five more to pray for."

As he spoke those last few words he slapped me on the shoulder again and said, "What are you going to do?" Meanwhile I was thinking, "I have no idea what I would do if that happened to me." But before I had even finished the thought, this big guy started jumping up and down, and he said, "I'm here to tell you that God did not call you to heal. He called you to pray." As he continued pouring out the gospel that night, emphasizing God's authority and our responsibility to pray and remain faithful, I knew that revelation was for me, and it has stayed with me through all the years. We are to pray the prayer of faith, believing God to heal. But, when all is said and done, it's all up to Him what He does.

Only God knows the hearts of men. He knows our lives and our needs, and more importantly He knows what He's trying to accomplish through us, short-term, long-term, now, and forever. We can ask, but only God can heal. That takes the burden off of us if He doesn't heal, but it should also take the pride away from us when He does. We can never take credit for what God chooses to do.

At that moment, I understood what God was showing me. And as painful as it was to hear that this sweet young boy had died the night before I called, I knew that God's will was being done in Ronnie's life and mine. It wasn't the answer I had wanted, but I know now that it was all within God's sovereignty. That discovery brought me right back into fellowship with the Lord, and I realized I had been given an incredible revelation of His power and a glimpse of His purposes.

I've come to understand that success cannot be measured over a short period of time. We humans tend to measure success in short bursts, but God doesn't see it that way. He measures success over the course of our entire lifetimes. When I was in jail at the age of fourteen, my life wasn't worth very much. Nobody would have given a nickel for it at the time. But the Bible says, "we know that all things work together for good to those who love God, to those who are the called according to His purpose" (Rom. 8:28). That means *all things*, not just a few. Let's face it, not everything that happens in our lives is good. Some things are horrible, painful, and cruel; but in the end God makes even those things—yes, all things—work together for good, if we will only let Him.

God uses *everything* in our lives to accomplish his purposes. The Lord said to Jeremiah, "Before I formed you in the womb I knew you; Before you were born I sanctified you" (Jer. 1:5). What an awesome thought! Not just that He knew me, but that He chose me and ordained me for a particular place and role in this world. At the Last Supper, Jesus reminded his disciples, "You did not choose Me, but I chose you and appointed you that you should go and bear fruit, and that your fruit should remain ..." (John 15:16).

This was such a powerful revelation for me, the idea that Jesus had chosen me from my mother's womb, knowing I was going to be kicked out of school in the first grade, that I was going to be thrown in jail, and that I would end up in all that mess in Miami Beach. Despite all the failings and disappointments of my life, nevertheless, he had chosen me. What awesome love. To realize that God could see through all of that and not give up on me was more than I could comprehend.

As I considered all I'd been through, all I'd done and not done, and all the changes I was still going through, I understood that God has a different way of measuring success. He can accomplish more in one minute than we can in ten lifetimes, but He measures our success over the course of a lifetime. Not over a few short years or even a few decades, but over our entire life.

I was working for Bob Smith and still going to the church up in Williamsburg, but I began to feel that there was another transition coming. It was time to move on, and I felt that God was telling me I had accomplished what I'd come home to do. Bob was in a good position now. We had built him a solid retirement, and he was making a good living. He could quit work any time he wanted to and be taken care of for the rest of his life. The Lord had used those few years to build up a lot of revenue in the business, and now I sensed that He was preparing me for a new chapter in my life.

So in 1977, I decided to move to Williamsburg. I was spending more and more time in the church, so it only made sense to move closer. As soon as I got relocated, I started another new business called DJ's Hairstyling Studio and Replacement Center. I ran a half-page ad in the newspaper introducing myself and our services to the community, and from day one we had instant business. We were the only ones up there doing hairstyling, and we were doing hair replacement work and making custom hairpieces for men and women. God just blessed that business tremendously, and, best of all, that's where I would meet my future wife and the love of my life.

Not only was the business growing but also a lot of doors were opened for ministry. God put it into some of our hearts to launch a ministry at the Eastern State Mental Institution in Williamsburg, and we went there with great anticipation. We started at Building 14—I'll never forget it—and within a year we were working with men and women in every building. People were coming to Christ, being healed and set free.

A short time later we started ministering in downtown Norfolk. That was an especially rough area at the time, with a lot of bars, prostitutes working the streets, gay bars, and adult bookstores on every street. In fact, that's practically all there was. So we would take teams to downtown Norfolk at 11:00 o'clock at night and stay until 3:00 o'clock or so in the morning. Sometimes I would stand on the street corner, preaching the gospel. But one night a big, tough-looking guy came up and pulled a knife on me. He threatened to kill me right there on the street, and I said, "Friend, what you want to kill in me you can't touch." He challenged me and then tried to argue about the Word of God, but before it was over that man ended up giving his life to the Lord.

We would also go into the gay bars, and I would share the love of God with them, one after another, from table to table and stool to stool. On one occasion I got into a conversation about Jesus with one young man, and I could see that the bartender was furious with me. He hated us and wanted us out of his club, so he called the police, and they came and dragged us off to jail. We stayed there a few hours, witnessing to the officers on the night shift, and then went on home.

The next weekend we went back to the same bar, and this time a big guy got so angry with me he broke a beer bottle on the bar and came after me with it. I was with my good friend, Bobby, and when we saw him coming we just knelt down on the floor in front of the jukebox and raised our hands to the Lord, thinking it was all over, and we started praying. As soon as he saw what was happening, the same bartender who'd had us arrested the week before jumped over the bar, took the broken bottle away from the guy, and I ended up leading the bartender to the Lord that night.

There have been so many times like that, and I'm constantly amazed at the way God works. But one of the funniest things happened on a night when I was buying a meal for a homeless man that I had run into on the street. We were sitting in a booth eating and a couple of my friends who had been witnessing on the sidewalk outside the restaurant came in and grabbed me. They said, "Dennis, you've got to come outside. There's a guy out here with nine demons, and they won't come out."

This was in the late 1970s, and a book had come out about that time called, *Jesus Taught Me to Cast Out Demons*, and all my Christian friends were reading it. I didn't read many books, but I did read the Bible, and I knew how Jesus and Peter did it, and I especially liked the way the apostle Paul did it. So I told my friends to stay with the homeless guy and make sure he was OK, and then I went to check it out.

When I got outside, there were at least six of my Christian brothers gathered around, standing with this guy with a bandana around his neck, and they were shaking him and commanding the demons to come out. They said, "Dennis, there are nine of them in there, and their names are Daniel, Jeremiah, Ezekiel, Rebecca ..." and they went on down the list, naming every one of the nine demons.

As soon as I looked at this man, I had my doubts. So I asked him, "Friend, what's your name?"

He said, "My name is Clarence."

I said, "Clarence, do you have any brothers and sisters?"

"Yes, Sir," he said, "nine of them."

"What are their names?"

"Daniel, Jeremiah, Ezekiel, Rebecca ..." and he went right down the list. Every name my friends thought was a demon turned out to be that poor man's brothers and sisters. So I said, "Clarence, you'll have to forgive us. My friends meant well, and they thought they were helping you." After that, we took Clarence down to the diner. We shared a meal together and everything was fine, but that was an example of how some people who mean well can go to extremes. That man didn't have any demons. All he needed was a little bit of love and a good meal.

By the late 1970s, I had built and managed several successful businesses. I had started out as a barber and hairstylist, and then I worked for a while in real estate and resort development. I had done well at each of those jobs, but the thing I knew best was the hair business, and one way or another I always ended up coming back to that, regardless where my life had taken me.

Ever since I had moved back from Bryce Mountain I was on a roll. I was doing what I knew best, and the studio in Williamsburg was a tremendous success. Almost overnight it became one of the busiest and most prosperous hair salons in the state, and as the business grew, I was constantly on the lookout for talented stylists. One day in the summer of 1977, an attractive young woman walked into the shop looking for a job. Patricia Abee, better known by her nickname, Cookie, was fresh out of beauty school, but it was obvious from the moment I met her that she would be perfect for the job. Not only was she beautiful and intelligent, but she had an incredible work ethic. She told me she had worked in real estate and interior decorating before that, but she had decided to go to beauty school and she was committed to learning the trade.

I liked everything about her from day one. She was bright, witty, and self-assured, but I didn't want to push her, so I just said, "Cookie, I think you'd make a great addition to the team here. But why don't you go home and pray about this, and if you decide it's something you'd like to do, then call me in the morning and let me know." With her background in real estate and interior decorating, I wondered why she wanted to get into the hair business. But she assured me that's what she wanted to do. A few years later she told me she couldn't wait until the following morning to call and tell me she wanted the job.

Cookie didn't have much experience in a busy studio like ours when she started, but within nine months she had the largest clientele in the clinic. Her personality, work ethic, and the quality of her work were exceptional. Over the next few years we came to trust each other and confide in each other, and we worked through a lot of problems together. We became best friends, but in all that time I never asked her out and we never dated. Frankly, I didn't want to risk losing her. I was afraid that if I told Cookie how I felt about her she might quit. In fact, neither of us wanted to say or do anything that might mess up the relationship, so it just continued that way for seven long years.

We had a tradition in the shop that when any of the staff had a birthday, I would take them all out to dinner at a nice restaurant. One day in the fall of 1984, we were headed back to the office after one of those birthday celebrations and Cookie told me she needed a ride back to her car. I immediately offered her a ride because I wanted to show her the new 280-Z I had just bought. But while we were driving back, something happened that changed our lives forever. Just as I was reaching down to shift gears, Cookie reached over to tune the radio and our hands touched.

If fireworks had gone off in that car it couldn't have been more surprising or more electric. We both looked at each other. Something amazing was happening, and I knew I had to say something, so I pulled over to the side of the road, and I said, "Cookie, do you feel the same way about me that I feel about you?"

Cookie smiled and said, "I don't know, Dennis. How do you feel about me?"

I said, "I love you. I've loved you for a very long time."

Then, with one of the most beautiful smiles I've ever seen, she said, "I love you too, Dennis."

I can't tell you how thrilling it was to hear those words. From that day we began dating, but I was determined to keep our relationship as pure and undefiled as it had been for all those years. Until that time in my life, I had never had a completely honest and respectful relationship with any woman. I knew nothing about true intimacy. Until I became a Christian, I behaved like a heathen, especially with women, but Jesus was changing me.

I had been transformed, and I didn't want any part of that old lifestyle to come into my relationship with Cookie, so I began to court her. I bought her flowers and candy, and took her to fine restaurants I'd never been to before. We talked about marriage, and we shared our hopes and dreams for the future. Then, after about ten months of this, something else happened that took me by surprise.

One afternoon while I was working back in the office, the Lord spoke to my spirit so clearly. He asked me a question: "Do you really love her?"

I couldn't imagine why the Lord would be asking me that. He knew how much I loved Cookie, so I said out loud, "Lord, You know I do. I've never loved anyone like this."

Then He said, "I want you to give her to Me."

At first I didn't understand what He meant by that, but over the next few days He revealed to me that He wanted me to let go of Cookie and give her to Him. I fought with that for a week or so, but it became very clear to me that God wanted me to let go of her because there was a work He wanted to do, and I was standing in the way. I was blocking Him. But for the first time in the twelve years since I had become a Christian, I told the Lord, no. I said, "Lord, I just can't do that. I can't let her go that easy."

The Scripture verse that best expresses what I was going through at the time is Psalm 32:4, where it says, "For day and night Your hand was heavy upon me; my vitality was turned into the drought of summer." God began to press down on me in a way I had never experienced it in my life. I was losing my composure. I was on a short fuse all the time, and I didn't understand what was happening to my personality. We were in a growth phase in the business, but I couldn't concentrate on my work. I was losing control of my life, and God just kept telling me, "Give Cookie to me."

I tried bargaining with Him, offering to give her up if he would just delay it until after her birthday, after Thanksgiving, or after Christmas. But the Lord doesn't allow us to bargain. I knew that eventually I would have to give it up and obey, but it all came to a head one morning when I walked into the office and kicked the trash can completely across the room. That really shocked my secretary who had never seen me behave that way before, so I left the office and drove away for a while, to clear my mind.

I knew I couldn't go another day without losing my mind, but Cookie's birthday was the next day so I took her out for a wonderful dinner after work. When I drove her back to her apartment, I told her I needed to talk to her about something, so we went inside, and as we were standing there in her kitchen, I asked her, "Cookie, do you love me?"

She gave me a puzzled look and said, "You know I do, Dennis. I love you with all my heart."

"Do you love me enough to let me go," I said, "so the Lord can do what He wants to in my life?"

She said, "I don't understand."

I said, "I know. It's hard. But God has been speaking to me for months now, telling me there's something He wants to do in your life, and I'm holding you back. He wants me to release you and give you to Him."

"What does that mean?" she asked, obviously puzzled.

"It means I have to let you go. We can't see each other anymore."

That night we just held each other, and we both wept. But I prayed and committed her to the Lord, and I let go. Cookie prayed for me, as well, and she agreed to let me go.

We continued to work together after that, but from that night we didn't date, we didn't go out to lunch or dinner, and we didn't talk on the phone. God didn't tell us that He was going to get us back together, but seven months later I was sitting in a restaurant in Newport News having dinner with a pastor and two elders from a church in Williamsburg. And while we were talking, the Lord spoke to me as clearly as anything I've ever heard. He said, "Go home and call Cookie. I'm giving her to you to be your wife."

As soon as I heard those words, I jumped up from the table and said, "Guys, I'm sorry, but I've got to go." I literally ran out of the restaurant, jumped in my car, and drove to my home about a mile and a half away. I ran into the house, grabbed the phone, and dialed Cookie's number as fast as I could. But when she answered the phone she was crying.

I said, "What's wrong, Cookie?"

She said, "Dennis, I just got filled with the Holy Spirit."

Cookie had known the Lord all her life. She had been raised in a wonderful Christian home by a godly mother and father, but God was drawing her into a much more intimate relationship with Him. She knew all about the Lord and served Him the best way she knew how, but because of God's calling on my life and what He was calling us to do together, He knew it would take a total commitment. It would take an intimate relationship with Christ to endure the storms that she and I would have to face.

Not many women could have endured all that we've been through over the years, but the most amazing part was how it all came together. Cookie had stayed home to watch a Christian program on television that night, and the message really touched her heart. At the end of the program, the minister asked for those who wanted to recommit their lives to Christ and be filled with the Holy Spirit to pray with him. So she prayed the prayer, and when she did she was baptized in the Holy Spirit. As we found out later, that was the very moment that God spoke to me and said He had given Cookie to me to be my wife.

In the everyday world, a man will find someone he wants to marry and then do whatever he can to convince her that he's the one. In a sense, he lays claim to her; or just as often she may lay claim to him. But in my situation there was never a doubt that God had given Cookie to me to be my wife. And He had given me to her to be her husband. It wasn't something we did, but something He did.

We got together that night, and the next day we went to see the pastor, to talk to him about our desire to get married. He said, "Dennis, I don't see any reason why you two should have a long engagement. You've known each other for seven years already. It's clear that you love each other, and God has called you to be together." So we set the date to get married, two months later.

As we talked about our plans for the wedding, we realized that neither of us wanted the wedding to be a big complicated affair. We didn't want to make it a big deal that required our families and friends to get involved. In particular, I didn't want to put any more responsibility on Cookie's mom and dad. We had done most of our dating in restaurants, and we'd done a lot of our ministry there as well, so after I went to her father and received his blessings, we decided to get married at one of our favorite restaurants in Virginia Beach.

All our friends and family knew that Cookie and I were engaged, but we hadn't discussed our wedding plans with them. We just invited all of them to join us for dinner one Sunday afternoon, and when they arrived at the restaurant Cookie and I were actually across the street watching them going in. Cookie was wearing a beautiful wedding gown and I was in my tuxedo.

When everyone was seated, the pastor of our church stood up and gave them a warm welcome. He said, "Because you're all so special to Dennis and Cookie, they asked you to join them here today. And now they have something special for you. They wanted you all to be with them as they become husband and wife." As soon as he said that, Cookie and I came in together and walked to the front of the room, and the pastor performed the ceremony. From beginning to end it was a beautiful experience. After all the excitement was over and all the guests came up and greeted the bride and groom, we enjoyed a wonderful dinner with our friends and our two families, who were meeting each other for the first time. Then we left for our honeymoon in Hawaii.

When we were still making plans for the wedding, I had warned Cookie that there was something she needed to know about me. I said, "Cookie, before we get married, I want you to know one thing. My life has never been normal, and it never will be. One day we might be living in a mansion, and the next day we might be sleeping on the ground in Africa. But I promise you this—if you marry me, our life will never be boring."

Cookie had known me long enough to know that our marriage would never be a sedentary affair. I'm always thinking about new things to do and new places to get involved, and this has taken us to all sorts of exotic locales. When we got married, we decided we wanted to consecrate our first vacation to the Lord. We were already involved in missions work through our church, so we decided to spend our first vacation together taking a team on a mission trip to the mountains of Jamaica, to help with a church plant. It wouldn't be a tropical vacation in a famous Caribbean resort; instead, we would spend this trip evangelizing in the villages that were hardest to reach.

The region where the village of Linstead, Jamaica, is located happens to be very rural, deep jungle, and rife with demonic forces. The members of our team spent time in fasting and prayer before we arrived, but when we got there we saw things we had heard about but never seen before. When we were in the villages we encountered spiritual forces that could easily have done great harm to us if we hadn't been covered by the grace and mercy of God.

Thirty days before we left Virginia, we began preparing ourselves for the trip. But just ten days before we left there was a major flood in Jamaica. The storms that pounded the island washed away thousands of homes on the mountainside, which meant that some of the places we had planned to go no longer existed. When we got there we made a few strategic changes, and we decided to drive up into one of the jungle areas to hold a crusade and do a church plant.

The roads were very rough, and there were places where the bridges were completely washed out. But as we were going up the mountain we drove past a prison. It was a dark and forbidding place with a sign on the outside that told us this was the Gun Court Prison. Gun crimes in Jamaica had become a major problem, so the authorities had converted this old facility into the place where killers and others who used weapons in their crimes would be punished. It was considered by most Jamaicans to be the most dangerous and most frightening place on the island. But as we passed, the Lord spoke to my heart and said, "I want you to minister there."

Cookie and I were standing in the back of the truck, so when I heard those words I pounded on the side of the cab and yelled to the driver, "Stop the truck." When he stopped, I jumped down and went over to the gates where a couple of guards were standing, and I said, "I'd like to speak to someone in charge."

After a few minutes a man came out of the main building with a puzzled look on his face, so I introduced myself and said, "We've come here from America, and we would like to share the love of God with the prisoners."

But the man shook his head vigorously and said, "No. You can't do that. No one comes in here."

From his tone I knew it was pointless to argue with him further, so I said, "OK, we'll come back later." Then I went back to the truck, and we continued on to the top of the mountain where the people we had arranged to minister to that evening were gathered.

Many of these people had lost their homes in the flood, and they had nothing. So after we greeted them and told them why we had come, my wife and some of the others drove the truck back to the capital city of Kingston to buy provisions. We had brought clothing and other essentials with us on the plane, but now they needed food, so Cookie bought rice, flour, and other things they needed. Our friends filled the truck with supplies and brought everything back to the village. They unloaded all the supplies, and later that evening we called everyone together at the schoolhouse where we held our first crusade on the island.

The place where we gathered was a dilapidated old building with a dirt floor and just one bare light bulb hanging in the middle of the room. Cookie and the group that went into town had already distributed all the food and supplies they brought back, but we quickly discovered that this wasn't what the people wanted. They just wanted to be comforted. They were afraid. So I stood up and began sharing the love of God with them, and at the end of the message I said, "God wants to reveal his love for you. For those of you who need healing, He wants you to come forward."

I waited a few minutes, but no one came. So I told them again that God wanted to bless them, and finally a young girl came forward with her grandmother who had been deaf in both ears for most of her life. Everybody knew this woman, and they knew she was deaf. But when I put my fingers in her ears and rebuked the deaf spirit, God instantly restored her eardrums and whatever else she needed to be able to hear, and immediately the old woman started yelling and jumping up and down, shouting, "I can hear! I can hear!"

After that there was a tremendous celebration, and we were all praising the Lord. The next person who came forward was a young woman about nineteen years of age who said she had severe pains in her chest. As I started to pray for her, the Holy Spirit said to me, "No. Wait." So I put my hands down, and when she looked up at me I could see the demons in her eyes. The instant I recognized what she was dealing with, she fell down to the ground like a sack of potatoes. My wife had seen the movie, *The Exorcist*, but she told me later that she had never seen anything like this, and she was justifiably scared. Most people have never been exposed to these situations, but believe me, they're real and you don't want to play around with such things if you don't know what you're doing.

When the girl fell, she threw her head back and made a terrible face, but I just kneeled down beside her, put my hand behind her head, and I said, "Open your eyes." When she did, we could see the swarms of demons that were in her. When Cookie saw it she jumped back. Then, suddenly, not one voice but many voices came from her mouth, and said to me, "We have to come out, don't we?"

When I heard that, I don't know why, but I started laughing. I said, "You bet you do! In the name of the Lord Jesus Christ, come out of her!"

The demons didn't resist. They knew they had no choice, so they came out, but when they did they brushed against Cookie. Evil spirits will always try to intimidate you, so they brushed against my wife on the way out, but I bound them in the name of Jesus and forbade them to do that anymore. Cookie told me later that going through that experience changed her forever.

When the meeting was over, Cookie and I were standing outside with the man who was the head of the Assemblies of God in Jamaica. I informed him that God had told me He wanted me to minister in the Gun Court Prison. "Oh, well," he said. "We've been trying to minister there for many years, but we can't get in. The commissioner is the only one who can authorize it, and he won't let anybody go in there."

Two days later we were in downtown Kingston, and all our team were out on the street, witnessing and praying for people's needs. So I told them, "I'm going to go and see if I can meet with the commissioner about the Gun Court Prison." I asked around and found out where the commissioner's office was located, and as I was going into the building I noticed that his name was McGarrett. I asked the receptionist if I could see the commissioner, and she said, "I'm sorry, but he isn't here at the moment. However," she added, "he should be back from lunch any minute." Hearing that, I said I would wait, and I took a seat on a bench just inside the door.

A few minutes later a distinguished black man came in and walked by me toward his private office. He paused and checked in briefly at the front desk, then went on back to his office. A couple of minutes later, he came back out and spoke to me. "Yes, sir," he said. "How can we help you?"

As I stood up I said, "Hello, Commissioner McGarrett. How's Dan-O?" Anybody who has seen the old TV police drama, *Hawaii 5-0* will remember the two main characters, Detective McGarrett and his young assistant, Dan-O. I'm sure the commissioner had heard that line many times, but we had a good laugh, and he said, "What can I do for you?"

So I said, "We're here visiting your beautiful country, and we want to share the love of God with your people. We drove past the prison called Gun Court two days ago, and I would really like to go back there and share the gospel with those men."

He shook his head and said, "That's a very rough place. You know they're all murderers. Every prisoner is there because they've killed someone."

"Yes, sir, I understand that," I said. "But that doesn't matter to me. I would really like to go there, with your permission."

He thought about it for a minute or so, and then asked, "When do you want to go?" I told him what day we would like to go, and he immediately took his pen and wrote out a pass for us and told his assistant to make the arrangements.

We had three days to wait before we could go to the prison, so the members of our group decided to spend most of that time in prayer and fasting. When the day finally arrived, we piled into the truck and made the long drive back up the mountainside, and everyone in the group said they felt led to go there. There were eleven of us in the group, but as soon as we got to the gates of the prison, seven of our people told me they were having second thoughts. They said they didn't think they ought to go inside, so I suggested they should go on back to the hotel, and we would come down there after we finished.

That left four of us, Cookie and me and two others, who went in to minister to the twelve hundred men who were serving life sentences in that place. We waited on one side of a long building, and right in front of us were iron bars. Beyond that was a large open dirt courtyard with a very simple basketball court. The guards had already arranged several rows of benches and chairs in the courtyard, and I could see that it was all set up for us to go in.

While we were praying and fasting, preparing for the visit, I had asked the Lord repeatedly, "Father, what do You want me to share with these men?" But He gave me nothing. Not a word. So there I was, with no idea of what I was going to say. When it was time to begin, the guards opened all the cells and prisoners began filing into the courtyard. When they were situated, I saw that there were at least three hundred prisoners sitting on benches or standing against the walls, staring at us. The rest of the prisoners—at least two-thirds of the inmates—decided they didn't want to come, so they stayed back in their cells. They could hear everything that was said, but these men were hardened criminals, and they didn't want any part of what we were doing.

Just as I stood up to begin, the Lord spoke to me. He gave me Psalm 139, which speaks of God's love for each and every person, how He formed us in our mother's womb, and knows us better than we know ourselves. So as I began speaking, I said, "You can't con a con. I know a bit about jailhouse religion." And from there I went on to share my own testimony, telling them how I got into trouble and wound up in jail with a nine-year sentence. I said, "I know what it's like to be in prison. Every man here claims to be innocent, but I want to tell you about a man who really was innocent, who did no wrong, who lived a perfect life, and yet they convicted him, beat him with whips, and executed him on a cross."

Then I started sharing from Psalm 139, which says, "Where can I go from Your Spirit? Or where can I flee from Your presence? If I ascend into heaven, You are there; if I make my bed in hell, behold, You are there. If I take the wings of the morning, and dwell in the uttermost parts of the sea, even there Your hand shall lead me, and Your right hand shall hold me" (vv. 7–10).

"No matter where you are, God knows you," I said. "Whether you're innocent or guilty, He knows." Over the next hour or so I walked through the whole thing with them. I told them about the love of God and how He knows our hearts and wants the best for us. I told them how their lives could be transformed by the love of God, and whether or not they ever left that prison alive, they would be in God's hands.

God gave me the words to speak, and they were exactly what those hardened prisoners needed to hear. Having been in jail myself, I understood the mentality of such men. I knew what it was like to be stripped of your dignity, to have everything you value taken away from you. At the same time, you're lying to yourself and everyone else about what you did or didn't do. Yet, there is One who knows everything about you, and despite the terrible crimes you've committed, He still loves you with a deep and abiding love, and He wants to give you a second chance. Even if you're eventually executed for your crimes, that won't change the way He cares for you. You may die in this life, but you'll have eternal life in heaven if Jesus is living in your heart.

They understood the message. Many of the men in that prison yard were sitting on the edge of their seats, just waiting for a chance to receive the Lord. And when I looked around, I could see the men who chose to stay behind bars inside the prison crammed up with their faces peering out at us. When I asked for all those who wanted to receive Jesus Christ as their Lord and Savior to stand up or raise their hands, at least 80 percent of the entire prison raised their hands and gave their hearts to Christ. So we prayed for those men and challenged them to get a Bible and learn His ways. Then I told them that there were ministers in Jamaica who would like to come into the prison to disciple them, pray for them, and teach them how to begin their new lives in Christ.

But those men weren't the only ones who were blessed that day. When we left the prison, the Lord spoke to me and said, "Do you see how I'm using everything in your life?"

I said, "Yes, Lord. Now I see." And I did see. I was deeply moved by the way God uses everything in our lives to achieve His purposes.

Chapter Four

A TIME TO BUILD UP

E
VER SINCE MAKING the move up to Williamsburg, God had really blessed our business. After talking it over with Cookie and a couple of our staff, I decided it was time to expand. I had gone from barbering to hairstyling, and from hairstyling to hair replacement. By this time things were going so well in the hair replacement business, I thought we ought to specialize in that, so I opened a new center in Newport News doing only non-surgical hair replacement.

We wanted to be able to offer a solution for everyone experiencing hair loss, regardless of what stage of hair loss they were in. So I developed a hair and scalp treatment program for clients who were thinning or just beginning to lose their hair. For those who came to us early enough, we could actually help stop their hair loss with the products and treatments we developed. And of course we were designing custom hair replacement systems for those who weren't good candidates for the treatment programs.

Throughout the eighties, we were doing thirty- and sixty-second commercials, as well as thirty-minute infomercials advertising our hair-replacement products and services on TV. A few years later we developed the process for a system that could eliminate the unnatural look of the standard hairpiece. For us to use this system, the client needed to have enough healthy donor hair around the side and back for this procedure to be successful. We would then do mini-grafts and micro-grafts to give the hair transplants a totally natural look in the front and along the hairline. Since they would still be balding on the back of the head, we would then design a custom hair replacement system for that area, and we called that *Transplacement*—a combination of the two procedures. I eventually patented that process in 1989.

Once the center in Newport News was up and running, we opened a second one in Williamsburg. Before long I was doing less and less hairstyling and moving more toward the hair replacement business. It wasn't a hard choice. In order to grow the business I needed to make the transition. So I began spending most of my time with the replacement centers, and before long we opened another new center in Virginia Beach.

That change of address, from one zip code to another, was actually a major change for the business. In 1980, when you drove across the Hampton Roads Tunnel from Newport News to Virginia Beach, it was almost like going to another world. Virginia Beach was much more upscale, and always at least five years ahead in almost anything.

When we opened the new center in the Pembrook area of Virginia Beach, it was successful from the beginning. Part of our success was due to the new product line we developed called Ultra Mane. We were the first ones to put commercials on television for a full line of hair products specifically designed for those who were just beginning to experience hair loss. We wrote the commercials, directed them, and went to the film studio in New York to have them shot. They were all very successful.

But once again I felt that a change was coming. Before they began the process, we wanted to be able to show our customers who had lost a significant amount of hair what they would look like after the replacement procedure. So we invented the first full-color video imaging system in the world. Everybody was trying to figure out how to make full- color imaging back then. In the early eighties, when personal computers were just coming into common use, the standard computers could only display black and white images. Up to that time, no one was producing computers that could display the full color spectrum.

By way of background, when IBM first came out with their Color Graphics Adapters (CGA) in 1981, the best computer monitors could display four basic colors: red, green, blue, and black. With the introduction of Enhanced Graphics Adapters (EGA) in 1984, they could display up to 16 different colors. Then with the Video Graphics Array (VGA) in 1987, and later the Extended Graphics Array (XGA), computer monitors could give you what we now call "true color," with 16.8 million colors.

But we were ahead of the curve. I knew we needed thousands of colors and all the various blends of colors in order to display hair colors accurately. In the early eighties, that was going to be a major challenge; but one day while I was wrestling with this problem, my younger brother, Freddie, asked if I would drive him and a friend down to a venue in Virginia Beach, where they could watch a closed-circuit broadcast of the Holmes–Cooney fight. It was going to be broadcast live from Caesar's Palace in Las Vegas and they really wanted to go.

My brother had been seriously injured in an accident and was confined to a wheelchair. He was a paraplegic and his friend was a quadriplegic, so after getting both of them into the car, I went with them to see the fight. It was an amazing show, displayed on a large screen in full color. But while I was standing there, I looked up at the three guns over our heads that focused the television image on the screen, in really amazing color, and suddenly it hit me: that's how you make color work. You have to be able to blend the Red-Green-Blue (RGB) spectrum to get true color.

The next day I started digging through all the research I could find to see who made the kind of equipment that would allow us to do that, and I found a company up in Reston, Virginia, called Scion Corporation, that had developed a high-resolution black-and-white system. They were one of the first to come out with 640 x 480 pixel imaging, which gave them the best clarity of any graphics adapters at the time. But they still weren't able to do it in full color.

So I called ahead and made an appointment, then I drove up to Reston and met with their executives, and I said I wanted them to work with me to develop a color imaging system for our industry. They liked the idea and agreed to work with us on the project, so we signed a contract. The next step, then, was to set up a time to meet with the full development team.

I'll never forget it. When I went into the boardroom, there were twenty or so of their top people sitting around the table, and they said, "OK, Mr. Jones. How do we make it?"

So I said, "It's simple. You already have a system using a graphics board that digitizes the image into sixteen levels of color. So here is what we have to do. We create a color wheel using a series of Kodak Wratten gel filters, arranged in three gradients: red, green, and blue. You then grab the image photographically. It goes into three separate graphics boards, one designated to capture the red, one the green, and the other the blue, and this digitizes all that information. Once you reassemble the image that has been passed through the color wheel, we should have full color."

As soon as I said it, the engineers started talking and making notes, sketching out dozens of possible configurations, to see what they could come up with. To start with, they agreed, it might take three separate graphics cards with the appropriate digital arrays to capture and recombine the images, but with further development they thought it would be possible to simplify the technology and reduce the amount of hardware needed. And that's exactly what did happen.

After four hours of head scratching, scribbling, and calculations, one of the engineers let out a yelp, and said, "We can do this!" I still have the color wheel we created. We made the first one out of an erector set, with red, green, and blue Wratten gel filters. That allowed us to render images of hairstyles in anatomically correct colors and superimpose those images on the computer monitor over the faces of our clients so they could see in advance how the various hair replacements we created would look before they made the decision to buy.

From that original concept came a wide range of new applications that had not been possible with the old technology, including the cosmetic computers used in high-end salons, as well as software applications that could be used by police departments and federal law enforcement agencies to track criminals and solve crimes. Over the next several months I traveled all over the country to technology exhibitions and trade shows with the new equipment. I did demonstrations at the federal COMDEX exhibition in Washington, D.C., in 1985, the International Law Enforcement Show in Salt Lake City, and many others.

Meanwhile, the hair replacement centers appeared to be doing very well. But while I was traveling to conventions coast-to-coast, I had turned over the management of both of our centers to a couple of men who had been with me for a few years, believing they would take care of the business until I got back in town. Whenever I checked in with them, they assured me that everything was in good shape. Business had slowed somewhat along with the rest of the economy during that time, but they always said, "No complaints so far, Dennis."

I'm sure they were doing their best, but, unfortunately, things weren't going as well as I had hoped. Then one day when I was back in town, I was sitting in my office, and an IRS agent showed up at the front desk demanding to speak to me. As soon as the receptionist pointed out my office, he came straight back and told me he was there to collect fifty-three thousand dollars in back taxes.

I protested and said that was impossible. We had always paid our taxes on time. The agent told me it was withholding tax for our employees that hadn't been filed quarterly. But, again, I said that was impossible. Our system had been set up years earlier to make sure that all our taxes were paid according to the book and on time. So at that point I called in the man who had been managing the centers in my absence and told him what was going on.

"Is this possible?" I asked. "Haven't we been paying the quarterly with-holding tax?"

He said, "Well, things have been a little tight, Dennis, and I just decided to wait on the taxes until you got back."

Needless to say, I was shocked to hear that. "A little tight?" I said, "What do you mean? If you were having problems, why on earth didn't you tell me?"

He hemmed and hawed a bit, then said, "Well, you were so busy, and you have so much on you. You've been on the road all the time, and we didn't want to bother you."

"Bother me?" I said angrily. "It wouldn't have bothered me, but now we're facing the prospect of being put out of business!"

When the agent heard all of this, he could see what had happened. We didn't have fifty-three thousand dollars on hand, so I couldn't write him a check on the spot. In fact, business at the centers had slowed down since I started traveling, and things were tight. But we were given seven days to come up with the full amount. If we couldn't do that, he said, they would confiscate all my property, sell off the equipment, bill me for any unpaid balance, and that would put me out of business.

I had no idea how I would come up with the money. We were in a major crisis, and there was no way I could raise that much cash in such a short period of time. But Cookie and I began praying about it, asking God to show us what to do. Then, two days later, I got a call from a medical doctor in Florida by the name of Chambers. I didn't recognize the name at the time, but he was the nation's leading medical hair transplant specialist. In fact, he told me he had pioneered hair transplant surgery back in 1959.

He was based in Clearwater, Florida, and he said that he had heard a lot about some of the hair care products I developed. I had worked with Upjohn on their Rogaine formula a couple of years earlier. Rogaine is a vasso dilator that is used to promote hair growth. It's like putting your hair on a life-sup-port system. As long as the individual continues to use it, the product helps promote blood flow into the hair cells, which helps to maintain life in the hair. My products, on the other hand, used no drugs or synthetic materials, and this was apparently what interested Dr. Chambers.

So he asked me, "Mr. Jones, are you the owner of these products?"

I said, "Yes, I am."

He said, "What's in them?"

I said, "It's a specialized formula I developed using all natural ingredients. But why do you ask?"

He said, "My medical clinics are the leading hair transplant centers in the world. We do a lot of transplants. Most of them are successful, but some clients experience better results than others. When I started looking into this, I discovered that some of the men and women who have used our services were having exceptional success. Normally it takes twelve to sixteen weeks for transplanted hair to start growing after the procedure. But, to my surprise, some of our clients' hair transplants were starting to grow back within three to four weeks. Some, in fact, were growing new hair almost immediately. When I asked what they were doing that made such a difference, it turned out they were using some of your products."

I said, "That's wonderful news, and I'm glad to hear it's working so well. But why are you calling?"

"I'm very interested in these products. I'm sure you can understand why. We need to talk. Can you come down to see me in Clearwater?"

The fact was, the IRS had already confiscated my personal and business bank accounts, and I didn't have enough left to buy a plane ticket to Florida. But I didn't want to say no, so I said, "OK, when do you want to see me?"

He said, "I would like it if you could come down this Friday." That was just three days away, which also happened to be the day my seven days were up, and I had to complete the payment to the IRS. I was still fifty thousand dollars short, but it might as well have been a million.

I knew I needed to make that flight, so I got busy and scraped up enough to get one round-trip ticket to Tampa, and then I spent all day Friday with Dr. Chambers at his home. We talked about the business and our mutual interest in the hair replacement and hair transplant business. We didn't spend much time talking about my products or the reason for my visit, but at the end of the day he said, "I really like you, Denny." The only person who ever called me Denny was my mother, but I didn't object.

He said, "I really want to do something with you and your line of products. Here's what I suggest. You bring your company in with my company, and we'll form one company covering all the bases. You be the president of the company, with a $250 thousand annual salary, and I'll give you 50 percent of the profits."

This was the best opportunity that had ever been proposed to me in my life. The offer included a very nice salary, half of the transplant business of the most successful operation of its kind, as well as a chance to franchise a string of transplant centers all across the country. But I was faced with a dilemma. The Bible says, "Do not be unequally yoked together with unbelievers" (2 Cor. 6:14).

This was when that scripture became real to me. I really needed this deal, but I had been with Dr. Chambers all day, and I had seen the way he lived, the way he talked, and I realized there was no way we shared the same philosophy of doing business. So I said, "You don't know me, but my wife and I are born-again Christians. We run our lives and our business, to the best of our ability, according to biblical principles. The Bible tells me I can't be unequally yoked with an unbeliever, and it's obvious you don't feel the same way I do."

He smiled and said, "Denny, me and the man upstairs have our own understanding."

I said, "Well, if you call Him 'the man upstairs,' it's clear to me that you don't know the Lord."

God does things so quickly. He can turn things around so fast it's astonishing. No matter how desperate we are or how dire the circumstances, He can transform the situation in an instant. Before I had even stopped speaking, the Lord put a business plan in my head, instantly. I'm not great with math in the first place, and I didn't really know if the numbers would work, but I said, "However, here's what we can do. You keep your business and I'll keep my business, and we'll form a separate corporation. That corporation will have one hundred shares of stock. You take thirty-seven and a half shares, I'll take thirty-seven and a half, and we'll sell the remaining twenty-five shares for five hundred thousand, and with that I'll build all the commercials, marketing tools, and branding, and we'll market my products under the name of Chambers Concepts." Then I asked him, "How does that sound?"

"Perfect," he said without the slightest hesitation, "and I'll put up the five hundred thousand."

But then I said, "There's one more thing. I must have absolute authority over the short-term, mid-term, and long-term decisions of this company. Without that, I can't do business with you."

"No problem," he said. "Is there anything else you want?"

"Yes," I said, "I'll need fifty thousand dollars today for what I've already put into developing the formulas and the products."

The words were barely out of my mouth when Chambers yelled, "Julie," calling to his secretary in the next room. "Bring me the checkbook." On the spot he wrote out a check for fifty thousand dollars and handed it to me. Cookie and I had prayed for an answer to our desperate need of fifty thousand dollars to save our business, and I had no way of raising that much money in such a short period of time. But God, who is rich in mercy because of His great love, supplied our need just in the nick of time.

For me, that was an incredible demonstration of the power of prayer. But here's what God taught me. A lot of us have a misunderstanding of what it means to be "unequally yoked." What it means is being yoked to someone, but you are not able to do what God is calling you to do when He is calling you to do it. If your work, your job, your business, or any other relationship keeps you from doing what God is showing you to do, you are unequally yoked.

But it goes further than that. Most people believe that the admonition not to be unequally yoked only means that a Christian should not be yoked with a non-Christian. But, in fact, two Christians can be yoked together and be unequally yoked. On the other hand, a Christian can be in business with an unbeliever and be equally yoked. What this teaching actually means is that believers must be in a position of authority and in a position to do whatever God calls them to do when He tells them to do it.

Only God could have put together a business plan like the one I proposed to Chambers. Here was a man living in a multi-million-dollar mansion. He had an expensive jet boat, jet airplanes, and was making millions of dollars a year. Who in the world is going to turn his business over to somebody he meets in one day and then write out a personal check for fifty thousand dollars with no questions asked? That can only happen when God is giving you His favor.

When I was willing to let go of it, telling this man that I couldn't be in business with Him because of my faith, and then insisting that I would need to have controlling authority over the business, I was saying that my commitment to the Lord was greater than my desire for financial success—even though I desperately needed it at the time—and God honored that. Without any premeditation on my part, He put the words in my mouth and made the arrangements.

Over the years, people have come to me for advice on how to start a corporation. Most of the time there will be two or three people who have agreed to start a business and they've decided to divide up the responsibilities so that everybody shares on an equal basis. But my first question is always, "Who has final authority?"

They'll say, "Well, nobody. I'll handle the business end, she'll handles the marketing, and he'll handle the day-to-day operations."

"Yes," I say, "but who has the final authority?"

"Nobody," they say, "we all share equally—a third, a third, a third."

"Then you're not going to make it." That's the best answer I can give them. Someone has to have the final decision-making authority in any business arrangement, so my question is always the same: who's going to have the final say when critical issues arise? Whoever God gave the vision to in the first place, most of the time that will be the person who ought to be making the final decision.

One of the greatest problems we see in the church is when people are unequally yoked. I have seen situations in some of our churches—sometimes even leading to break-ups and church splits—in which the senior pastor and an associate pastor ended up in a power struggle. In many cases, the associate pastor was never called to be an associate in the first place; he was called to be a pastor. But in his desire to lead the flock and make decisions that were not his to make, he ended up dividing the flock. The only way one man can serve another man's vision is to be totally submitted to it. If he can't do that, he'll end up causing problems, whether it's a business, a church, or whatever organization he belongs to.

In this world, money rules. But in the kingdom of God, God rules. His Word rules. And the one to whom God gave the vision, that's the one who has to have the final say. If they don't, they're unequally yoked. When you put a yoke on the neck of an ox, the animal has to bend his head down. He is submitting his will to the authority of another individual. By the same token, when you put on a yoke in a personal relationship or cooperative venture of any kind, you have to bow down. But before you do that, you need to know to whom you're bowing.

In my agreement with Dr. Chambers, I spelled it out in the contract that I would have absolute short-term, mid-term, and long-term decision-making authority. I could have sold the company the next day without anyone's permission if I had wanted to. That wasn't my intention, of course, but I needed to have the authority to do so. I put myself in a position of authority even though my partner was an unbeliever.

When I returned home to Virginia, my wife and I put a plan together and made some improvements in our product line, then we put a kit together and called it the Chambers Concept. We launched the new line on January 1, 1986.

We did $1.3 million in sales the first month, fresh out of the chute. God's blessing was on it. We also opened up nine medical hair transplant centers with Dr. Chambers.

God had taken me from barbering to styling, and from non-surgical hair replacement to surgical hair transplantation. At that point we had entered the medical world. In the process of setting up our centers around the country, I was training doctors on our hair and scalp treatment programs. I was negotiating contracts, signing lease agreements, buying furniture and equipment, creating a nationwide marketing campaign, and setting up centers all around the country.

One of our first new centers was in Newark, New Jersey. Obviously, he had a different lifestyle than I did. When he entertained, he went all out, and he had the wherewithal to do it. The ballroom in his home was bigger than my whole house. He really was a big shot. He was the most famous medical hair-transplant physician in the world at the time, and I made the arrangements for him to appear on television with Oprah Winfrey, Geraldo Rivera, Phil Donahue, and all the major talk shows.

Whenever we would travel out of town on business, I would frequently call ahead and make arrangements in whatever city or town we were in, to preach in a local church on a Sunday night or to participate in a mid-week service. While I was doing that, however, Dr. Chambers would be doing, lets just say "other things." He might even skip the business trip altogether. There were many occasions when we lost touch with him for three or four days at a time.

This went on from 1986 to 1989, and then one night I had another dream. In the dream, I saw Chambers and a group of young women in a jet plane. There was another guy on the plane as well. They were flying somewhere together, and all of a sudden the plane just blew up. The Lord told me through that dream to go tell Dr. Chambers that the fire of God was going to come down on him if he didn't turn his life around. But he also said to me that it was time for me to go, and if I stayed with Chambers I would be burned up right along with him.

I told Cookie what I had seen and how real it was. So we prayed about it for a couple of days, and we felt the Lord was really leading us out of that relationship. It wasn't an easy decision, however. By that time we had made millions of dollars through the business, and we were living very well. The Lord had really blessed us, and we were able to start church plants, to support missionaries and ministries of one sort or another, and to donate to individual charities that we came across in the course of doing business. We felt we were being used by God to make a difference in ways we had never experienced before.

We had paid off our mortgage and put away enough to carry us through the first quarter of the year, but there wasn't a whole lot left after that. That's just how we lived. It would be a big deal for me to walk away from this new business, but the Lord didn't leave me any options. He was telling me it was time for a change. But I also knew that if He were closing one door, another door would open.

So I called Dr. Chambers and I said, "I need to talk with you." This wasn't something I wanted to say over the phone, so I flew down to Clearwater and he met me at the airport. I sat down in the backseat of his personal limousine where he was sitting, and after a brief greeting, I said, "You know I love you like a brother." By this time, that was true. You couldn't help but like this man, and I had developed warm feelings for him. Then I said, "We've come to the place in our relationship where you know who I am, what I believe, and where I'm coming from."

He said, "Yes, that's true, Dennis. I know where you stand, and you've been a good business partner. I believe I can trust you."

"Thank you," I said. "I'm glad you feel that way." I was glad he trusted me, even though it wasn't always a two-way street.

I said, "We're at the place where I need to ask you one last time: please, give your life to the Lord. Repent of your sins. The way you're living now, you're heading for a life of destruction."

He listened to me, but he wasn't taking any of it seriously. He just shook his head and said, "Denny, I've already told you: me and the man upstairs have an understanding."

"And when you talk about Him like that," I said, "it tells me you don't know Him. But the reason I flew down here is to tell you what God showed me in a dream. He showed me that if you don't repent and turn to Him, the fire of God is going to come down on you, and when it does it's going to destroy you. And He also showed me that if I'm with you at that time, I'd be burned up as well. So as of this moment, we can no longer be partners."

"So what are you proposing?" he asked.

"Either you can buy me out," I said, "or I'll buy you out. Your choice."

I already knew the principle I was proposing to him. If you look at the story of Abraham and Lot in the Book of Genesis, you can see how God wants us to deal with a situation like this. When God told Abraham to leave the land of Ur with his wife and children, He told him not to take anyone else with him, but Abraham took his nephew, Lot. At that point, he was in business with his nephew, and for a time they prospered together. Their lands and herds and families continued to grow, but before long Abraham found out his nephew was stealing from him. Lot's people were stealing from Abraham's herds, and even killing Abraham's people. So the Lord told Abraham it was time for the two tribes to go their separate ways.

Here's the principle. When you find that you're unequally yoked with a business partner and you have to get out of the relationship, you will need to make an equitable split. Abraham said, in effect, Lot, take your people and your herds, and you can either go east toward the sea and the fertile valleys below and I'll go west toward the barren lands, or you can go west and I'll go east. Your choice. Abraham, the elder and the one who was being led by God, let his nephew choose which way he would go, knowing that Lot would probably choose the fertile valleys to the east. But that's how the choice ought to be made.

If you're willing to accept that, God will take you to the next level of blessing. If you're not willing, then it's going to take a lot longer to get there. In my situation, I told Dr. Chambers, "Either you can buy me out, or I will buy you out," and he said, "I want to buy you out." I told him that would be fine, but in the contract I stipulated that he could keep the product line—which already had his name on it anyway—but I would retain the right to be the sole and exclusive manufacturer of those products for five years.

When I said that, he looked at me and said, "Dennis, I'm a surgeon. You know what surgeons do with cancers? We cut them off. You've become like a cancer on my little finger, and I'm going to cut you off."

I said, "That's fine, I'm going back to Virginia now and I'll see my attorney tomorrow. In a day or two I'll send you a new agreement and tell you what it will cost you to cut that cancer off."

We hadn't left the airport, so I just opened the door and got out of the limo. Then I walked back into the terminal and took the next flight back to Norfolk. That was a tremendous lesson, and when I told Cookie what had happened, she just laughed. There's a chorus we sing in church sometimes that says, "He blessed us going in, He blessed us going out." That's how we felt, and we left that company with no regrets. Not only had the company experienced tremendous financial growth while we were there, but we had gained so much along the way and learned that God is faithful in every situation. And, best of all, I knew it was the right thing to do.

We left the business in 1989, and over the next two to three years some of the medical hair-transplant centers we had started closed their doors. In addition, some of the owners and suppliers Chambers was using had taken advantage of him. Then one day in 1999, Cookie got a call from her mother, who lives not far from us in Virginia, and she asked Cookie, "Did you see the front page of the newspaper this morning?"

Cookie said, "No, we hadn't looked at the paper."

Her mother said, "Wasn't that Dr. Chambers that you and Dennis worked with, the doctor down in Florida?"

Cookie said, "Yes. That's his name."

Then her mother told her what she read that morning. Dr. Chambers was returning to Florida from Troy, Michigan, on his private plane. On board were Chambers and five other young adults plus the pilot. They were on approach, coming into Boca Raton, Florida, flying low, and apparently the wing of the private plane clipped the top of a building. The plane burst into flames on impact and crashed in the parking lot. Everyone on board was killed, and the bodies were all burned. That was a sobering moment for all of us, and it crossed my mind that I could easily have been on that plane if I hadn't listened to the warning from the Lord.

I don't want to dishonor Dr. Chambers' memory. I really mean it when I say I loved him like a brother. But that experience was an incredible testimony of how God protects us. Some people may not know for sure that it's God speaking to them, but even if it's only intuition, they need to listen. If God speaks to us and we ignore what He is saying, He will eventually stop speaking. But if we will listen, trust Him, and strive to be obedient, God will guide us through even the most difficult circumstances; and He will do it in ways that will bring us into a closer relationship with Him. And as Scripture says, He will guide our footsteps in the way that we should go. (See Psalm 32:8.)

Chapter Five

A TIME OF TRANSITION

THE YEAR 1985 was a major transition year for Cookie and me. God was taking us from non-surgical hair replacement into a brand new field. I believe the reason for my experience with Dr. Chambers was to introduce me to and teach me in the medical hair transplant industry. It was a new world for us in the beginning, and in my wildest dreams I never thought I'd be involved with that. It was an amazing journey from being a seventeen-year-old boy working in a barbershop to the now thirty-eight-year-old man with a string of successful businesses.

The Bible says, "A man's gift makes room for him, and brings him before great men" (Prov. 18:16). I know that to be true. If we're faithful to use the gifts and talents He gives us, He will continue to bless and multiply what we have. Just think about the parable of the talents in Matthew 25. The servants who invested and multiplied the talents their master had given them were given more, while the servant who buried his talent without investing it had that one talent taken away and given to the servant who made the most of what he was given. And that's a principle of life, which I believe flies in the face of the direction we see our country going in today—wanting to redistribute wealth by taking away from those who have worked hard to achieve and giving to those who have not.

When I first got into the medical hair transplant business, everybody was doing twenty-five millimeter plugs, and they looked like plugs, like baby doll hair. I was sitting in the office with my wife one afternoon and the thought came to me, what if we took that standard plug of tissue and hair and we cut it into fourths and did mini-grafts? When I discussed this with one of our surgeons, he thought it was a great idea, and he got all the physicians to start doing mini-grafts, which looked so much more natural. From there we went to even finer precision, with the one-, two-, or three-hair grafts they're doing today, and it's totally natural looking if it's done by a skilled physician.

Whenever God has made changes in my life, I've noticed that He always does it in two's. For example, I started developing the Ultra Mane products in 1984, which was the same year He gave me the idea for the video imaging system. In 1985, the same year we made the transition from non-surgical hair replacement into the world of medical hair transplants, God sent me on my first mission trip to Africa. God had blessed us in our business. We prospered, and we had given money to the work of the church, but we were disappointed that so little of the money we were giving actually got to the ministries we were supporting. So we decided to try a more direct approach in our giving.

We found out that in some cases as much as 85 percent was being eaten up with administrative costs, and less than 15 percent was actually getting to the people we wanted to help. We didn't want to be a party to that, so Cookie and I started praying about how we could make a more useful contribution. Within a matter of days, the Lord put a man in my path who was a pastor from Nigeria, named Jonathan Ikegwuonu. Jonathan and I became friends, and he asked if I would go with him to conduct an evangelistic crusade in his country. Cookie and I prayed about it, then after considering what it could mean, I agreed to go, and I went with Jonathan to a village in western Nigeria called Nnewi.

That was the first mission trip where I would have the privilege of using my personal resources to help spread the Word of God in a foreign land. I had the privilege of purchasing the lumber to build the platform, as well as the generators for electricity, the keyboards and all the other musical instruments, and everything else we needed to do the crusade. Then I had the privilege of preaching the crusade. That was my first evangelistic crusade, and it was one of the most amazing experiences of my life.

When everything was set up and ready, we went all through the villages inviting the people to come to a healing service. The first night only about two hundred people showed up, but God did incredible miracles that night. By the third night there were more than thirty thousand, and it just continued to grow each night. By the end of the seven days I was there, thousands of people had come to the Lord, but they didn't have a church in the area to disciple them. I was really burdened in my heart about that, so I called my wife and said, "Cookie, here's what I feel the Lord wants us to do. Let's buy some land here and give it to the church. Let's build a world outreach center here in Nnewi, and from there the leaders can do church planting all across Nigeria.

Cookie liked the idea, so that's what we did. We bought five and a half acres of land. With this land, the local people were able to start growing their own vegetables. We bought chickens so they could raise them for food, and then they built a three-story headquarters building for the world outreach center, right in the middle of the jungle. It was all built by hand. Every brick was made by hand, and the structure was held up with bamboo scaffolding until it dried. We have pictures of that facility, and it's a beautiful testament to the work God did in that place.

I had ministered for years on the streets in Virginia, through personal evangelism and preaching in churches, but that was the beginning of our outreach ministry. I felt that God was calling us to reach out to the rest of the world. Multiple churches were established through that effort in Nigeria, and it's still ongoing. But that was just the beginning.

At that time I realized God wanted to use my life and not just my money. A lot of Christians in the business world think that God only wants to use their finances. But I believe he wants more than that. The "kings and priests" concept from the Old Testament is an example of how I believe leadership should be established in the churches today. It is clear that God called some to be priests, and He called others to serve Him in the marketplace and in everyday life. The priestly responsibility was to pray and seek the Lord, to minister to the people, and to take care of the widow and the orphans. The king, on the other hand, would go out and conquer and bring back provisions for the people, to provide for the storehouse and the work of the Lord.

That's an example that should be used today, because most pastors tend to feel they're responsible for everything, when, in fact, there are competent businessmen and women and community leaders in the churches who can help expand and extend the ministry in many different (and in most cases more effective and efficient) ways. If the pastors would call on these people when they feel God is leading them to do a new work, they could accomplish a lot more than they can by trying to do it all on their own.

But it's important for businessmen and women to know that they can do more than just contribute financial support. All those who are redeemed and anointed by God are called to be ministers in one way or another. Not all are called to be preachers or teachers or evangelists, but all are called. Some are called to be pastors and shepherds of the flock, while others are called to let the light of Christ be seen and experienced in and through them in everyday life. All these various roles are interdependent, but we also need to understand the qualifications and the limitations upon the calling that God gives to each one.

King Saul, who preceded David as king of Israel, violated his calling. He was called to be a king but he decided to take on the priestly role, which led to his downfall. When the prophet Samuel didn't show up, Saul took it upon himself to offer the sacrifice; but when he did, God told him that from that day the throne of Israel would be taken from him. He had stepped over the line, forgotten his true calling, and entered the realm of the priesthood without God's blessing and authority.

Businesspeople today, like the kings of old, are called to provide for the storehouse, but we are also called to be ministers of the gospel in the market-place and around the world. We can get into places as business people that pastors cannot. There are many countries that aren't open to clergy, but business people can often go in and out freely. So this is another way that God can use our lives and not just our money to accomplish His purposes and establish His kingdom around the world.

I believe God wants to bring us all to the place where he can trust us. If God knows He can trust us, then He can trust us with the gifts of the Holy Spirit, signs and wonders, and miracles to minister to the needs of others, wherever we find ourselves in life. If He can trust us, He can also put hundreds of millions of dollars in our laps, because He knows we'll use it the way He wants us to. The Bible says, "No good thing will He withhold from those who walk uprightly" (Ps. 84:11). There's nothing that God will withhold from us if He knows we can be trusted. But before God can bring us to the place where He can trust us, He first needs to know that we trust Him.

The truth of the matter is we often say we trust God when in fact we really don't. When our back is against the wall and it appears there's no way out, do we trust Him, or are we really fearful? Do we really believe He will come through for us? There will be times in life when we feel like we're drowning in our circumstances, but if we will wait and trust the Lord He will always come through. But there's also something else that has always bothered me: there have been times in the midst of difficult circumstances when I gave up on God and didn't trust Him to see me through, only to be embarrassed and ashamed later after He brought me through the situation with victory. It was only after the fact that I realized He had been there all along. Even though I had given up on God, He never gave up on me.

In some cases we realize only later that God has been working for years to get us to the place where He can supply all our needs. In the middle of the storm we may think we're going to drown, when God is calling us to stay the course. He is always there, but we may not see that until we come out on the other side. Perhaps the most memorable statement of this truth is the scripture that millions of Christians have taken to heart: "Trust in the Lord with all your heart, and lean not on your own understanding; in all your ways acknowledge Him, and He shall direct your paths" (Prov. 3:5–6). There is such reassurance in that promise, but it takes genuine faith and courage to live by it.

I think, for example, of Christ's own disciples on the Sea of Galilee. They were crossing to the other side of the lake and Jesus was lying there in the back of the boat, fast asleep. He wasn't worried. He was just lying there peacefully with His head on a pillow. But when a storm came up and the boat started tossing in the wind, the disciples who, by the way, were seasoned fishermen and knew the lake like the back of their hands, were suddenly terrified. So they woke Him up and said, "Teacher, don't You care that we're perishing?"

Unfortunately for them, that was the test. You see, Jesus wanted to know if they trusted Him and by their reaction they showed that they didn't. You have to wonder what they expected Him to do. Did they think Jesus would cry out in terror, "Every man for himself!" Would He start shouting, "Swim for it!"? Not likely. Instead, He calmed the storm by simply speaking the words, "Peace, be still!" And when the wind and waves immediately ceased, the disciples must have been terribly embarrassed.

Jesus said to them, "How is it that you have no faith?" How many times had they witnessed the power of God? Healing the lame, the blind, the lepers, and feeding the multitudes. Yet, they were apparently still unconvinced. But they said afterward, "Who can this be, that even the wind and the sea obey Him!" (Mark 4:36–41).

Jesus could have stilled the storm at any point, but He waited, and this is instructive. God often waits until the eleventh hour and fifty-ninth minute to intervene in our situation, but He always comes through if we simply trust Him. We can't have a relationship with God without trusting Him, and He's going to test us until the very end. When God gives us a vision or calls us to perform a certain task that call is going to be tested, and we may fear that it's not going to work. Are we going to quit? But here's the point: If you stay the course, the same word that tests you is the word that delivers you into the vision, the calling, or the blessing that God has laid on your heart.

~

When people ask me how to start a business, I tell them the best book to read isn't the newest bestseller by some Wall Street tycoon but the Book of Nehemiah in the Old Testament. This is the way my wife and I have lived our lives and run our businesses for many years. By way of disclaimer, this principle cannot be experienced unless you really want to do business God's way and follow after Him: unless you're willing to do whatever God calls you to do and to pay whatever price it takes. Every test that God gives us is intended for one purpose: that is, to bring us into a more intimate relationship with Him. Unless that's what you truly want in your heart of hearts, you probably will not be able to experience the blessings of this incredible principle.

No one can truly know Jesus without going through times of suffering. I don't care who you are. Jesus was "despised and rejected by men, a Man of sorrows and acquainted with grief" (Isa. 53:3). Until we learn to know him in times of pain and sorrow, we will never know Him as the resurrected Christ. We'll never know Him as the Victor until we know Him as the suffering Savior, because that's where we learn to trust Him. We meet Him most fully in those places in our hearts that no one else can touch but Him. When we're in a place of real suffering, when no one else understands, and when we're despised and rejected, He is there. That's where we can really come to know Him.

When I share these principles with people, I often say, "Don't try to walk my walk. You have to walk your own walk, being who you are, where you are, in your own relationship with God." But I believe this is the model that the Word of God has given for those who want to start a new ministry or a new business. When God called Nehemiah to return to Jerusalem and rebuild the wall around the ancient city, Nehemiah didn't go down to the bank and take out a loan. The Bible says that He sought the Lord.

Just about every time God gives us an idea to start a church, a ministry, or a business, the first thing we tend to say is, "Where's the money?" Or we may think, "If I only had this much money I could do great things." In our human reasoning we tend to think it's all about the money. But that should not be the deciding factor. God owns the cattle on a thousand hills; the silver and the gold belong to Him. He can provide the funds to anyone He wants to, at any time.

The Bible says that when God called Nehemiah to rebuild the walls, the first thing he did was to seek the Lord for wisdom, understanding, and knowledge. Solomon said that wisdom is the greatest thing, but with wisdom we are also to seek knowledge and understanding. If we want to start a new endeavor, it's our responsibility to go and get the knowledge. More than at any other time in history, knowledge of every kind is available to us at a moment's notice today, over the Internet, in libraries, or from official sources all over the world. But we have to seek it, and we have to have understanding to use it properly.

The Bible says, "Commit your works to the Lord, and your plans will be established" (Prov. 16:3). Too often we pray, "Lord, I just commit my plans into your hands," and I sense God saying, "What plans? You have no plans." Once we have the knowledge, we can begin to understand. And with understanding, we can formulate our plans. Knowledge gives understanding, and then God gives us the wisdom.

The second thing we see in this story is that God brought the people to Nehemiah. I have experienced that over and over again. God brings the people into my life to help me accomplish certain goals. Jesus said, "many are called, but few chosen" (Matt. 20:16). I believe the difference between being called and chosen is waiting on God. Most of us are not willing to wait. God will bring the people. Every time there's been something that God has been involved with in my life, He has brought the people. It may seem to be coincidence, but I like to say that coincidence is God's way of remaining anonymous.

This is the way Cookie and I have chosen to live: until God brings the right people and the money needed for the endeavor, we're not going to budge. It's really very simple. You wouldn't ask your son or daughter to go across the street to buy a bag of donuts without giving them the money to do it. Yet, many people will say that God is calling them to build a church or a business, and they don't wait for Him to give them the money to do it. They start building on their own, without God's guidance, and before you know it, they've fallen into what I describe later in this book as "the deception of compromise." In most cases they wind up deeply in debt. And that's also why most businesses fail within the first twelve months.

In the story of Nehemiah, we see that not one penny of Israel's money was used to rebuild the walls; it all came from heathen nations. When God told Solomon to rebuild the temple, not one penny of Israel's money was used. The Bible says that the amount of silver that the people brought to help build the temple was piled so high in the streets that Solomon had to tell them to stop. They had all the money they needed.

If God wants me to do something, I believe He will provide me with the resources to do it. We can get off to a false start and do it on our own if we want to; but most of the time we will suffer for that. If we're willing to wait upon the Lord, He will open up doors, anoint our efforts, bless them, and the work will succeed beyond our wildest dreams. I've found that to be true over and over again in the businesses and ministries I've built.

Another important principal we need to learn is that who you are in life is more important that what you do. Sometimes when I've counseled businessmen, I've asked them, "Who are you?" And they will say, "I'm a businessman," "I'm a doctor," "I'm a teacher," or whatever they do for a living. And I say, "No, that's what you do. I want to know who you are as a man." On one occasion I delivered a message to a group of pastors, and I asked them, "Who are you as men? I want to go around the room and have each of you answer that question."

So we did that, and each one of them told me their job. Some said they were pastors, teachers, apostles, prophets, or whatever role they filled in their congregations. But I said, "I'm sorry to inform you, but that's what you do, not who you are. That's merely your vocation; that's how you make a living. I know that's the way we're raised, to believe that our job is who we are, but that's not who we are at all. If that's who you are, then what happens when you lose your job?"

Too many times when people find themselves out of work, they lose their feeling of significance, their identity, their purpose in life. Think about the professional athlete. Today he's famous, travels all over the country playing his sport and earning millions of dollars for doing that, but then he has a serious injury. Or maybe he's involved in an automobile accident and suddenly his career is finished. If you ask him then, "Who are you?" he may not know.

If your job is your identity, then you're in for a rough ride when you have to start all over again. God wants us to find our identity in Him, and the only way to do that is to come into an intimate relationship with Jesus.

I always look for a scriptural basis for principles like this, and Jesus is the best example of all. He said, "the Son of Man has come to seek and to save that which was lost" (Luke 19:10). He said He had come to give His life as a ransom for many (Matt. 20:28). He knew what He was called to do, but when it came time to do it, it was very difficult, and that's how we feel much of the time. When it comes time to do the hard things that God is calling us to do—which is the greatest introduction into our relationship with Jesus— we hold back and resist the calling.

The apostle Paul said it was his desire "that I may know Him and the power of His resurrection, and the fellowship of His sufferings, being con- formed to His death, if, by any means, I may attain to the resurrection from the dead" (Phil. 3:10–11). Nobody would volunteer for suffering. But if we understand that we come into a closer relationship with God through our suffering, why are we so quick to reject the suffering? We do everything we can to keep from experiencing pain in our life because we've identified our- selves as our vocation rather than as the children of God.

Of course, nobody would go out looking for ways to suffer, and nobody says we have to merely accept suffering without trying to avoid it. When Jesus was in prayer in the garden of Gethsemane, He prayed, "Father, if it is Your will, take this cup away from Me ..." He didn't want to go through the agony that was awaiting Him. But He knew who He was; He knew what He had been sent to do. So when He prayed, He said, "nevertheless not My will, but Yours, be done" (Luke 22:42). He surrendered the difficult situation He was in to the will of the Father, and that's how we have to learn to live our lives. We have to be willing to surrender our difficult circumstances and trust them to Him if we want to come into that intimate place of fellowship with Him.

It's generally the hard tasks that give us the best opportunity to know Him more fully. We can run from them or we can embrace them; but if we embrace them, we may go through times of pain. When that happens we need to remember that pain opens the door into a closer relationship with Him, if we let it. We shouldn't be afraid of that, but because so many will do anything to avoid any pain or suffering we end up saying, in effect, that we're not willing to trust Him completely. But if we want to grow in Christ, it will be important for each of us to focus on who we really are as a person and not just what we do. The tougher the challenge, the greater the opportunity to know Christ. And nothing is more fulfilling than that.

Chapter Six

MY WORLD IS EXPANDING

I TOOK MY FIRST major mission trip to Africa in 1985. When I began doing those crusades, I was truly amazed—it was such an incredible experience. There's nothing like standing in a field with forty to fifty thousand people when signs and wonders and miracles start happening. People are praising and glorifying God, and you can feel the presence and power of the Holy Spirit at work.

I thoroughly enjoyed those experiences, and building the world outreach center in Nigeria was a blessing. When we began doing the crusades, instead of going from church to church, we started working directly with the indigenous pastors who took up the mantle and carried the gospel to the people. At that point the Lord started leading me to Ghana in West Africa, to undertake a new work with a pastor named Alfred Nyamekyeh. Alfred was a true apostle's apostle, a very humble man, but a powerful man of God who moved in the supernatural with a ministry of signs and wonders.

Alfred had about 4,500 people in his church at that time, and I first went there to participate in a conference to train pastors and business leaders. I felt that God was leading us to bring pastors and business leaders together to establish churches in unreached areas of Africa. It is difficult enough to get people in America to partner in that way, and it had never been done successfully in Africa before that time. But this was a challenge that Alfred, my friend Howard, and I were eager to undertake.

The idea was for the pastors to accept the spiritual oversight over these works, and then to ask the business leaders to partner with them and accept financial oversight over the new church plants. We would bring them in for training, teach them how to marry people, bury people, and fulfill all the basic functions of a minister. In the process, we helped start a school there, and a big part of the mission was training the pastors, teaching them how to start a new church and pastor the flock.

We held our first training conference in West Ghana in 1989. When we shared the vision we had used in Nigeria with the leading Ghanian pastor, he brought together a group of about three thousand pastors and twenty-five hundred business leaders from all across the country. During the five-day conference, I trained the business leaders during the day while Dr. Howard Foltz, the founder of Accelerating International Mission Strategies (AIMS), worked with the pastors, training them how to carry out their missions work. Then during the evenings, Howard and I would take turns leading the evening session, teaching the pastors and business leaders together.

That was a turning point for me. The first night while Howard was preaching, I was sitting on the platform with the other conference leaders, and the Lord spoke to me. He said, "I don't want you doing any more crusades right now. I want you to train leaders." I heard what the Lord was saying, but I really resisted it at first because I loved doing those crusades. The presence of God was so powerful in our meetings, with such an outpouring of signs and wonders, but God was saying, "That's not what I want you to do." He wanted me to train and raise up pastors and business leaders to support the work of His kingdom. That was a struggle for me, but I said, "Lord, if that's what You want, that's what I'll do."

In general, the indigenous pastors have an advantage over missionaries coming from abroad because of their native understanding of the languages and cultures. However, we found that we were able to reach many more people during the early part of the crusade because we were a novelty. The people would come because they were curious to see what we were like. In some areas, the locals had never seen a white man before; but when we came into their villages the people always showed us great respect.

But we also learned that some of the evangelists who had come to Africa to conduct these enormous million-person crusades actually did very little to help the people. One of the leaders of the African church—a man who had helped set up crusades for some of the best known preachers from America and Europe—told me, "They come here and they use us. They leave nothing for the church in Ghana or Nigeria, but they get their video footage, take it back and put it on television, and they raise money for themselves."

More than once I found myself having to apologize to the African churches for the false doctrines that had been taught to them by the evangelists from America. One of the teachings that virtually crippled the churches in Africa for many years was the prosperity doctrine that was being preached in the United States at the time. Some of our preachers took that message to Africa and taught it to the pastors, and it had a pernicious effect.

The prosperity doctrine taught that if you've repented of your sin and you're walking with God, you're never going to suffer. You're never going to be sick, and you're always going to prosper. But that's not Christianity. The Bible says that, although Jesus was the Son of God, "yet He learned obedience by the things which He suffered" (Heb. 5:8). And if Jesus learned through suffering, so do we. That's one of the ways we learn to walk in obedience. I mean, life is full of trouble and no one is going to escape without experiencing some measure of hardship.

God may have used the church to get us saved, but He's going to use the world to mature us. We're never going to learn spiritual maturity within the four walls of the church; we're tried and tested out in the world by going through the hard places—through illnesses and stresses of many kinds. We're all going to experience those things, and to tell people that suffering is a sign of God's disfavor, or evidence of sin in your life, is a terrible thing to do. Yet, because they had been taught this false doctrine by some of our ministers, they believed it. I know of cases where, if a pastor got sick, he might not even show up at his own church because the people would naturally assume the pastor was either engaged in sin of some kind or he was weak in faith.

So when I spoke to the church leaders I apologized for those false teachings and showed them from the scriptures why that doctrine was terribly wrong. And we taught them the full gospel, showing them what God intended for believers to experience. As Job expressed it, "Man who is born of woman is of few days and full of trouble" (Job 14:1). So what really matters is how we respond to that. If we're sick, God can heal us, but it's up to us to trust Him and have the faith that He will do it.

I also reminded them of the story in which Jesus healed the man who was blind from birth. His disciples asked Him who had sinned, this man or his parents, that he was born blind. And Jesus said, "Neither this man nor his parents sinned, but that the works of God should be revealed in him" (John 9:3). There are times when God allows us to be tested through adversity, knowing that faith and endurance can teach us lessons that prosperity and success could never do.

As we began to teach all these things, I shared my vision with the leading pastor and told him I wanted to bring the pastors and business leaders together at one time. When they were assembled, I told them that once they had identified fifteen unreached (people) groups and had fifteen pastors who were trained and committed to go and live among the people and disciple them, then we would hold a conference. We would bring pastors and business leaders together for one week, and at the end of the week we would pray over them, equip them, and team each pastor up with a businessman who would provide financial support and oversight for his ministry. At that point we would send them out to start the new churches.

The pastor I worked with thought this was a wonderful idea, because up to this point most of the churches in Africa had been dependent on the American church for financial support. In many cases they had never been taught the importance of tithing or the benefits of giving to the work of God; they were looking to America and to Christians in other countries for financial support. But on the final day of our conference, we called those fifteen pastors to come up to the platform.

I challenged each of the pastors to come forward and commit themselves to work with and support one of those fifteen men. Then I asked the business leaders to commit to the amount of financial support they felt led to contribute to those ministries, and when we tallied it all up, there was enough money given on the platform that day to support all fifteen church plants and their pastors for the next eleven years.

I believe that was a turning point for the church in that part of Africa. Suddenly they realized that God could supply all their needs. They didn't need the churches in Europe and America to be their benefactors; they had all the resources they needed. They just needed a way to marshal the resources from their own community to support the work that God had called them to do.

The Lord had already confirmed that He wanted me to train the pastors and business leaders rather than to preach in the crusades, and that was disappointing to me at first. I loved doing the crusades, and I loved preaching to the people. But God told me He had something else in mind. That didn't mean I wasn't to preach in other situations. I still feel the call of an evangelist. But the Lord made it clear that I was to focus in the area of my greatest success and strength, as a businessman who serves the Lord.

I am still a businessman, but businessmen can also preach. Unlike those who are called to be full-time pastors or evangelists, I'm not called to be a pastor, and I have no need to be supported by the church. Unlike those who are called to be pastors, dependent on a local church for their support, I have the means to provide my own support. With the calling that God has put on my life, I can trust Him to provide whatever I need to fulfill that call, and remain His free man. Like the apostle Paul, who worked as a tentmaker during his missionary journeys, I earn my own living and I'm able to provide for my own ministry so that I am not indebted to anyone, and no one is indebted to me. This is the way I feel God has called me to live.

Over the years many people have told me I ought to be a pastor, but I tell them that's not my calling. I've been an elder in my church and served on apostolic boards and councils in the past, but whenever I'm asked to serve in that capacity today I generally say, "I'd rather just be your friend." God has told me that in this season of my life He wants me to be His free man so that I can speak freely into any life or circumstance.

Like many others, I'm called as a businessman to the marketplace, but that doesn't exclude me from the gifts of the Holy Spirit, from being able to preach, or from moving among the nations apostolically to help build and establish churches. And it does not exclude me from being able to speak prophetically and teach the Word of God. I am free in Christ to do whatever He wants, wherever He wants.

I rejoice in this calling. I have seen as many people get saved, as many people get healed, and as many marriages restored in that little conference room in my office as most churches experience. Whether it's in a church pulpit on Sunday morning, a clearing in the jungle in a remote African village, or in a corporate boardroom, there are no limits to Christ's ability to change hearts and lives, if we will only make ourselves available.

I believe the Holy Spirit desires to restore the five-fold ministry to the church of Jesus Christ. He wants to see the pastor, the teacher, the prophet, the evangelist, and the apostle working side-by-side and in harmony to fulfill the ministry of the church to this world. When these five offices work together as they should, the world will see the full ministry of the Christian church.

Even though we have many individuals who not only profess but also market themselves as functioning in all five of these roles, Jesus was the only one who truly fulfilled all five offices. He was the Great Shepherd, a prophet and apostle, the greatest evangelist who ever walked the earth, and they called him Teacher. He had the full package. Nobody else has ever had that. But if the leaders in our churches can put away their pride and ambition and embrace the five-fold ministries and giftings that God has placed in others outside of their own churches, coming together in the unity of the Spirit, then and only then will the world see the church of Jesus Christ as it was meant to be.

I have never experienced true revival in America—my prayer is that we may see it one day very soon—but I can say that I have witnessed a true outpouring of the Holy Spirit in Russia. From 1989–1990, when the Berlin Wall came down and the Soviet Union was beginning to crumble, the nations of Eastern Europe were moving rapidly toward democracy. The Communist governments never gave up, of course. They had held the people of those nations in bondage for seventy years. But for whatever reason, they began to loosen their grip for a season, allowing the spread of freedom and democratic ideals in a way they had never done before. And that provided a tremendous opportunity to reach the people of those nations with the gospel.

One hundred years earlier, in the 1890s, the great medical missionary to the Far East, Hudson Taylor, had prophesied that there would be a great revival in Russia shortly before the Second Coming of the Lord. It would be an explosion of the gospel, he said, like nothing the world had ever seen. But he warned that it would only last a short time. There would be a window of opportunity, but eventually the window would close. At that point, God's Spirit would begin to move in China, which was where Taylor served and where he died. He said the Spirit of revival would stir the entire world, and then Christ would come.

When I first began paying close attention to what was happening in Russia, I learned that Pat Robertson and the executives at the Christian Broadcasting Network (CBN) had negotiated with the Russian government to broadcast the animated story of Jesus, called *SuperBook*, all across Russia. That was a truly remarkable event—as great in many ways as the collapse of the Berlin Wall. More than one hundred million Russians watched that program.

That was nearly half the entire population of the Soviet Union. And of that number, more than twenty million people responded to the gospel, sending cards and letters saying they had prayed with the host to receive Jesus Christ as their Lord and Savior.

Those who responded said they wanted to know God, but it was all so new to them. After seventy years of atheist indoctrination, they had been stripped of the Christian faith that had once been so strong in that country. So they asked, "What does it mean? How can we learn more about Jesus?" So many letters poured in addressed to CBN in Kiev that at one point the post office decided to leave all their mail bags at the CBN headquarters, telling them: "Take your mail, and we'll come back tomorrow and pick up whatever is left over." It was that overwhelming.

At that time I was serving as chairman of the board for Accelerating International Mission Strategies (AIMS), working closely with Dr. Foltz to equip missionaries in developing countries. While Howard and I were in Nigeria leading a pastor's conference, we were thinking about how we could help the ministry move into Russia, and how we could assist with the revival that was taking place over there.

When we got back to the states, we arranged to meet with Pat Robertson, and we said that if CBN would send a mailing to the millions of people who had responded, we would take a team in there to help build a base for evangelism. First, we would section off the various regions of the country, and we would take groups of pastors and business leaders to build churches and schools and bring the gospel to the people. The folks at CBN liked the idea, so we came up with a plan. We decided to reach out to pastors and business leaders in the United States, Germany, and a few other countries, asking them to join us in Russia. We all knew that this would be the best chance we would ever have to plant new churches and house churches in that country, and everyone was eager to help.

When we got to Russia, we only had ten days at a time to accomplish all our goals, so we had to work fast. We assembled approximately 250 pastors and business leaders in Moscow, and then we launched a program to provide in-country orientation for the pastors in Kiev. As soon as they were trained, we brought them back to Moscow where they would be introduced to the local culture. The Russian pastors would teach them about their culture, and the American and European pastors would teach the Russians about their culture. Then we would send them out in teams to do church plants. It was an amazing time.

We rented movie houses, theaters, opera houses, and churches that had been shut down by the Communists, and that's where we planted the churches. After we had trained the pastors, we began working with the business leaders who had made a commitment to support the new churches. For four thousand dollars we could rent an opera house for a year, and that would provide the financial support for the pastor and his wife and family, and also provide all the Bibles and literature they would need for an entire year. It was one of the best investments I've ever had the opportunity to make.

For seventy years, the people of these communist nations had been told there was no God. Most of what the Russian people had known about God and the Bible had been forgotten, but they were hungry, and their hearts and minds had been opened. Prior to our arrival in that country, CBN mailed brochures to every household in every city we went, telling them when and where the meetings would be held, and the people came out eagerly, filling the opera houses and theaters to the rafters.

I will never forget the first night that I preached to a Russian audience. I simply gave the gospel and the response was overwhelming. The message was very basic, Christianity 101. We told them, "In the beginning, God created the heavens and the earth." It was a message we would teach to children, and they sat there like little birds waiting to be fed. They were starved for the truth. We told them how God sent His Son to draw all men to Himself, and how Christ came and died for their sins. When we asked those who wanted to receive Christ to stand, everyone stood.

I remember one evening in particular. It was an audience of at least ten thousand, and I spoke for over an hour and shared a simple gospel message. When I was finished, I said, "Now, all those who want to receive Jesus Christ as your Lord and Savior, please stand." As soon as the interpreter spoke the words, all ten thousand people jumped to their feet. So I said, "No, I don't think you understand. Please sit back down. Here's the way you've been living your life. You've been drunk on vodka, you've been mistreating your wife and family, and living in sin. When you accept Jesus Christ, you are changing directions and going the opposite way for the rest of your life. You're committing your life to Him. Now, all who want to receive Jesus Christ as your Lord and Savior, please stand," and, again, all ten thousand people in that auditorium leaped to their feet.

You could have put a child on a stool to give that appeal and they would have come. They came forward, weeping. They were starving for the truth. I've never seen anything like it before or since.

One of the next places we went to was the city of Alexandrov, located on the River Seraya, north of Moscow. We were told that the gospel had not been preached openly in that city for more than six hundred years. There was, however, a little underground church where the gospel was still being preached. When we arrived, we met two of the most precious older women I have ever known. Their names were Nina and Vera. They had come to the Lord when they were girls—aged fourteen and sixteen at the time—and they had a small church in their home. The house was very simple, with a dirt floor, and their church consisted of eleven women who had been praying their entire lives for God to bring the gospel back to Russia.

In the beginning, they said, they had to meet outdoors in the woods because it was against the law to have a Bible or to preach the gospel under communist law. Their grandfather had been the pastor of an underground church years earlier—at one time, they told us, there had been many of these secret churches. But to be safe they would meet in the woods at night, and when those two old ladies told me how their grandfather had made a hole in the ice in the river for them to be baptized, it brought tears to my eyes.

Many of their family members had suffered and died for the faith. They told me of the price they had paid over the years, and what it had cost them to profess Christ in those difficult times. Their brothers were killed, and many had been persecuted and imprisoned for refusing to deny their beliefs. Now, suddenly, the gospel was open and available to them for the first time in their lives.

There I was, a businessman from America, sitting in their humble home, and the interpreter said they wanted me to minister to them. I thought, "What can I possibly say to minister to these women?" So I said, "You should be ministering to me." But they insisted that I speak to them from the scriptures, and I have to say, I've never felt so inadequate as I did at that moment. But the grace of God allowed me to encourage them, to minister to them, and to bless them that day.

We went to the opera house that evening, and as we went in I could feel the presence of demonic forces—they were very strong all around us. The spiritual warfare was so strong that I could hardly keep a thought in my head. It was the most difficult time I've ever had ministering in my life. Yet, the people hung on every word. When revival comes to a people, they may not know who God is but they're hungry for the Word of truth. And even when you stumble, it doesn't matter, because they're not interested in you, they're interested in how they can get to know God.

So, again, I shared a simple message: I said, "God loves you." And I could see it begin to break through in their hearts. At first they reacted with anger, not because of my message, but because of what it meant. They had been lied to and told there was no God for all those years, and suddenly they realized that, yes, there is a God. They resented the government for lying to them, but then there was weeping and a deep sense of conviction. When they were given an opportunity to accept Christ as Lord and Savior, they jumped up out of their seats, just as all the Russian audiences had done. They were so excited to know that God loves them and wants to forgive them.

It was bitter cold, and there was little or no heat in the building. Many of them were wearing five or six layers of clothing to keep warm. When they came forward during the invitation, my wife said they were like little birds waiting for someone to feed them. It was one of the most humbling experiences of my life, and when we got back to the hotel that night I was weeping so hard that I couldn't speak. I told Cookie that God was using the Russian people to break my heart.

In America we tend to take the gospel for granted, and as a result our faith is often so pale. Many people in this country are so numb to the gospel that they reject it without thinking. But the people we ministered to in Russia and Eastern Europe who had been denied the truth of God's Word their entire lives yearned to hear the truth; and when they realized they could actually have a relationship with God, they reached out for it with all their heart and soul.

When we would give them a Bible, they would start reading it instantly. They didn't wait until they got home. They wanted it right then. During that week we sent teams of pastors, teachers, and business leaders out to speak to the people about Jesus, and when they came back they were like the disciples that Jesus sent to preach in the villages in the New Testament (Luke 10:1–24). They were praising the Lord, overwhelmed by the reception they had received, and almost unable to comprehend the way the Spirit had worked through them. But everyone had the same testimony.

"Everybody came to Christ," they said. "They were so hungry for the gospel. We could barely get the message out before they responded." And it was that way all across Russia.

The most memorable disappointment of that trip, however, came when I had gone to preach in one of the small villages up in the Ural Mountains. I stayed with a small family who told me they lived on potatoes, cheese, and tomatoes. They couldn't remember ever eating a piece of beef. But the day after I had preached in that village, they took me to the local bazaar, which was like a small flea market in the middle of town. There were vendors at all these little tables selling their goods—embroidery, wood carvings, pottery, and all sorts of things they had made by hand—but right down the center of the aisle were slot machines, lined up one after the other. And every slot machine had a picture of Mt. Rushmore and the four American presidents, and said "The American Dream." How sad to think that this was their image of America.

The hardest part of preaching the gospel in Russia was that many of them believed that Jesus is an American god. They didn't think of Him as a god for the world or for Russia. And one of the first things we had to overcome was this idea that Jesus was only for Americans. So I assured them that the gospel of Jesus Christ was being preached in Russia long before there was ever a place called America. Jesus belonged to Russia long before the explorers discovered the New World. He is a God for all peoples and all nations. He is the God of the universe. This was something they could understand, and they were glad to hear it.

When we went into Moscow on a subsequent trip, we brought several teams together and they were all spread out to several cities and towns in the region. I was going to be planting three churches at that time, so I would be preaching at eleven o'clock in one church, at three o'clock in the afternoon in another church, and then at seven o'clock in the evening at the third one. The Russian pastors who were going to become the pastors at each of those churches would be with us during the service.

I preached for three successive days, and on the third day I would introduce the pastor, telling the people that this man would be there to minister the gospel and to shepherd the congregation. "His job," I said, "is to pray with you, to bless you, to marry your young people, to baptize new believers, and to teach you about Jesus." They had never had anyone to care for them that way. The building we were meeting in would be their new church, and when they returned each Sunday they would hear the gospel in that place. So, instantly, there were hundreds—and in some cases thousands—of people who belonged to each of those congregations.

Fortunately, the people understood that the freedom they were experiencing at that time might not last forever, so we established hundreds of house churches as well. Since that time, the government has shut down almost all of the seven hundred churches we helped organize. The government has been putting pressure on churches all across Russia, but the house churches are still thriving and growing. At last count there were more than ten thousand house churches in that country.

On another memorable occasion Cookie went with me to St. Petersburg where I would also be preaching three services each day for several days. After the third or fourth day, the pastor told me, "Rev. Jones, the congregation wants to meet your wife." Now, Cookie is wonderful with people one-on-one, but she doesn't like being in front of large groups. But I told her, "The people want to meet you, Cookie, so you need to stand up and give them a greeting. They just want you to speak to them and say a few words at the service tomorrow. That's all." After a little persuading, she reluctantly agreed to do that.

In the meantime, the pastor said, "Rev. Jones, you've been preaching every service. Let us preach tonight and you and your wife can take the night off and rest." I said that would be wonderful, so Cookie and I decided to sit in the back of the church. I said I would listen and Cookie wanted to take some photographs. It was very cold in those churches, and our feet would get so cold that we decided to wear our long underwear. I wore mine under my suit, but since Cookie was wearing a long dress like most of the Russian women, she decided she would wear hers—which were covered with red, yellow, and blue flowers—and pull the legs up to her knees so they wouldn't show.

When we got to the church we took our seats in the back, but after a few minutes I heard the pastor saying, "Brother Dennis and Cookie Jones." When we heard that, Cookie said, "What are they doing, Dennis?"

I said, "It sounds like we're on." Everyone started applauding so I grabbed Cookie's hand and we started toward the front, but as we were going up the steps her long underwear started sliding down her legs, and eventually came all the way down to her ankles. Cookie immediately started pulling my arm, holding me back. She said, "Dennis, I can't go up there! My underwear has slipped down!"

But there were hundreds of people waiting for us to go up on stage, so I said, "Cookie, in five minutes I'm going to minister to these people. I don't have a message and I really don't care about your underwear right now. It's going to be alright, so please come on!" As we walked up the steps to the platform, some of the people in the front rows could see those flowers, and they chuckled and smiled. They knew we were cold. They were cold too, but they were used to it. So as we stepped onto the stage, I took the microphone and said, "Before we share with you from the Word of God tonight, I want you to meet the love of my life. This is my wife, Cookie."

They gave Cookie a warm round of applause and at that point she took the microphone and shared the most wonderful greeting. She said it was such an honor to be there. She said she had been praying for them for so long, and to be able to stand there and see them face-to-face, to see the love of God in their faces, was the greatest honor and privilege she could imagine. They gave her a standing ovation, and after that nobody was the least concerned that the legs of Cookie's flowered long johns were now visible for all the world to see.

Chapter Seven

THE WORLD IS OUR PULPIT

THE MISSION TO Russia was an eye-opening experience for me, but the church in China is experiencing incredible spiritual growth today, just as the great missionary, Hudson Taylor, prophesied more than a century ago. Revival and an awakening to the gospel is taking place there on an even greater scale than anything we saw in Russia. We were told that as many as fifteen to twenty thousand people were coming to faith in Jesus Christ every day. I have since heard reports that the actual numbers may be more than double that—as many as a half-million new believers every month. Having the opportunity to go and minister to those giants of the faith was one of the greatest privileges of my life.

When our ministry learned of the needs over there, we knew we had to go. We made arrangements to meet with some of the leaders of the house churches in a remote area of China. When we flew into Beijing in the summer of 2006, we were concerned that we would be under surveillance most of the time, so we decided to go in two teams. One team would remain in the city, highly visible, visiting the churches in the capital city and learning more about what was happening there. In the meantime, my partner and I would leave quietly, and we would be taken to another location far from the city to find out what was really happening in the underground churches.

Not surprisingly, we were delayed at the airport for several hours. We were checked and double-checked, from one end to the other, but we eventually made it out with those that had been sent for us, and that was the beginning of one of the most incredible adventures of my life. We were taken first to another large city in Hunan Province. Then after a day or so we were taken to a safe house in the countryside where we met some of the leaders of the local churches.

We were told that a group of secret believers had a restaurant where we could meet and encourage some of the pastors and teachers who went out to evangelize in villages and towns all over the country. While we were there, however, our hosts discovered that someone had seen what was happening through the windows, and they had called the police. The restaurant was busted and several of the brothers were taken to jail and, in many cases, mistreated. Fortunately, my partner and I got out just in time, but some of the others weren't so fortunate.

They told us that one way of avoiding detection they often used was to take groups of itinerant preachers on public transportation, driving all over the city in plain sight, while they trained those young pastors how to take the gospel to the people. They were hiding in plain sight, but even that wasn't always foolproof. Even in some of the smallest cities there were eavesdropping devices in the rooms, so many of our meetings had to take place outdoors where no one could listen in on our conversations.

Then one day we were told that a car was coming to pick us up. The car would come at night and drive us for several hours to a safe house much further away, in an undisclosed area. When the driver arrived, he told us to keep low and out of sight as he was leaving the city. Then he drove most of the night, to the place where we made contact with the leaders of the churches.

I will never forget the sight when they opened the gates of the compound and we went inside. There were high concrete walls all around the courtyard, and over on one side was a kitchen where all the cooking was done. They were using huge clay pots that were hundreds of years old. There was no running water, no toilets, and very little in the way of conveniences. It was, without a doubt, the most primitive place I've ever been in my life.

It was late at night when we arrived so they wanted to feed us. From experience, I've always been careful of eating local foods. I would never want to show disrespect for my hosts, but the change of diet and the differences in the water and sanitary conditions in those remote places can be very dangerous for a westerner, so I was very selective in what I ate. Basically, I stayed away from anything that hadn't been boiled in water. My partner, however, was much more gracious, and he ate what he was served.

By morning he came down with a severe case of diarrhea. He began vomiting, and over the next few days he was so ill we weren't at all sure he would survive. He was so sick, I had to carry him to the latrine area so he could go to the bathroom. He couldn't even stand up on his own. But we all prayed for him and God was gracious. He was still weak for several days, but he recovered enough for us to continue the journey, ministering to the people and being ministered to by them.

When they cooked for us, we would eat the fresh-baked bread, which was wonderful. And even though I stayed away from regular meals, I didn't go hungry. Whenever I travel, Cookie always wants to put little snacks into my luggage. Most of the time I tell her I don't need them, but that doesn't stop her. She puts little love notes in my socks, my Bible, or my briefcase, and on this trip she slipped in several packets of crackers and some of those little packets of tuna in foil envelopes. I was surprised to find them in my luggage, but I thank God for that. It was a blessing, and that's how I was able to go for a full week without eating the indigenous food.

The men who worked at the compound had cut down a tree to make beds for us. These beds were simply slats with a blanket stretched across them. They were rough, but they were the best they had. The men slept on the ground, head to toe, row after row, while we slept in a little room with a single light bulb overhead. There were cobwebs everywhere. The next morning we woke up at five o'clock to the sound of praise and worship. When we walked into the room, we joined them in singing, and then they went into a time of prayer for more than an hour and a half, fervently praying for China, for America, and for the rest of the world. This was serious prayer, and the Spirit of God just filled that place.

Many of the men had scars where they had been cut, burned, and tortured for their faith. Some of them were missing parts of their ears or fingers, or there were scars where their noses had been split open. It was incredible what they had suffered, and I felt I had never been so privileged in my life to be able to stand before them. It came to my mind that what's happening in China today is very much like what happened in Jerusalem in the Book of Acts. It is such a powerful and miraculous time.

Here we were, Americans, coming from a life of luxury—men who had enjoyed the best our country has to offer—finding ourselves in that place with all those humble men that I would have to call giants of the faith, and they were looking to us to instruct them. One thing that became real to me at that time was how rich we are in this country, not only in physical wealth and opportunity, but with freedom of worship, and the riches of the kingdom of God that have been lavished upon us for our entire history.

When you consider what the church in America has been given and compare that to the constant struggles and the life-and-death dilemmas of believers in places like China, it's just overwhelming. We ought to be on our faces before God, thanking Him for the blessings we enjoy in this country; but we ought to be praying fervently for all those who are struggling, suffering, and dying for the cause of Christ in remote places all around the world.

Whenever I think of that, I also think of the scandals that have happened in the church in this country: things like the "shepherding movement" of a few years ago, for example, that turned so many people away from the church forever. It started off with some of the best Bible teaching that has ever been available to the church. I remember times when we would think nothing of driving a hundred miles or more for a good Bible study. Sadly, that's no longer the case. Most of our American Christians can't even make time for a Wednesday night Bible study unless the church promises to feed them.

But think of all the wealth that God has lavished on the church in America, and we take it all for granted. When you encounter people who have nothing—not even Bibles—but they cherish every Word of Scripture and literally risk their lives to learn more about Jesus and the gospel, it really changes your perspective. In many places in China there aren't enough Bibles to go around, so they take them apart, page-by-page, and pass single pages around among themselves. After a few days they trade pages, and they devour every word, one page at a time, until they eventually have access to the entire Bible. Many of these people have memorized entire books of the Bible that way, one page at a time. And to think that here in America, and in other so-called Christian countries, we have Bibles sitting around on the shelves gathering dust.

Thinking about all these things, I was struck by the wealth that God had given us here in America. Standing before those brave men in the wilderness, with the privilege of teaching them the Word of God, showing them how to establish their churches and how to build an infrastructure of support, was the most unbelievable privilege. But I thank God that he had given me the opportunity to use the knowledge I had gained in the business world to minister to those courageous leaders. It was a challenge, but it was also a tremendous honor.

My companion and I had the chance to give them instruction and standard Bible teaching on the Holy Spirit, the doctrine of healing, and other essentials of Christian theology that we've grown up with in this country. Most of those men had never heard the teaching we were giving them, but they drank in every word and copied down everything we said with their notepads and pencils. The second night we were there I was teaching them about faith giving. I'm sorry to say, the American church has taken it upon themselves not to teach Christians in many of these Third World countries about the doctrine of giving. Because they're poor, they think, "How can we expect them to give part of their earnings to the church?" But by withholding this essential doctrine of the faith, I believe we've been robbing them of the blessings and promises that God has for those who give.

The Old Testament prophets spell it out for us. Malachi 3:10, in particular, spells out in detail the promise of blessing that overflows into our lives when we honor God with our tithes and offerings. By not teaching this doctrine, we have been depriving believers in these remote places from experiencing the supernatural hand of God, bringing financial and spiritual blessings upon them, into their lives, their ministry, and their churches.

As I prayed about this one night, the Lord spoke a simple thing to me. The church in China—just like the church in Africa, Russia, Haiti, and all the places where I've ministered—has always looked to America and the West for financial support. But the Lord showed me something very simple that night. Here was a church of more than fifty million people, scattered all across China. If they understood the concept of giving, even if they gave less than 10 percent of their earnings to the church, it could revolutionize what they're doing.

At that time, I was told, the average income for Chinese workers was twenty to twenty-five dollars a month. Even if they could only tithe the equivalent of a dollar a year, that would give the church more than fifty million dollars each year, making them one of the wealthiest churches in the world. And they didn't even realize it because they had never been taught the doctrine of giving.

So we called the leaders into that little room and shared this idea with them, and it made me think of the kinds of meetings the apostles must have had when the gospel was first being preached in the first century. Here we were in a dimly lit room, in a place that was so remote that the authorities would never think to go there, and we shared with them that God had laid it on our hearts to teach them about the principles of giving. We said, "You've been deprived of one of the most foundational truths of the faith. It is a doctrine that will make it possible for believers to give to the work of the church so it can expand, grow, and fulfill your vision for the church in China."

"Up till now," we said, "you've looked to believers in America and other nations to provide you with the financial support you need. But the day will come when that will no longer be possible, and you will not be able to depend on America. You need to learn to be dependent upon God. Jesus said He would supply all your needs according to His riches in glory, and God wants to prove Himself to you. He wants to prove to you that He will give you everything you need to accomplish the things He has put on your heart to do."

They had already paid such an incredible price for their faith, but they had never been taught about the blessings of Malachi 3:10–11. So I read it aloud: "Bring all the tithes into the storehouse, that there may be food in My house, and try Me now in this," says the Lord of hosts, "if I will not open for you the windows of heaven and pour out for you such blessing that there will not be room enough to receive it. And I will rebuke the devourer for your sakes, so that he will not destroy the fruit of your ground, nor shall the vine fail to bear fruit for you in the field" says the Lord of hosts.

Then I said, "Do you realize that a tithe of one dollar a year from each of these faithful believers would give the church such a vast sum of money you would be able to take care of all your needs without needing to depend on the western churches?" The doctrine of giving is the door to an awesome blessing, but they didn't know anything about it. Because of a false sense of compassion, they had never been taught this essential truth. So I shared what God had shown me, and what it would mean if each household could give just a dollar a year. Even if they gave only half of that, I said, fifty cents a year, which would provide $26 million a year.

I said, "These are beliefs that many of you have gone to prison for, and that some have given their lives for. But now God wants to provide what you need, to prove to you that He can supply everything you need to accomplish this work."

There is such an important lesson in this. If the church in China continues growing at the present rate, and if believers prosper to the point that they can give as much as one dollar a month, that could mean as much as $600 million per year going to the work of evangelism in China. Without a doubt, the Chinese church would be the wealthiest church in the world.

～

It is obvious that God's vision for China is huge, and the elders and leaders of the church in that country are so eager to grow. They are willing to endure every kind of threat and humiliation to serve Him faithfully. But what struck me most forcefully was learning that their goal is not simply to evangelize China. They fully intend to spread the gospel all the way to Jerusalem and around the world. And I believe they will do it.

As a result, God is blessing China. The church in China is growing beyond anything we can imagine. But it's important to understand that there are actually two churches in China today. One is the church the communist leaders allow the West to see. That church is open to the public, and believers there can worship freely. I've been to the authorized church in Beijing. I'm glad it's there, and I'm glad it's open to the public. But the kind of freedom we enjoy in the West is still very much controlled by the authorities. The true church, however, the church that is growing, prospering, and overflowing with signs and wonders, is the underground church, and that church, to this day, is under intense persecution. The same things that Jesus did when He was walking the earth, those things are happening in China today. But that church has to remain underground for the time being. It's not allowed to come to the surface, but it is powerful and radical, and they don't hold back on any of the gospel.

During our stay there, my partners and I were able to establish a warm and trusting relationship with the five Chinese uncles—that's what they call the senior leaders of the house churches. Those five uncles oversee fifty-two million Chinese Christians, all part of the underground church movement. Under them are the 120 regional leaders who oversee ten thousand individual church leaders. Anyone who doubts the intensity of the persecution of the believers over there needs to see the conditions the members of those churches are forced to endure, and their leaders often suffer the brunt of it.

You may hear people talking about how the church is growing and thriving in China, and how they're building churches in all the major cities, but that's not the whole story. We need to remember that the church that is above ground for the rest of the world to see is under strict control by the communist government. Members have to register as Christians, and every Bible is counted and registered with the state. Anyone who tries to avoid those controls will be subjected to the government's will. But outside the cities, and in homes and restaurants and secret places all over China, the true church is alive and thriving, growing bolder and stronger every day.

Before returning to the capital, my partner and I were taken to the far north of China, close to the border with North Korea, where we learned about a whole new level of persecution. We were told that thousands of Chinese people attempt to cross the Tumen River into North Korea each year. Many Chinese Christians go there with Bibles and food to help their families and those persecuted people on the other side of the border. But if the military guards catch them, they send them back. And if they're caught with Bibles, the soldiers shoot them in the head and throw them in the river. Thousands of people die that way every year, but we never hear a word about that in this country.

Over the years I have had the privilege of taking part in missions outreaches in many places, but experiences like those in China, Russia, and West Africa changed the way I think about church growth and revival. Not just because of the differences in lifestyles I observed, but because of the way God reaches out to those who seek him. Miracles and demonstrations of His love are happening in all these places, and I've been the beneficiary of those blessings as well. An experience that my friend, Howard Foltz, and I had in Africa shows how remarkable, and unexpected, those blessings can be.

On this occasion, we were on our way back home to America after a week of ministry and teaching in Nigeria. Howard was scheduled to fly out one day and I was to follow him the next. As it turned out, I completed my work a day early so I decided I would try to get out on the same flight. That meant I would need to get down to the airport as quickly as possible to make arrangements for the flight that would depart later that evening.

Now, there are a lot of Christians in Nigeria, but it can be a very dangerous place. There are soldiers with rifles and machine guns all around the airport at Lagos—it's an intimidating place. And everywhere you go, there are officials, policemen, and government employees at checkpoints trying to extort more money out of you. They're everywhere. So when I got to the airport, I went upstairs to try to get a ticket, and they told me the flight was over-sold. It always is, and there were no tickets available. But they said I could go back downstairs and see if the gate attendant would put me on the waiting list. So that's what I did.

When I spoke to the agent downstairs, he said the waiting list was already full. He might be able to book me part way, he said, but not all the way back to New York. By this time the Nigerian Christian brothers who brought me to the airport were getting angry, but I said, "Please, don't worry, and don't be upset. Either God will put me on the flight or He won't. Either way," I said, "I have a seat on the flight to New York tomorrow night. So we don't need to worry about it."

Actually, I was trying to live up to what I had been teaching them, which is not always easy. I wanted to set a good example and help these brothers to trust in the Lord's guidance. When we got back upstairs, I spoke to the man at the counter and he told me they could get me to London but there were no open seats for the flight to New York. According to the rules, he said, he couldn't put me on the flight, but he called down to the agent I had spoken to earlier and said, "Mr. Jones has convinced me that if we can get him to London, God will make a way for him to get back to America. So please see if you can get him on the flight to London tonight." At that point I went back to the hotel to finish my packing.

Howard and I arrived at the airport around nine o'clock that evening; the flight was scheduled to leave at 11:30 p.m., as it did every other night. Unless you've been to a country like Nigeria, I doubt you've ever seen anything like it.

It was pandemonium and utter chaos as far as the eye could see. There were people yelling and fighting; guards were waving their weapons and threatening the crowds, trying to push people back from the doors to the terminal.

With the help of our Nigerian friends, we made our way through the crowds. When we got to the gate, Howard presented his ticket and they said everything was fine. His bags were checked through, and he would be able to board and take his seat as soon as the flight was ready to go. When I showed the attendant my ticket, he said, "You'll have to wait. There are no seats." Once again he said, "We're over-booked. This flight is over-sold, and we have no tickets."

I just smiled and said, "Thank you." Then I went over to stand with Howard. But when I did, another gate attendant who had been standing at the counter caught my eye and waved for me to come over. When I did, he said, "Are you on this flight?"

I said, "No," and told him my situation, that I hadn't been able to get a ticket through to New York.

So he said, "Would you like to be on this flight?"

And I said, "Yes, very much. My friend is on the flight, and I'd like to go with him."

He said, "OK, you stand right there." He pointed to a spot near the boarding ramp.

It was getting later and later, and everybody was getting edgy. Some passengers were beginning to board the plane and others were milling around, not quite sure what was happening. I could see that Howard was getting a little tired and wanted to get on board. I've never taken a pastor or minister to anyplace, other than Nigeria, where they were afraid they wouldn't get out. None of us knew if we were getting out or not, but there were groups of people behind the counter trying to bribe the gate attendant to get a seat on the plane. Eventually, everyone with a ticket was told to get on board, and the boarding area cleared out quickly. There was one man and one woman at the counter, still yelling at each other, but I just stood there quietly in the middle of the room.

Finally, the agent who had told me where to stand looked over and waved for me to come up to the gate. When I got there he said, "Do you have any luggage?" I said yes and showed him my bag. He said, "OK, I'll take care of it." So he took my bag, handed me a ticket, and said, "You're all set."

When I approached the boarding ramp, I checked my ticket and was surprised to see that it was a first-class seat. Then, just as I was arriving at the final gate to the plane, the man who gave me the ticket came running up to me and asked, "Mr. Jones, is your bag on board the plane?"

"I don't know," I said. "Someone took it."

So he said, "Come with me," and we walked back downstairs and outside to the tarmac, and I saw that my bag was not on board. I pointed it out to him, and he physically put the bag in the cargo hold himself.

At that point, he walked me back upstairs again and said, "Where's your friend?"

I said, "He's already on board."

Hearing that, he told a young man to go on the plane and get Howard. That was a surprise to both of us, but when they brought Howard back off the plane, I said, "Please give him the seat in first class. I would like for my friend to have that seat."

But the agent said, "Oh, no, no," and he said something to the same young man, who then ran back onto the plane and did something. When he came back, the young man said it was all taken care of, and then he handed both Howard and me our tickets and told us to go aboard and take our seats in first class.

I had prayed about it, and I had already decided I wasn't going to be upset, regardless what happened. But when I realized we had been given first class seats all the way from Lagos to London, and then on to New York, I was stunned and amazed. But as soon as I got to my seat, I realized I had to speak to that gate attendant one more time. So I ran back up the gangplank and caught him as he was walking down the terminal, and I said, "Please, sir. You've got to tell me. Why did you go to all this trouble to show me this great kindness?"

Then, with a gentle smile, he looked at me and said, "God told me to."

His words brought tears to my eyes as I realized that, once again, I had experienced the unmerited favor of God. But I also knew that God was teaching me this lesson. Depending on how we respond to the circumstances of life will determine our success or failure. I had never seen that man before, but God spoke to him and, bless his heart, he did exactly as he was asked.

Chapter Eight

THE MEANING OF SUCCESS

AFTER MY BUSINESS experience with Dr. Chambers, Cookie and I went through a major period of transition, waiting to see clearly the direction we would be going. When I first started in the hair-transplantation business, I didn't know anything about the medical end of the business. But by the time Chambers and I parted company I knew it pretty well. Through all the development and marketing experience I had gained in the field, I felt like I understood it about as well as anyone. Over the past few years I had developed patents and techniques that helped to revolutionize the industry.

After considering all the options, we decided to start a new company named the Professional Hair Institute (PHI), and we opened our first medical hair transplant center in Virginia Beach. One of the first things I did was to get in contact with an orthopedic surgeon in the area who had told me he wanted to get into the hair transplant business with us if there was ever an opportunity. We told him what we had in mind, and once he was trained in the procedure, we brought him into the business as a partner. From the first day we opened the doors, the Lord really began to bless us.

Over the next thirteen months we opened eleven transplant centers. We were doing business in twelve states, and our affiliates included people with whom I'd had relationships going back to my hairstyling days. When they heard I was going into the medical hair transplant business, they said they wanted to get in it with me. So we formed a company unlike anything we'd ever seen. The Lord gave us the concept. It was a type of revenue sharing that, to my knowledge, had never been done before.

When we opened the centers, we worked with our affiliates in setting up all the furniture and equipment, including all the related medical equipment, and we provided all the advertising, marketing, and everything else necessary to make the business a success. Then we brought the physicians, nurses, and support staff on board and provided them with the training they needed. It was very successful, and before long many of these men and women became very wealthy. Every one of our centers was successful, and everyone was prospering.

The profit-sharing arrangement we had created was working very well, but right at the pinnacle of our success, some of the physicians got together and decided they wanted a higher percentage of the profits for themselves. According to the laws that regulate the medical profession, only physicians can have patients. It is illegal, of course, to practice medicine without a license, and only licensed physicians can have patients who pay for their services. So some of the doctors who were working with us made this an issue, and threatened to stop everything if they didn't get a bigger share of the profits.

According to our contract, we owned the business. From our headquarters in Virginia Beach, we managed all the staffing, equipment, marketing, advertising, legal, and support functions. We had signed agreements with the doctors who performed the procedures, but since only physicians can have patients, the men and women who came to our centers were legally clients of the physicians.

When this all came to a head, I began to understand how greed really works. I came to the conclusion that there's a greed button that kicks in at around $250 thousand. Most people's thinking begins to change when their personal income hits that level. When they reached that point, some of the physicians wanted not only what they had, but what we had as well, and when that happened, the entire structure of the corporation was suddenly in jeopardy. Their demands affected all the operational procedures we'd put in place, including staffing, overhead costs, marketing, and all the related issues, and that made it impossible to run the business the way it had been designed.

I made it clear to the doctors that if they changed the revenue plan we had worked out, then PHI could no longer exist, because there had to be enough revenue in the system for us to develop all the advertising and marketing materials, the thirty- and sixty-minute infomercials, the full-color brochures, and all the related materials we were providing to the affiliates. But they didn't care about that, and they gave us an ultimatum. Either we increased the percentage of revenues going to the doctors, or they would pull the plug, shut down the existing centers, and open their own competing businesses. At that point I knew it was the beginning of the end.

After everyone had enjoyed six years of amazing success in the new business, we had come to another major transition. There were a lot of lessons to be learned through that experience that really showed me how the Lord works, and how faithful He is. It was one more example of the importance of trusting God with each step in our lives, and then doing the right thing.

The process we went through was involved, painful, and confusing at times; but when we saw how the dots were connected, Cookie and I really saw the hand of God at work. When we're in the middle of a transition, it's often difficult to see how what your doing has anything to do with where you thought you were going. And that's when your faith is tested and you just have to put the full weight of your faith upon Him.

One day when Cookie and I were working in the conference room at our corporate offices, I told her I felt the Lord was moving us in a new direction and that PHI was about to come to an end. I was sure the Lord was leading us to something else, but at that point I didn't know what it was. So we committed all this to prayer and continued to work while we waited on the Lord. Then one afternoon a few weeks later my secretary came around to my office and told me there was a gentleman at the front desk who said he had a two o'clock appointment with me.

She handed me his business card, which said his name was Horace Furumoto. I told her I didn't know the man and, so far as I knew, I didn't have a two o'clock appointment with anyone. But when she told me he insisted that he had scheduled an appointment, I said, "In that case, tell him I'll be with him in just a few minutes."

I went out and introduced myself to this very distinguished seventy-year-old Japanese-American gentleman and invited him to come back to the conference room. When we were seated we simply chatted for a few minutes and got to know each other. Along the way I learned that Horace Furumoto was one of the foremost developers of surgical laser technology. He had invented the dye laser back in 1959, which was interesting to me because it was the same year that my former partner, Dr. Chambers, had started doing transplants.

Dr. Furumoto, who was involved in nuclear weapons research during the war and spent several years after that at NASA, held 283 patents on laser technologies, and started a company called Candela, which is one of the top cosmetic laser companies in the world. But after a management shakeup at Candela, he started a new company called Cynosure, and along the way developed the leading technology for laser hair removal in the world. Early on he had developed use of the ruby lens for lasers, then later came up with the alexandrite laser, which was ideal for laser hair removal.

Dr. Furumoto told me he had developed the technology for photo-thermolysis, sometimes called photoepilation, to remove unwanted hair using a laser. He also told me that he owned a laser manufacturing company but was considering moving his focus into a new area. And then he asked me what I would do in his situation. Without hesitation I laid out a basic business plan, just off the top of my head. I said these new technologies would only be good for so long. This is a field in which technology changes rapidly, and when it does, any entrepreneur in the field will find himself with a smaller and smaller share of the market. The answer, I suggested, would be to find a way to take the technology directly to the consumer.

After we had talked like that for forty-five minutes or so, I said, "By the way, Horace. Why are you here?"

"I know that people in the industry are trying to find ways to go around your patent," he said, "and I'm here to do the honorable thing. I'm here to ask you to sell me a license to use your patent."

That was certainly puzzling. I had a number of patents at the time, but none of them was directly related to what we had been talking about. So I said, "With all due respect, Sir, who do you think you're talking with?"

He said, "Mr. Mehl."

I said, "I'm sorry, but my name is Dennis Jones." As soon as the words left my mouth I could see that he was terribly embarrassed. He was a distinguished older gentleman from a Japanese family and a culture that is generally reserved and polite, and he was clearly shocked to find out that I wasn't the person he thought I was. As it turned out, Thomas Mehl, the man he thought he was talking to, was in business in Gainesville, Florida. So Dr. Furumoto wasn't even in the right state.

I don't know how he got to my office, but apparently he had been referred by someone who had come across some of our literature and thought I was Thomas Mehl. So after apologies were given all around, he left. I had spent a fascinating hour or so with a very wise and knowledgeable man, but I didn't understand any of it at the time. Meanwhile, it was becoming increasingly clear that things weren't improving with our business.

A couple of months after that meeting, I was working at home one day. Cookie and I were both feeling very discontent with the business, and we were having no end of troubles. One way to know you are discontent is that you start becoming critical of others. You find fault with your employees, your customers, your suppliers, and even yourself. You start getting critical of everything, which is the sign of a discontented spirit. When we saw what was happening, Cookie and I agreed that we didn't like living that way, so we started praying about it.

I was sitting at my desk one afternoon. I had been complaining. Cookie was complaining. The employees were complaining about how the business was going—or perhaps I should say *wasn't* going—and I was feeling about as unhappy as I've ever been. But I was sitting there in my leather desk chair, leaning my head back, and I prayed silently, "Lord, what do you want me to do?"

No sooner had I spoken the words than the Lord opened my eyes, and He gave me an open vision. What I saw in that vision changed my life. He gave me a glimpse of what heaven was like before He created man—before he created heaven and earth or anything we know. As this incredible scene played out in my head, I saw millions of angels and heavenly beings all over the place, as far as the eye can see. And then the Lord had me focus on Lucifer. I saw Lucifer going from one angel to another, backbiting against Jesus, criticizing Him, being critical of everything, and sowing seeds of doubt, discord, and discontent.

The Lord was showing me that this was the origin of discontentment. What I saw was the first manifestation of the sin of discontent. See, Lucifer wasn't satisfied with his job; he wanted Jesus' job. Because he could not have it, and because of pride and the spirit of discontentment festering inside of him, he was going all around, creating chaos among the angels. I wasn't shown the part where he convinced a third of the angels of heaven to join him in rebellion against God, which we know about from Scripture, or how he was cast out with the fallen angels. But the Lord spoke to me this way.

He said, "Son, don't ever be discontent again. To be discontent with your present circumstances is to be discontent with Me, and is a sin against Me." That's what He said, and He revealed to me that there are three aspects to this sin. First, to be discontent with your present provision when the Bible says God will provide for our needs according to His riches in glory (Phil.

4:19) is to say that God has not and will not do as He promised, and He will not provide for our needs. That is a reproach to God.

Second, to be discontent with our present circumstances is to say that we are discontent with His grace. We're no longer walking in grace, acknowledging His grace, or in a position to receive grace when we have a discontented spirit. Third, and worst, when we're discontent, we're no longer acknowledging God's sovereignty over our life. We're no longer looking to God for direction, and we feel alone, separated and totally dependent upon ourselves. If you believe that God is in control of your life, then you also have to believe that He is allowing whatever takes place in your life to happen. Before you start complaining about your circumstances, you may need to make sure that your heart is in the right place to receive God's blessings. And you may need to make some changes. But if you're walking in His grace, how can you be discontent with what He has given you?

I now believe that one of the greatest sins we commit as Christians is allowing the spirit of discontentment to take control of our lives. As God showed me that day, the root of that sin goes all the way back before the creation to the first rebellion against the Creator. The Bible says that the root of every sin is pride, but I realize now that the root of pride may very well be the spirit of discontentment.

The apostle Paul said it this way: "Now godliness with contentment is great gain" (1 Tim. 6:6). If that's true, then godliness without contentment is of little or no gain. If we're not content, there can be no gain whatsoever in the eyes of God. But Paul also tells us he has found the key to living successfully. Now when I first read those words, I realized I really needed to pay attention to whatever the apostle was about to say. When the apostle Paul, who wrote thirteen books in the New Testament, says he has found the key to successful living, I want to know what he has to say.

He says, "I have learned in whatever state I am, to be content: I know how to be abased, and I know how to abound. Everywhere and in all things I have learned both to be full and to be hungry, both to abound and to suffer need." And then he adds this wonderful postscript, saying, "I can do all things through Christ who strengthens me" (Phil. 4:11–13).

The apostle Paul says that the key to success when times are hard is to be content. That's the key. Most of us are discontent most of the time. We're discontent with our position in life, with what we have, with what we don't have, with our job, our finances, our food, our spouses, or even our relationship with God. In every area of life it's so easy to fall into a pattern of discontentment. As long as we're discontent, we will never come under the grace of God or experience the fullness of what He has for us. Life will be a constant struggle, and we will never realize the fulfillment of our dreams and visions. God can't take us to the next level until we learn to be content with what we have and where we are.

As any sailor will tell you, when you're in the midst of a storm, you don't put up new sails. You pull in your sails, batten down the hatches, and ride it out. The wisdom of the world tells us to do something. Even if it's wrong, they say, do something. The famous line of the athletic shoe company says, "Just do it!" But that's not God's way. He says to wait. Or as the psalmist says it, "Wait on the Lord; be of good courage, and He shall strengthen your heart; wait, I say, on the Lord!" (Ps. 27:14).

Until we can see God's direction clearly, we shouldn't go. But the thing that's going to get us to the place where we can go and move us to the next phase of blessing and advancement in our life is coming to a place of contentment. Until we do that, God will never move you to a higher level. That would violate the principles of His Word. This applies to Christians and non-Christians alike. If you try to move ahead with a spirit of discontentment, you'll end up with a lot of false starts and false conclusions.

Some people become so unhappy with their job that they leap out of the frying pan into the fire, just to make a change. They get so angry they quit without any plan for where they'll go next. How absurd that is. For someone who is discontent with his job to quit that job without having another job lined up is just stupidity. And when they find themselves out of work, growing more and more desperate by the day, they have the nerve to say that God hasn't provided for them.

When I look back on the times in my life when the budget was really tight and I was struggling to get by, it was never God's fault. He is always ready to provide for us if He can get our undivided attention. When I counsel young couples going through tough times, it's amazing how often they complain about how bad things are when they've been spending every penny they make on their own amusements.

When I see that, I say, "Look what's happened. You don't have money to pay your bills now, but over the last twelve months what have you bought? Did you really need that new flat-screen TV? Did you need that new stereo? Did you need all those expensive new toys? God provided the money, but you used it wrongly. You haven't used it the way God wanted you to use it." More often than not, the root of their problem is a discontented spirit. They're always wanting more, more, more, and it's never enough. But I tell them, "Listen to the words of the apostle Paul who holds out the key, 'I have learned in whatever state I am, to be content.' And these words are equally powerful: 'godliness with contentment is great gain.'"

But back to my story. As I was sitting there in my leather chair on that stress-filled afternoon, God spoke to my heart with a message that said, in effect, "Dennis, why do you act as if you're out there on your own? You say you believe in Me, yet you're constantly discontent, thrashing about as if it was all up to you. You're not acknowledging My sovereignty in your life. You seem to think you're on your own. Haven't I been with you since the day you were born? Yet, you don't seem to recognize that I care for you."

As those words sank into my heart, I was humbled and embarrassed, because I knew it was true. I had been discontent and angry because everything seemed to be going wrong in my business. But as soon as I caught my breath, I walked down the hall to where Cookie was working and I said, "We need to talk." Then I closed the door and told her what the Lord had just shown me. We held hands and prayed, "Father, we repent for being discontent and for allowing a discontented spirit to control our lives. We ask you to please forgive us for our ingratitude and discontentment. We purpose not only to stay in this job and be faithful, but also to be content for the rest of our lives. And, Father, please forgive us for our ingratitude and discontentment."

We poured our hearts out, and almost immediately I could feel a change come over me. When God's people come face-to-face with their own disobedience and seek God's forgiveness, it's always a radical change. I've seen lives radically changed by that simple act of honest confession and repentance. This is especially true when it comes to marriage. When you're discontent with God, you can't be content with your spouse either. The relationship between a husband and wife is a model of the bond between Christ and the church, and when your heart is out of favor with God your marriage is bound to suffer.

Cookie and I opened our hearts to the Lord that day, and two days later I was at home reading the Bible, and something just popped out from the passage I was reading. As I thought about it, I felt the Lord speaking to me again. This time He said, "There is a place I want to take you, but you're not ready to go."

That surprised me and I said, "Father, that's not acceptable. Whatever it is in my life that's preventing you from taking me where you want me to go, show me what it is so I can take care of it."

What He showed me was that there was a deep root of discontentment in my heart that went all the way back to my childhood. Over the years, I had gone from having nothing to having plenty, but there were many hurts and disappointments along the way. I had come to a place where I felt I had to have more and more. But that day, as I was sitting there with the Word of God in my hands, I repented for all those emotions and asked for His forgiveness. And at that moment I felt a tremendous sense of release.

As I was sitting there, praying and meditating on what God had shown me, He said, "All right, it's time for you to go." Then He said, "I want you to call Sy Sperling at Hair Club for Men. He's going to buy your business."

Well, that was a huge surprise. I hadn't even thought about selling the business at that point. But I went to the office and told Cookie what had just happened, and we both knew this was going to be huge for us. I had been in the hair business since I was sixteen years old. Now, after all I had been through, God was saying that He was taking us into something new. Until we were content, He couldn't take us, but after we acknowledged the sin of discontentment and repented, we were ready for a new adventure.

Once that happened, I called Sy Sperling. I had spoken to him three or four years earlier about the video imaging system we had developed, but we hadn't spoken since that time. When I called at about 11:45 a.m., he said, "Dennis, this is unbelievable. In just over a half hour, at noon, my people are meeting with real estate people at the Kroger Center in Norfolk to talk about opening our new hair replacement center in the Tidewater area. It sounds like we need to get together."

Within seventy-two hours, and after being in the hair business for more than thirty years, we had a contract drawn up and signed, all the employees were taken care of and we had shaken hands on the deal. Just like that, in just three days time, we had turned over the keys to our operation to a new owner. It happened so fast it was almost unbelievable, but we knew that God had made all the arrangements, and He walked us right through that door.

When God said He was taking us to a new place, we didn't know where we were going or what we would be doing, but we were ready, and He took us right where He wanted us to be. At that point Cookie and I weren't sure what was next, so we decided to take a break, and because we're both avid golfers, we thought that would be a great time to go and play golf for a while. So that's what we did.

A couple of weeks after that, I got a phone call while I was out on the golf course at Hilton Head. I didn't recognize the number, but I answered it, and the guy on the other end said, "Is this Dennis Jones?" I said it was, and he said, "This is Tom Mehl. I understand that you're a Christian businessman, and you're doing missions work in Africa."

I said, "Yes, that's right."

He said, "I'd like to talk to you about how I can help you do that. Could you come see me? I'm in Gainesville, Florida."

I said, "Yes, Tom. I'd love to do that."

Tom Mehl, as I had discovered during my brief conversation with Horace Furumoto, was the man who owned the patent for laser hair removal. I hadn't realized it before, but he was a Spirit-filled Christian to whom God had given the idea of a system of hair removal. As it turned out, this was the patent for which Horace Furumoto had been trying to buy a license when he came to see me.

So I went down to meet with Tom Mehl at his office in Gainesville, and it was a very impressive facility with high-tech security and elegant furnishings. It was obvious these people were living large. My appointment was for 9:15 a.m., and I only waited a few minutes before his secretary took me back to Tom's office. He was a big man with a full beard and a full head of hair, as white as mine. When I went into his private office, there were chairs set up for five members of his team. There were three phones on his desk—red, white, and black—and when I came in he was on two of them.

As soon as I took my seat, the Lord spoke to me about Tom. It was a very clear message for him. So when Tom finished his call and reached across the desk to shake my hand, I said, "Tom Mehl, the Holy Spirit has a word for you." I went ahead and told him what the Lord had said to me, and it was a hard word that reached down and touched an area of his life that God wanted to address. When I finished, he told the five members of his entourage to leave the room.

Tom and I stayed there, and I ministered to him from 9:15 until 4:15 that afternoon when he drove me back to the airport. During that time I shared biblical principles of business with him, and it was clear that the Lord was working. God had so much for him. Tom really loved God, but in many ways he was serving Him on his own terms. There was a lot of conflict, and he had been abrasive to many people in the industry, but we talked about those things the entire day, and we never got around to the work in Africa.

When I got to the airport, I checked in at the gate and we took off a short time later. All this time I was thinking about the events of that day. But just as we were breaking through the clouds, the Lord spoke to me again, and He said, "Tom Mehl is going to ask you to come work with him, and I want you to go."

~

When I got home that evening, Cookie asked me how the day had gone and I told her all about the meeting, and I said, "The Lord told me that Tom is going to ask me to come to Florida and run his company." What I didn't know at the time was that his company had lost millions of dollars the previous year. They were bleeding four to five million dollars a quarter.

The strength of the business was that he owned a billion-dollar patent in surgical laser technology. In the fall of 1997 when this all happened, the laser hair-removal business worldwide was bringing in about a million dollars a year. Today it's an estimated $8.5 billion industry, so the business was about to explode. The real growth was just starting, but Mehl's company was spending at least a million dollars a month while generating less than ten thousand dollars a month in income. It appeared to me that some of the managers were more concerned with keeping the stock moving than in building the company.

Cookie and I just relaxed that weekend, but at nine o'clock on Monday morning the phone rang, and it was Tom Mehl. His wife's name was Cookie also, and he said, "I told Cookie about our meeting, and we prayed about it the whole weekend. I want to ask you to come back to Gainesville and do three things. First, I want you to come and mentor me in my Christian walk. Second, I want you to help me get my company functioning on solid biblical principles. And, third, I want you to come down and help run this company for me."

I already knew that call was coming. The Lord had given me advance warning. But I just said, "Tom, I'll pray about it. That would be a big move for us, so if you'll give me two weeks, my wife and I will pray about our decision and I'll get back to you."

So that's what we did. Cookie and I prayed about it. I went to meet with a pastor I trust, and after we prayed about it he said he thought Tom's offer was of God. I then went to see my friend Howard Foltz, and he counseled with us about it. Both of them confirmed that this was the right move. Tom's offer to come to Florida was what the Lord wanted for me at that time. So after Cookie and I listened to their counsel, we decided to go. That was the beginning of the Sona Corporation that Cookie and I would build, although we didn't know it at the time.

According to the terms of our agreement with Tom, I wouldn't have to sell our home in Virginia. He got an apartment for me in Gainesville. I flew down to Florida every Tuesday morning and returned home to Virginia late every Thursday evening. That was the time I had committed to it. In return, I had a substantial salary with comparable travel and expense allowances, plus a large share of corporate stock. When Tom showed me the actual condition of the company, I wasn't disturbed in the least. Obviously, it was in bad shape, and I realized immediately that there were many things in place that were bleeding the company dry.

Fortunately, I like solving problems, and this was something I thought I could do. But as I was flying down to Gainesville for the first time, planning to start work on Tuesday morning, I began to pray, and I said, "Lord, can I really do this? You told me You wanted me to accept Tom's offer, but I've never turned a public company around before. Do I have the experience? You know I don't have the education, and I've never studied formal accounting. Is this really going to work?"

I began to doubt myself. It was exciting to be launching a new stage of my career, but I wanted to be able to help this man and I needed to have the confidence that I could really do what he was asking me to do. The Lord spoke to me so gently, and He said, "Study Joseph's life." So I pulled my Bible out of my briefcase and started reading. What I discovered was something I had read many times before, but it had never meant so much to me as it did on that occasion.

Here was a boy, the apple of his father's eye, who had a dream in which he saw his brothers bowing down to him. Innocently enough, he told them about the dream, and they were immediately angry because he apparently thought he was better than they were. They reacted with jealousy and envy, which almost always leads to even greater sins—sometimes even murder. So they took Joseph and threw him into a pit and left him to die. When they saw a caravan coming along the road, they decided to make a little money by selling their brother into slavery.

So Joseph was taken into slavery for many years, but God was with him the whole time. He eventually got a good job as steward over a rich man's household. He had authority over other servants, and he was treated with respect. It was a really good job until his boss's wife accused him falsely of rape, and he was thrown into prison where he remained for fourteen long years.

Do you know what his next position was? Joseph went from being a prisoner to become the president and CEO of the entire known world. When I saw that I thought, "How in the world did he go from the dungeons of Egypt to the highest office in Pharaoh's palace?" Joseph didn't even have a seventh-grade education. He had no education at all. He spent most of his life in slavery or in prison, yet God promoted him to the most important position in all the land. So I said, "Lord, where did he get that ability?"

That's when the Lord revealed to me this simple truth: success or failure in every area of life will be determined by one thing, and that is by the decisions we make. The only way we can make the right decisions is to have the wisdom of God when we make them. Whether it's success in marriage, in business, in ministry, or whatever else we're doing, we cannot make wise decisions without having access to the wisdom of God. And God only gives wisdom, understanding, and knowledge to those who will truly seek Him and learn how to develop an intimate relationship with Him.

This was encouraging to me—just as it ought to be encouraging to everyone, regardless where they may be—because we all have the same access to the wisdom of God. The Bible says, "If any of you lacks wisdom, let him ask of God, who gives to all liberally and without reproach, and it will be given to him" (James 1:5). If we will make an honest effort to seek the Lord and come into an intimate relationship with Him, God will give us the wisdom to make the right decisions, and those decisions will promote us to the next level of our life. That's the real meaning of success. God does not measure success by our bank account; He measures success by the measure of Christ that He sees formed in you and me.

This is a message I've carried around the world—to Russia, China, Africa, Jamaica, Haiti, and everywhere else I've ministered—that no matter who you are or where you happen to be in your life at any given time, if you will seek the Lord and ask Him for wisdom, God will give you the wisdom, understanding, and knowledge you need to make the right decisions for your life. Those decisions will determine your circumstances, and the way you respond to your circumstances will ultimately determine your success or failure.

So I was encouraged and I realized that, so long as I looked to the Lord for counsel, I was qualified to do that or any other job He called me to do.

Chapter Nine

TRANSITION IS A JOURNEY

W HEN I TOOK on the challenge with Tom Mehl, the Lord gave me an idea of how to do something that had never been tried before in the laser hair removal world. It was a successful business model we had learned when we were in the hair transplant business. We owned all the lasers, so I decided the best way to build the business was to set up revenue-sharing agreements with our customers. So I developed and implemented our entire marketing and advertising program around it with radio and TV commercials and a series of thirty-minute infomercials. We had two packages, one for physicians to reach out to potential clients, and another inviting prospective medical practices to join the program.

What I was proposing was revolutionary. For anyone joining our network, we would provide the laser at no cost. At the time that was a $135 thousand piece of equipment that we would install in their facility, along with a service agreement, maintenance, laser lamps, and everything else they might need, along with complete advertising, marketing, and training. When the program was ramped up, I was giving seminars virtually every Saturday in major cities across the country. We would have as many as 120 doctors and nurses at a time going through these seminars. I had never done anything like it before, but after preaching to hundreds of thousands of men, women, and children in our evangelistic crusades, it was a piece of cake.

We reached out to physicians all over the country, telling them that laser hair removal was the emerging industry, and they could get into without a lot of upfront capital investment. The only financial requirement was to commit the money necessary to promote their own business each month, and they would pay us 50 percent of their revenue for the equipment and services we provided.

From that point, it was a revenue-sharing agreement. If the centers didn't make any money, they didn't owe us a cent. But whatever income they made at the end of the month, they would pay us 50 percent. From October 1997 to February 1998, when we participated in the American Academy of Dermatology Conference, we reduced expenses from $1.5 million a month to a little over $600 thousand a month, and took corporate income from roughly $10 thousand a month to over $400 thousand a month. At that point I knew we were becoming a viable business.

The second week I was there, Tom Mehl introduced me to his pastor and I started developing a close relationship with him. I also had the privilege of preaching and ministering on many Wednesday nights in his church. But Tom's company had been so top-heavy in employees, I had to let a lot of people go, and many of them were the same people I was ministering to at the church. Tom was a big openhearted guy and if anyone came to him and said they needed a job, he would find a place for them, whether he needed them or not. Once we cut the company down to size and got rid of this big financial drain, we were able to start turning the company around. It was one of the hardest things I've ever had to do in business, but it was necessary and it was my responsibility.

In my agreement with Tom I said I would come to Gainesville and do my best to serve him faithfully in all three of the areas he described in our first phone call. I would do everything required to turn the business around and, with the Lord's help, bring it back into a profitable position. But I also said that if at any point I found out that what the organization was doing was in opposition to the Word of God, and if they persisted in doing that thing after I'd shown them what the Word has to say, then I would have to leave the company. I was open and straightforward about that, and Tom agreed.

It wasn't long before our success was making headlines all over the country. For a time, we were the talk of Wall Street, and there were industry stories about how the company was growing. It was all good, but when the investors who had helped him start the company saw what was happening they decided to up the ante, so they came and offered Tom a cash infusion of millions of dollars in exchange for a bigger chunk of stock. There was just one hitch. If they gave him the money, they would bring in their own CEO and CFO. I would remain as president, they said, but their handpicked guys would actually be in charge, and they would control the purse strings.

The handwriting was on the wall, and I told Tom I thought that was a bad idea and he shouldn't do it. It was only the second time I put my finger in his face, but I said, "Tom, if you do this you will regret it. As sure as God took the kingdom away from Saul, He will take this business away from you. You don't need to do this. God is turning things around, and good things are beginning to happen. The business is on track, and the last thing we need now is for a group of venture capitalists to come in here and change everything."

After making my case, I left and went home on Thursday evening, just as I always did. But over the weekend, Tom met with the investors and he took the deal. I told him it was a bad idea and he shouldn't do it, but by that time he had already decided to go ahead. So I said, "Tom, as soon as the other guys come in, let's set up a meeting with them. I will do whatever it takes to put everything in order for you, but it's time for me to go. I've done what the Lord sent me here to do, but we had an agreement and you've chosen to go in another direction. What you're doing is wrong. They're going to take your company over and you're going to lose it. But I don't want to get into a fight with you over it. I still have a lot of respect for you, but as soon as I speak to the other guys and work out a schedule to properly transition my responsibilities, I'm out of here."

When the principals of the investment group arrived, I told them, "I know your vision for what you want to do with this company is different than the track Tom and I were on. So before we start butting heads, why don't you just buy out my contract and I'll go on down the road?" Over the next couple of months, we worked out an agreement and came to terms, and I left the company. Two months later Tom learned that he had cancer, and he went to the hospital for a series of very complex treatments. With Tom sidelined and in failing health, the investors did end up with his company, and about six months later, while I was on a mission trip to China, I learned that Tom went home to be with the Lord. It was a sad ending to what we had started together, but it pleased me to know that God had blessed Tom's company during my short time there.

The new owners came in and took over, but I was never paid what they agreed to pay me—not that I was terribly surprised by that. They found ways to hold back the payments they had promised, and by the time they finished making changes and shaking things up, there was nothing left. So Cookie and I got nothing out of that arrangement. It was all gone.

We hadn't anticipated that things would fall apart so quickly, and we hadn't saved a lot of money. For years we had been using our resources for ministry, and we deliberately put ourselves in a position where we would be dependent upon God for whatever we earned. So Cookie and I were suddenly at loose ends once again, and we were asking, "What do we do now?" Neither one of us knew what to expect, but I had already made plans for another mission trip to Africa, to participate in a training conference for pastors and business leaders, and I felt like I needed to keep that commitment.

We had recently purchased some new furniture, so before leaving for Africa I wanted to finish moving the furniture into the house. Unfortunately, as I was helping to move one of the heaviest pieces I wrenched my back. I found out I had torn two muscles in my lower back, and it was incredibly painful. When the doctor looked at it, he said there was nothing he could do. When I went to see a chiropractor he told me there was no way I could fly to Africa in that condition. I was already walking with a cane, and the only thing I could do was either lie down or stand up; I couldn't sit.

Cookie was very concerned for me because she could see that I was determined to get on that plane. She knew there was no way I'd be able to take such a long flight in that condition. But I told her I knew the Lord wanted me to go. We prayed about it, and even though Cookie had urged me to change my plans, I was getting ready for the trip. Then, about twenty-four hours before I was scheduled to leave, the phone rang, and it was an old friend that I hadn't seen in many years. He was the older brother of another friend I had worked with up in the mountains.

When I told him I was just about to leave the country, he said, "Dennis, I just called to say that my brother really needs you."

I said, "What's wrong?"

He said, "He's gotten hooked on drugs." We had both been on drugs in the sixties, but we had both come clean since then. His brother had given his life to the Lord, he was very active in the church, and he had gotten married to a sweet girl and had five wonderful children. He had been doing really well, but his brother told me that he had found himself at the wrong place at the wrong time. He took one snort of crack, and he was immediately hooked all over again.

"Dennis," he said, practically pleading with me, "would you please come help him?"

"OK," I said. "I'm getting ready to leave tomorrow. But as soon as I get back from Africa I'll go see him." He was grateful for that. He was relieved that I would go and visit his brother, even if it would be a couple of weeks before I could do it.

The next day Cookie drove me to the airport, still nervous about the trip. But neither one of us had expected what happened next. When I walked down the concourse, I was leaning heavily on the cane; but the moment I stepped through the door of that airplane, God instantly healed me. As soon as I stepped onto the plane I felt it, so I told the flight attendant, "Excuse me. I'll be right back." And I turned around and ran back to the concourse where Cookie was still waiting, standing there with tears in her eyes. I handed her the cane and I said, "Here, Baby, you can take this. I won't need it. The Lord just healed me. All the pain is gone!"

I didn't have time to spare, so I went back to the plane and took my seat. But as I thought about it, I realized that God had withheld the healing until I showed I was fully committed to do what He was asking me to do, regardless of my physical condition. And he confirmed it with His blessings. I made the trip to Africa and I never felt any further pain in my back. But while I was there, I felt the Lord speaking to me about my friend, and He said, "I want you to go help him."

During my prayer time I was asking the Lord, "What do you want me to do now? The business you put me in is gone. I believe the deal Tom made with the investors was misguided, but it was his decision. Cookie and I are free of all that now, but what's next? Where do you want us to go from here?"

The Lord gave me one scripture, and as I have applied this principal in my life, I've been able to use what I learned to help many people who find themselves in the same predicament. After Jesus appeared to Peter and a group of disciples after the Resurrection, He went away for a while and they didn't know when He would return; but He told them to wait in Jerusalem until they received power from on high, and further instructions. They were waiting on the Lord who had risen from the dead, but what really got my attention was Peter's response. He said, "I go a fishing" (John 21:3, KJV).

You can imagine the conversations that Peter must have had with his wife. "Peter," she might have said, "you've been walking with the Lord for three years now, and I know that our family's needs have always been met. But Jesus is not here now and you have a family to support. You have children to feed. What are you going to do now?" Well, Peter did what he had to do while he was waiting on Jesus to open the next door ... he went fishing.

The Lord really opened this principle up to me. When we're waiting on

God, do something, provide for your family. Make a living. When God is transitioning you from one place to another—moving you from point A to point B—don't just sit back and do nothing. Earn a living; provide for your family. It doesn't matter whether it's flipping burgers at the local fast-food restaurant—even if it's short-term. It doesn't have to be a lifetime vocation. While you're waiting on God to show you what to do next, go fishing, do something. Just earn a living.

~

That's what God showed me. So when I got back to the United States, I called my friend and told him I'd like to come up to his place in Williamsburg for a visit. He sounded like he was in good spirits, and he said he would love to see me. So I drove up there and met him in a restaurant. We spent four and a half hours together, and he told me all about what was happening in his life. He had always been very open and honest with me.

He told me what happened and how he had fallen back into drugs, and he said he was having a hard time with it. His wife had left him, and his children were all gone. Then he looked at me with tears in his eyes and said, "Dennis, I can't believe that Jesus loves me so much that he would send you up here to work with me."

At that time he was selling timeshares at another new development, and I had absolutely no intention of working with him. I had only come to see him out of my love and concern for an old friend, and as a favor to his brother. It's true, I had worked with him in the resort development project up in the mountains, but I wasn't interested in selling timeshares. I had been around it in the past, and I was pretty sure selling used cars would have been a lot better. But when he spoke those words, it was as if God were speaking directly to me. This was what He wanted me to do and I knew it, so I said, "Yes, He does. He loves you that much."

He said, "Well, come on, then. Let me introduce you to the owner."

I got in the car with him and we drove over to the office, which was in a trailer at the timeshare development. I met the owner, and after my friend left I talked to him for a while. I was straight up with him. I said, "When I drove up here to see him, I had no intention of doing this, but I believe this is where I'm supposed to be. I have a lot of experience in sales, and if you want me to come on board, I only have one condition. My wife works with me. We work together in everything, and she will be a blessing to you. But I'm really here for one reason: I'm here to help my old friend through a hard place. I don't know how long I'll be here, but I'll honor you while I'm here, and I'll be as faithful as I can."

He said, "Dennis, I'd love to have you here, and I'd be more than happy for you and your wife to work together as a team." After that, we shook hands and embarked on another new adventure.

When I got home that night, I knew it was going to be a big surprise for Cookie, and this is really a tribute to her. Imagine coming home and springing something like this on your spouse. When I pulled in, she met me at the door and said, "How did it go with your old friend?"

I told her it went very well, but then I said, "Honey, what would you think about selling timeshares?"

"Timeshares?" she yelped. As soon as I said the words, she looked at me like I was completely out of my tree. She said, "Dennis, I don't want to sell timeshares! I've never sold anything in my life."

I said, "Well, we own timeshares, don't we? We know how it works. When we went to Malaga and Marbella on our vacation to Spain, we used two weeks of our timeshare, and you loved every minute of it."

After she thought about it for a minute, Cookie agreed to listen; and when I told her what happened with my friend, she said, "Well, if you feel that's what the Lord wants us to do, then that's what we'll do."

We live in Chesapeake, Virginia, which is just under a two-hour drive from Williamsburg, so the next day we had to be up and out of the house by six o'clock in the morning in order to be at the timeshare by eight o'clock. This would be our routine every day. We listened to praise and worship music all the way up there, and by the time we arrived we were ready for anything.

We showed up ready for work and met all the team members, and someone mentioned that the sales manager was making between four hundred and five hundred thousand dollars a year. That was very good money, but what we discovered was that timeshare sales was one of the highest paid jobs in America at that time. Only pharmaceutical sales was higher.

Shortly after we arrived every morning, there would be a sales meeting, and the sales manager would give us the story of the day, which most of the time turned out to be some fish story he had concocted to convince the visitors to buy timeshare. Cookie and I didn't like that way of doing business, so I told them we would be using our own sales approach, and we didn't want to use those stories. The manager said he didn't like me challenging him that way, so I went back to one of the owners and said, "We want to work for you, but we're not going to try to deceive our customers. We own timeshares, too, so we know how it works, and we've had some of the best vacations of our lives through exchanges. We'll study the materials and make the best presentation we can. But give us thirty days to do it our way, and if we don't produce enough for you in that period of time, then we'll just leave."

He said, "Fair enough, Dennis. Let's see how it goes."

To make a long story short, I was salesman-of-the-month the very first month we were there. God just gave me a platform. After a couple of months, I was asked to share in some of the morning sales meetings, and I agreed. I started off each morning with a verse from Proverbs. I said, "If the wisest man who ever lived wrote this book, then let's see what he had to say about sales." It was all right there.

I began to share principals with them that could produce good results in their lives and their business goals, but I said they would only be successful if they did it with honesty and integrity and with the right motives. I told them that I knew a lot of people in sales. Some were Christians and some were not, but many of them failed by making the same clumsy mistakes, and they didn't have any idea why they were always so unsuccessful.

Over the years, I've known a lot of Christians in sales who go to church, read their Bibles, and spend time in prayer, and yet they're broke most of the time. And one of the reasons why they're never successful is that, without even knowing it, they're practicing the art of witchcraft. Sounds crazy, doesn't it? But on the same altar they pray on in the morning, asking God to meet their financial needs, they find themselves going to work practicing witchcraft and wondering why things never go well.

By definition, witchcraft is the attempt to manipulate the mind into believing something that is not true. If you exaggerate the benefits of your product or service to "get the sale," or if you lie about it or embellish it, you are trying to manipulate the mind to believe something that is not true. At that point you're practicing the art of witchcraft without even knowing it. And then you wonder why you just can't seem to make ends meet. And you question God, "Why aren't You blessing me"?

So this was what I shared with the sales team. I said, "If I was the sales manager here and you worked for me, I'd fire every one of you. The reason I'd do that is because you're so weak you can't make a sale by telling the truth. Some of you think you have to lie and exaggerate to make a sale." In fact, some of the stories these guys would come up with would make even the most unscrupulous used car salesman look like an altar boy. One of the guys was telling his customers that Disney World was going to be opening a new theme park just down the road. It was a total lie, and he knew it. Not everyone was like that, but that's one reason why the people in that business had such a bad reputation. What Cookie and I wanted to show them was that you could do it God's way and be successful.

Our approach was completely different, because we wanted our customers to know exactly what they were getting. In fact, I prayed with every customer I ever had, with only one exception. I led several people to the Lord while I was there. But let me tell you about one incredible experience Cookie and I had with three women from Texas—two sisters and their mother—who had come to us looking for information on timeshares.

While Cookie was talking to them, she learned that there had been generations of cancer in the family. A grandmother and a sister had already died of cancer, and the mother and a daughter were battling it. When she heard that, Cookie said she felt the cancer might have generational ties, and she said, "My husband is working inside the trailer, and I'm sure Dennis would be glad to pray with you and ask the Lord to bless you and protect you from that disease." They said they would like to do that, so Cookie came and asked me to go out there and speak to these women.

I was glad to do it. So there we were in the parking lot, talking and praying, and all the other salesmen were standing in the trailer next to the window watching what was going on. I was explaining about generational sin, and I told them there are curses that can follow a family from generation to generation. But Jesus came to break that curse and set people free. He went to the cross to break the stranglehold of sin on our lives, but it was apparent that there was something in their family history that could have very well brought this disease upon them.

When I told them that Jesus wanted to touch them and heal them, I could see that this was all new to them. These were good Baptist women and they'd never heard anything like that before, but when I prayed for them the Spirit of God touched them, and they started falling on the ground, one by one, right there in the parking lot. It was getting late and when the guys looking out the window saw that, they freaked out. They started yelling, "Call 9-1-1! Our customers are dropping dead in the parking lot! What's he doing to them?"

But Cookie said, "No, no! Don't worry. They'll be fine." In fact, God had healed those women. They were healed of cancer right there in the parking lot of the timeshare.

Cookie told me later that the time we spent working at the timeshare was one of the best experiences of her life. We went to work dressed like it was the most important job in the world. I wore a nice suit and tie, and Cookie wore a nice dress or a suit every single day. Up to that time the other salesmen usually showed up in casual slacks and a golf shirt. Most of them lived in the little motel next door and spent every evening in the nearest bar. Meanwhile, we led nineteen people to the Lord, gave away nineteen Bibles, and literally saw the lives of many of our customers and sales associates transformed. Marriages were saved, people were set free from alcohol and drugs, and Cookie turned that shabby little trailer we used for an office into a thing of beauty. That's one of Cookie's gifts. She can make a barn look like a palace, and the improvements she made in that trailer lifted our spirits and changed the way we all did business.

The whole experience was a testimony to the faithfulness of God. It was the only timeshare I'm aware of anywhere in the world that started closing on Sunday mornings so the employees could go to church if they wanted to. Whenever there was an event at the office, they would say, "Dennis, would you lead us in prayer?" They had never done that before. These were some of the most hard-core sales people we'd ever seen, and this was totally foreign to most of them. But God showed His love for them and did miracles there.

Ironically, many of our Christian friends were surprised and disappointed with Cookie and me when we told them where we were working. They would say, "How can you be in that business? That's not an honest way to make a living." That was the reputation of timeshare sales at the time. But, in fact, we saw it not just as a business but also as a ministry, and the Lord used that time to teach all of us some very important lessons.

I've known honest and dishonest car salesmen, honest and dishonest timeshare salesmen, and even honest and dishonest pastors. It's not the profession that determines if it's honest or dishonest, it's the person doing it. I do know this, however. When light hits darkness, it can change people's lives. As far as my friend was concerned, it took a few more years for the Lord to get him back to where He wanted him to be. But He got his life straightened out and ended up moving to Thailand, where he worked at a major resort, and he started a Christian ministry in his home. After a rough start, I'm happy to say he finished well.

But after seven months at the timeshare, I began to sense that change was coming. Then one day while I was standing out on the porch of the trailer, my cell phone rang. When I answered, the voice on the other end said, "Mr. Jones, this is Horace Furumoto. Do you remember me?"

This was in March 1999, exactly two years after Dr. Furumoto had shown up unannounced at my office in Chesapeake. I told him I certainly remembered his visit in March 1997, when he ended up in the wrong place. After we had a good laugh about that, he said, "Do you remember what we talked about in your office?" I said I did. So he said, "Would you come and talk to me and the members of my board about putting some kind of partnership together?"

Now, as background to what began to happen at that point, Cookie and I saw what we believed to be a new industry emerging and had formed a small company in 1997 called Sona Laser Centers. We incorporated it, had business cards printed, and did everything we needed to do to form this new company. But once everything was in place, we sought the Lord and waited for His guidance. We didn't feel the time was right to launch the company, so we put Sona on the shelf and waited for two years for God to bring the people and the finances we needed to make it happen.

Here's the amazing thing. When Horace Furumoto walked into my office in 1997, I knew nothing about laser hair removal; but now, after an amazing two-year journey, during which the Lord prepared me and equipped me for a major change, I knew everything I needed to know about the laser world to meet with Horace and his board.

I had been in the hair business all my life, but after putting hair on people for more than thirty-five years, I was about to get into the business of taking it off. I would still be in the hair business but from another angle. In fact, ABC did a story about me at one time. The reporter said, "Mr. Jones, you've been putting hair on people for thirty-five years and now you're taking it off. What's the story?"

I just said, "Well, I'm still in the hair business."

When Dr. Furumoto invited me to come to his headquarters in Boston, I made the reservations and flew up there the following week. I met with him and his board, and I shared our vision with them. I said, "If you're serious about making this work, here's how we ought to do it. The first thing you need to understand to make this business model work is that it can't just be about you. This vision is a different model from anything that's ever been done in this industry, and it's all based on sharing the revenue. The only way the revenue plan will work is if everyone shares in the profitability of the business.

"It must be a win, win, win for everybody," I said, "or it will fail, because God will not bless a business if only one wins and everyone else looses. If you try to build something that will benefit you without benefiting your franchise partners, then it will fail. Our entire focus as a company must be about building the success of the laser centers. If they're successful, you'll be successful."

Our goal, I told them, should be to build centers all over the country and make all of them successful. We'll build a national turnkey franchise and provide our partners with all the lasers, equipment, training, marketing, and guidance they need to be successful.

As soon as I said that, they asked, "What's it going to take?"

I said, "I will need $1.5 million. With that I can build the model."

That day they bought 40 percent of a vision. That's all it was at that time, a vision, but they were willing to pay me $1.5 million dollars to be a part of it. Of course there was some negotiating going on, but once again I insisted that I maintain majority ownership of the company.

If there's one thing I've learned, it's that whomever God gives the vision to, that's who should have the final authority and control. I'm always amazed at how many business people are willing to sell control of their vision just to get started, rather than waiting on God. Most of them soon regret it. Anyway, I sold them 40 percent of the company for $1.5 million. With that investment, we built prototypes of the ideal laser center in Portland, Oregon, and in Virginia Beach—those locations were our Jerusalem. Then we opened a second center in Richmond, Virginia, which, following the same biblical model was our Samaria; then Newport News, our Judea; and finally the uttermost parts of the earth, which was our center in Charlotte, North Carolina, and beyond.

With the help of my dear friend and corporate officer, along with a terrific staff, we were building an incredible infrastructure so we could support all these centers with a network that we would expand into every part of the country. Then, after we proved the model, we franchised it. We put our franchise plan together in four and a half months. We built the franchise Sona Laser Centers, and over the next eighteen months the Lord took that business to one of the largest laser hair-removal centers in the country.

There were some problems between Sona and Cynosure at various points, as I had anticipated, but I assured them our business model was working and we didn't need to change anything. Many of our franchises were in a positive cash flow position from the first month, and we were setting records in the laser hair-removal business like no one had ever seen before. Our success was incredible, and we were written up in *Entrepreneur* magazine. The picture on the cover was a red-hot chili pepper, and that's what we were. We were doing extremely well and the business world was taking notice.

We developed pre- and post-laser treatment products, along with a line of thirteen specially designed skin care products. Once the business was up and running and making a profit, we found that there was also business inside the business by providing products and services for all our centers, and this was a bonus for the franchise owners. As a result of all these developments, revenue took off to such an extent that the laser company benefited as well. Thanks to their relationship with Sona, it helped the laser manufacturers to take their company public.

I thought it was a win-win-win situation. If you're a Christian businessman and you're going to do business God's way, there can be no losers. If there are losers at any point, then something's wrong. Everybody has to win. In our centers the customer won because they got a good service at a good price, and they went away happy. The franchisees got into an emerging industry with incredible upside potential and they were making money. The laser manufacturers were happy because they were making more money through the revenue-sharing agreements than they could have made by simply selling the equipment outright. And, finally, we were doing very well as Sona Corporation, with virtually no limit to new expansion.

Between franchises and territories, we had sales commitments for 162 franchises, and I was the only salesman. I wanted to handle all the franchise sales myself, because I wanted to look every potential franchise owner in the eye. I wanted to be sure we were equally yoked, and that the prospective partners understood our vision, how we worked, and what we were trying to accomplish. I made no apologies for what I believe, or the fact that I was going to run the business based on biblical principles. Even though years later I would be mocked and criticized for it, and even had it used against me, that's who I am and I knew it was the right thing to do.

The amazing thing is that almost all of the franchises had positive cash flow by the second or third month of operation. Many doctors who were doing laser hair removal at the time in the cities we were opening up in, if they were bringing in ten to thirty thousand dollars a month in sales they were dancing all the way to the bank. And we had some centers that were doing more than three hundred thousand dollars a month, first month out of the chute.

We went in to dominate the market in every city, and God just blessed and prospered that business. For me, personally, it was an amazing journey. The first time I met Horace Furumoto I never imagined I would have anything to do with laser hair removal, but because of the journey God had taken me on, I was suddenly one of the foremost experts in laser hair removal in the world. When I was with Tom Mehl, we had almost every laser manufacturer in the world, from London to Tel Aviv, coming to us to negotiate licenses to use our technology. And because of that, I learned not only about the ruby lasers that we were selling but also the alexandrite lasers, and just about every other technology available on the market.

But the lesson Cookie and I learned through all of that has been very important to us ever since. In the midst of a time of transition, it may be impossible to figure out where you are or what's happening to you. You may not see how the things you're doing have anything to do with where you wanted to go or what you thought you'd be doing. But if you have committed your life to the Lord, you have to be dependent upon Him to show you the way.

First, you have to come to a place of contentment. Once you're content, God will put things into motion, taking you to the next step. But here's something else I learned. Life has a definite flow to it. Normally, God doesn't take a man or woman from what he or she has been doing all their life into something totally unrelated. But if you're faithful to follow His guidance and do the best you can, one step at a time, you may be surprised to find out that He has been building something bigger and better than you could ever have imagined.

When Horace Furumoto came to my office in Virginia, he was a long way from where he meant to be. He was supposed to be meeting with Tom Mehl in Florida, and he thought he'd made a big mistake. But three years later, there we were, in a very successful business together. The Bible says, "In all your ways acknowledge Him, and He shall direct your paths" (Prov. 3:6). The fact is, when Horace showed up unannounced, I could have blown him off. But because I took the time to meet this man and listen to him, God opened a new door.

That door was confirmation for us, once again, that depending on how we respond to the circumstances of life will determine where God takes us next.

Chapter Ten

WALKING ON WATER

I N THE MIDST of everything that was happening at that time, I received a
call from a dear friend who owned the Sona franchise in Dallas, Texas.
He said that a friend of his, who was an officer of a local bank, wanted to
meet with me, so I agreed to fly down to Dallas. As it turned out, he actually
wanted to introduce me to a man who had founded several successful corporations, and was one of the past officers of the International Franchise Association. He was listed in *Who's Who in Franchising* and had helped to create
and build many of the biggest name franchises in the country.

This person wanted to talk to me about Sona. But before meeting with
him, we set up a conference call so we could get to know one another. His
secretary sent me a copy of a book this guy had written so I could get a feel
for who he was. When it arrived, the first thing I saw was his portrait on
the back of the book, and in that picture he had his hand resting on a stack
of books. So I pulled out my magnifying glass to see what sort of books he
thought were important enough to use as props for his portrait, and I saw
that the book on the top of the stack was the Holy Bible.

When the call eventually came through, we exchanged pleasantries for a couple of minutes, but then I said, "Let me ask you this. I noticed that in your portrait on the back cover of your book, you have your hand on five books, and the top book is the Bible. What does that mean to you?" So he began to share with me that he was a born-again Christian, that he loved God, and he tried to run his businesses according to the Word of God.

Well, that was exciting news, and I thought this might be of the Lord. Maybe God was doing something here. We would just take it slowly and see what happens, but I thought I ought to at least see what he wanted. We tried to get together several times, but there always seemed to be calendar problems, but I didn't foresee anything to make me suspect that there might be problems down the road. In fact, I seemed to be getting positive confirmation that this was something God wanted me to look into. Maybe He was putting something together. But it was quite a while before we finally sat down together.

⌒⌇

There were many interesting coincidences along the way. He would call to set up a meeting, and I would say, "No, I can't meet that day. I'll be in Dallas." Then he would say, "Really? So will I." I would say, "I'm staying at the Marriott Hotel." And he would say, "Really? So am I." That's how we finally got together, and that happened several times. We would meet, have dinner, and have a pleasant evening, but for whatever reasons we never really talked about business. We would spend a couple of hours talking about our interests, our families, and all sorts of things, but never business.

On another occasion, he called and wanted to meet. He had never been to our corporate offices, so he suggested a time to get together, and I said, "I'm sorry, but my wife and I will be in Miami that week." He said, "Really? So will I." So we ended up getting together again, and these seemingly serendipitous connections kept happening, giving me stronger and stronger confirmation that maybe the Lord was putting something together.

We finally ended up spending some quality time together in Virginia

Beach. He flew up and we spent a long lunch together. We really hadn't talked much about business up to that point, but during this conversation I asked him, "Are you interested in partnering with Sona? Are you interested in buying all or part of Sona? I'd like to know your level of interest in the company."

He said, "Any or all of the above, Dennis. But there's just one thing I must tell you. Because of who I am and the positions I hold, I can't be a minority shareholder in the business. I would have to have controlling interest of any partnership agreement I sign. Would you be willing to agree to that?" I said, "Well, if God works it out that way and we see that it's of the Lord, I wouldn't have a problem with that. I will support the vision as long as it's something I can agree with."

At that point he began to describe his vision. He said he had built franchises all across the country and at that point he had also opened thousands of franchise units in Europe. His concept was that I would continue to expand Sona Corporation in the U.S. while he and his associates would begin building Sona all across Europe. He was thinking about taking the Sona concept to a level we hadn't thought much about up to that point.

I told him I would think about that and pray about it, and Cookie and I devoted a lot of time to seeking the Lord about his proposal. The thought came to my mind—and to this day I believe it was the Lord speaking to me—that God had used Moses to lead the nation of Israel to the Jordan, but He used Joshua to take them into the promised land. What that said to me was that I had taken Sona from start-up to the place where it was at the time, but here was a man who could take it to a level beyond anything we had previously considered. He could make it a worldwide franchise, which was, in fact, my ultimate goal, and I thought this might be the best thing for the franchisees, the laser manufacturers, and the company.

Because of my background and my lack of formal education, and no doubt because of some of my own insecurities, I felt this man was more qualified to do it than I was. At the time I didn't think about this, but I know now that the one to whom God gives the vision is the person best qualified to carry it out. It's not the one with the greatest accolades or finances, but the one to whom God gave the original vision.

Nevertheless, this conversation continued for nearly a year, talking back and forth about how to make it work. Our agreement was that I would continue to be president of the company; he would take over as CEO, and at that point he and his associates would start setting up operations in Europe.

We eventually came to terms and signed the document, and within a matter of weeks I was informed that I was to no longer have any direct oversight over the employees, and I was no longer to contact our vendors or franchisees. They said, in effect, we'll take it from here. We had more than one hundred employees at that time, and most were personal friends. I had led many of them to the Lord. But I was essentially stuck back in my nice, comfortable office suite with not much to do. Our contract stipulated that Cookie would remain on staff for at least another year, and I would stay for two years. But it didn't take long to realize that what we had agreed to was not going to happen.

I was still free to take mission trips—that was part of our agreement—and I made plans to return to Africa for a leadership conference, as I had done previously. So my dear friend Howard and I went over there, and while I was in prayer one day I felt that the Lord spoke to my spirit, and He said it was time for Cookie and me to leave Sona.

It had only been about seven months since we signed the contract with the new owners, but when I got home I told Cookie I felt the Lord was telling us that our time at Sona was coming to an end. Two days later I got a call from the guy who had set the whole thing up, asking me, "Is there any way you and Cookie can come down to Nashville to meet with a group of us? There are some things we need to talk about."

I'd already seen how the new organization did business. When we signed the agreement with them, it was agreed that the original center in Chesapeake would remain open, and none of our employees would lose their jobs unless they couldn't perform their duties. But within thirty days they had already let some of our people go. Then, little by little, they began letting others go, and moved the corporate headquarters to Nashville.

Before going to Nashville, I told Cookie that this would be the time when the Lord was going to set us free from this alliance we were in. So we went down there, and when Cookie and I were seated across the table from the new CEO, he immediately began trying to sell me on the idea of leaving the company early. Cookie and I looked at each other, and we were thinking, "Praise the Lord!" But he continued, saying, "Here's the problem, Dennis. So long as you remain with Sona, some of the employees' and franchisees' allegiance remains with you, and that's making it difficult for us to run the business."

It's true, I had built close personal relationships with all our staff and most of the franchisees. That has always been my practice. If the child of one of our people would go to the hospital, they would call and ask me to pray with them. Those who were going through marriage problems, even if they were at the point of divorce, would come to see me for marriage counseling. I had prayed for and counseled many of them through some very difficult situations, but the new guys felt that was hindering their ability to run the company the way they wanted to.

Actually, what he said made a lot of sense. I knew it was true that he could never be accepted as the leader so long as I was in that position and had the allegiance of many of the employees and franchise owners. No one can serve two masters. So we agreed to leave, and they bought out my contract. When Cookie and I left the company, we were still the largest shareholders with the largest stock holdings of any individual. The day we left Sona the company was strong, healthy, and financially solvent. But the new owners had a different vision.

Before long the revenue-sharing plan I had created was terminated. That had been the heart of our success, but they didn't want it anymore. The financial structure I had set up benefited everyone and allowed us to function as a debt-free company. We had a great relationship with our vendors and were current with all of them. We had well over a million dollars in cash in the bank and our stock was valued at ninety thousand dollars a share. Eighteen months after the new group took over, they had burned through the capital reserve, they were millions of dollars in debt, there were nine lawsuits against them, and the stock was worth pennies on the dollar.

Needless to say, that was devastating to me, because this was a company I believed God had put into our lives so that my wife and I could carry on with the missions work and church ministry He had called us to do. That was to be our support base for the rest of our lives, because we never wanted to take income from anyone else for the ministry we do. We've never accepted donations from any church or individual, and I believe that's the way the Lord wants it. I've felt a bit like the apostle Paul in that regard, since he continued to pursue his career as a tentmaker wherever he traveled. But suddenly that vision was coming to an end, so we began looking for what the Lord would do next.

God had not called me to be a pastor. I was a businessman, and my tent making was to support the ministry that He had called me to do. But we awoke one day to find our financial security gone. What was supposed to be a multi-million-dollar payback within three to five years turned out to be a small fraction of what the company was worth when we sold it.

The venture capital company saw the direction the company was going, and within two years they turned the operation over to one of the franchisees we had brought into the business—a very qualified and capable man—and asked him to take over the reins. Today Sona is alive and well once again, and growing under the leadership of this gentleman, who had originally owned and operated the franchise in Charlotte, North Carolina.

Needless to say, I learned many important lessons from that experience. We all want to know the will of God for our lives. The Bible says that those who are born of the Spirit are led by the Spirit. If the Spirit of God is alive in us, we are being led by His Spirit; and if we're out of the will of God, we'll soon know it. He won't let us wander too far without a warning. At other times, however, we may not realize that we're in the will of God. The Bible says, "The steps of a good man are ordered by the Lord" (Ps. 37:23), but most of the time we don't see how or where the Lord is taking us. It's only when we look back, sometimes years later, that we can see that He was leading us all the way, and step by step.

Another thing I learned was that, even though it can be the will of God for a group of people to go into business together, that doesn't mean it's going to work out the way we'd like. The Bible says that the Lord is "not willing that any should perish but that all should come to repentance" (2 Pet. 3:9). It's also not the will of God that any of us should sin. That's not God's will; yet, He knows these things are going to happen, and He loves us anyway. Even though it may be the will of God for two people to go into business together, as humans we're more than capable of messing up a good thing.

We can start out with the best of intentions, but if one or the other gets greedy, or selfish, or overly ambitious, not willing to submit to one another in the fear of God, then we can destroy what God had intended. But one of the hardest lessons I learned comes down to this: even though it's the will of God and we're doing our best to follow the will of God, that doesn't necessarily mean it's going to happen the way we would like. As I've said repeatedly, since the first page of this book, how we respond to the circumstances we encounter along the way will determine the amount of success or failure we experience in this life.

Through our circumstances God is able to take us to a place of reflection, where we will be able to analyze what's happening in our hearts and minds and where we can assess our attitudes and motives. This is where we come to terms with who we really are. God is able to take us through some of these things. Through the hardships and repercussions we're faced with, He can deal with our doubts, fears, and other issues we didn't even know were there.

After we left Sona, I asked myself, why did I sell the company? Was it because of my insecurity, feeling that I didn't really have the ability to carry it all the way? If so, that wasn't God's fault. "We know that all things work together for good, for those who love God" (Rom 8:28). God can take any man with the gifts and talents he has and accomplish all that God has intended for him in this life.

Another thing I realized is that God will never ask a man to do more than he already has the capacity to do. When God called Moses out of Egypt, Moses said, "O my Lord, I am not eloquent ... but I am slow of speech ..." (Exod. 4:10). Moses was frightened to be given such authority, to deliver the Israelites from centuries of bondage under Pharaoh. But God said He would use the staff that Moses carried in his hand to deliver the nation of Israel.

God will always take whatever we have in our hand and use it to accomplish everything He wants for us in this life. One of the biggest problems we have is that we underestimate the power of God. We underestimate how involved He wants to be in our lives. There's so much He will do through us if we will only let Him be involved. But sometimes we have to go through circumstances that take us to the very depths of despair, but if we let it, it will bring us into a new level of intimacy with Him, and from there He will take us to the next phase of our life.

It took me two years to admit to myself what I had done. I realize now that I had concluded falsely that it would be easier for someone whom I believed to be more qualified to take the reins and build the company than for me to do it myself. We have to be very careful not to quit before God tells us to. We have a tendency to sell ourselves short, and that was my mistake. I decided that I had achieved as much as I needed to, and it was time to sell. But that wasn't true. Sometimes we tend to get tired before the job is done. We start to feel weary of all the day-to-day headaches, and we look for the easy exit. But the Bible says, "let us not be weary in well doing: for in due season we shall reap, if we faint not" (Gal. 6:9, KJV). We can't quit in the middle. When we do, we sell ourselves short.

When all was said and done, the people I had trusted to come in as my business partners nearly destroyed the business. When God gives you a dream or a vision for a new enterprise, it is for you, and it does not belong to anybody else. When someone tries to take that dream and do something with it that God did not intend, it just won't work. That's why we see so many cases like this in the business world. Someone has a dream and builds a good, solid business, and at some point a major corporation comes in and buys them out. Then, within a year in many cases, the whole thing collapses and that good idea is gone. Many big corporations may know how to run a billion-dollar company, but they're incapable of running a smaller one, where people still have to roll up their sleeves and get the job done.

This was the lesson I learned: when someone tries to take something that God has given to someone else and tries to use it in a way that dishonors the original motives and spirit that God intended, it won't work. But there's one more thought that comes to mind as I recall these events: If I had gotten all that I was promised and immediately began traveling the world "fulfilling My dreams," chances are I would not be writing this book, and I would not have the opportunity to share all the lessons I have learned through that experience. So, here too, God is using this experience, and all the others I have described in these pages, hopefully, for a greater purpose.

For a period of time I felt that Sona was the culmination of everything I'd worked for my whole life. But when that was all gone, Cookie and I had to look in another direction to see where God would take us. But the one thing we knew was that we could trust God. He is sovereign in our lives, and we knew He had a plan. Jesus never said to His disciples, let's go half way across and drown. He said, "Let's go to the other side." And we were prepared to go to the other side even if we had to swim for it.

I told someone in the wake of that affair that what I'd been dealing with the past couple of years was like spiritual water boarding. We've all heard the term water boarding, from all the controversy over the interrogation techniques used by the CIA with terrorists captured on the battlefield. With spiritual water boarding, sometimes you find yourself in a place where you think you're going to drown, but you're not. You feel like you're drowning, but you don't. God is in control of your life, but He is taking you through a profound and possibly painful experience, to the point that you think everything in your life is about to be removed or destroyed.

You may not see any hope of a change. Nothing seems to be going the way you thought it would. You're at the end of your emotional reserve and you think you're going to drown, and then God comes through and saves you. What's so sad is that after God delivers you, you look back, and suddenly you're embarrassed because you discover that He was working behind the scenes all along. You didn't see Him, and, worst of all, you really didn't trust Him. And I'm afraid that was our situation, when all the time He was teaching us to walk on water.

⁓

Despite the Sona debacle, we still had options. For several years we've owned a little company called Creative Technologies. We had kept it going all during the Sona experience, and we maintained the corporate office in Chesapeake. That little office has been a creative incubator for us. It's where we've started most of our businesses. It was always a place where I could go to think creatively and solve problems of one kind or another. Even when we had the big building next door that we built for the Sona headquarters, I would come over by myself to think and plan. It's a place for reflection, where I can think and pray and meet the Lord.

When the new owners moved Sona's corporate headquarters to Nashville, several of the people who had worked with us for many years in that company came back with Cookie and me to the little office. So, with our faithful staff of friends, Evan, Theresa, Jeannette, and Ashleigh, we began revving up our product line with the pre- and post-laser products we had developed. We also had a one of a kind specialty product that we had developed from an idea God had given me back in 2000.

We owned all the formulas, and we had the patent for a specialty product we called Meladine. It's the only FDA-approved product on the market that allows a physician to effectively perform laser hair removal treatments on non-pigmented hair such as white, gray, and blonde. The Lord gave me the idea a few years ago when we first went into the laser hair removal business. As the laser hair removal market began to explode, it became obvious that, even though the lasers were effective in the treatment of pigmented hair, there was not a laser on the market that could treat non-pigmented hair, which was approximately a third of the entire market. As I committed my ideas to the Lord and began to pray about it, the solution came to me. We worked with a chemist to formulate the precise chemical compound, and today Meladine is the only product in the market that makes this process possible.

We had done very well with that product over the years, and now that Cookie's and my focus was back on Creative Technologies, we began to pursue what was still tremendous upside potential in the market for Meladine products, and have continued to build our business over the past few years. Neither Cookie nor I have drawn a salary in all of that time, but the Lord has provided for our needs, and he has provided just enough income to keep up with inventory demands and pay the staff. But, in the midst of all this, a new opportunity came our way when I got a call from a colleague in North Carolina.

She is a long-time friend and a chemist who has worked with us on many of our new product developments over the last thirty-five years, including all the skin-care products we developed for Sona. When she called, she said, "Dennis, there's a little factory down here that manufactures and fills lip balm for other companies. I just learned that it's on the market, and I think you could get it for a pretty good price. If you're interested, we could end up manufacturing all your products through there."

When I told Cookie about the call, it didn't take us long to realize we needed to take a drive down to North Carolina to see for ourselves what it was all about. I had the distinct feeling that, once again, the Lord was preparing the way for a new adventure. I had just finished telling the staff in January 2008 that my vision for the coming year was for us to be in control of our own destiny and be in a position to manufacture all our own products by the end of the year. So, after coordinating with the folks in North Carolina, Cookie and I made the four-and-a-half hour drive down to see the operation for ourselves.

The little town of Rockwell, North Carolina, population barely two thousand, looks like Main Street, U.S.A., ironically as though it could have come from an actual Normal Rockwell print. Right next door to the plant was a quaint old church, and directly across the street was the sheriff's office. When we went into the plant, there were twelve women working there. It wasn't a large operation but we were generally impressed with the facilities. The production line was going full steam, churning out tiny tubes of lip balm. We didn't know it at the time, but they were fulfilling one of their last orders.

After meeting with two of the owners, we learned that FillTech Incorporated had been started by four women, each owning an equal share of the company. Everyone knows that anything with two heads is a monster; but anything with four heads is a disaster! Two of the original owners had walked away from the company unexpectedly a year earlier. Since the company had never been computerized, there was very little documentation of the company's history or its performance, which made it very difficult to get our hands around the nature of their business.

We were assured they still maintained national manufacturing accounts and that the company was profitable. But after a two-hour meeting, we decided there were still too many unknowns, and decided to decline the purchase offer presented to us. We headed back to our car, but as we were walking across the parking lot, I asked one of the owners if we could take a look inside the manufacturing plant.

She said that would be OK, so we went inside and saw all twelve employees standing at conveyor lines, working as hard as they could work. Most of these women had been working for FillTech for most of their working years, all were working through a temporary staffing service, and most of them were earning minimum wage with no benefits. But we couldn't help but notice that they really knew how to do lip balm. It was hands-on for everything, and every piece they turned out was a work of art.

North Carolina had been hit very hard by recession over the past several years, and most of the businesses in Rockwell were struggling. Many of the textile mills and furniture mills that had made North Carolina famous had closed down years earlier, and almost everything had been outsourced to

China. The tobacco industry had been destroyed by the environmentalists and trial lawyers, and real unemployment in the state was more than 17 percent.

As we entered the plant, Wanda, the plant manager, walked over to meet us. After we introduced ourselves, she asked, "Are you thinking about buying the plant?" Up to that point, this was the farthest thing from our minds, but when we saw the look of fear and uncertainty in her eyes, I responded by saying, "If we were to purchase the company, Wanda, the first thing we would want to do is to convert all of the temporary workers to permanent employees; and, secondly, we would put a profit-sharing program in place so that every employee shares in the success and growth of the company ... we either sink or swim together."

She simply nodded, but I could see my comments had come as a surprise to her. So I asked if she thought any of the women would have a problem with these changes. With tears running down her face, Wanda looked at me and said, "You mean you would want us?"

Both Cookie and I responded by saying, "Yes, we would!"

At that moment, God dropped a burden and a new sense of excitement into our hearts, not only for the twelve women at FillTech, but also for the town of Rockwell. Wanda's words broke our hearts, and we could hardly speak after that. When we left, we were both in a quiet and reflective mood on the long drive back to Virginia. But after a while, Cookie said, "You know, Dennis, we've done missions work all over the world all these years, but there's a mission field right here in North Carolina."

After another three hours, and as we were getting close to home, I felt the Holy Spirit speaking to me. He said, "Son, I'm giving you an opportunity to be a part of building a community." At that point I knew we were supposed to buy that plant. To make a long story short, we went home and mortgaged our house. Then we went back down there and bought that little plant.

We felt that we were being given an opportunity to take part in helping to build and change an entire community, and by doing so, we would be making a real difference in people's lives. Over the last twenty-eight years, I had traveled to Russia, China, and Africa doing missions work, but on that day Cookie and I realized that Rockwell, North Carolina, had become our new mission field.

Shortly after our visit to Rockwell, we began the due diligence process, and on May 23, 2008, we became the owners of the new FillTech USA. Our next step was to begin putting a management team in place. The day we returned home from Rockwell, a long-time friend and business associate whom we hadn't heard from in many months called. Out of the clear blue, he asked if there was anything that we were involved in that he could be a part of—he said he was looking for a change of scenery for himself and his family.

When I told him about our new venture, he was genuinely excited and asked if he could be a part of the new team at FillTech USA. With his wife, Elaine and two young daughters in tow, Scott Hughes moved from Portland, Oregon, and set up residence in North Carolina, taking on a new assignment as FillTech USA's Chief Operating Officer. As we promised Wanda on that first encounter, we implemented a profit-sharing program, met with each worker one-on-one, dissolved their old contracts with the temporary agency, converted each of them from temporary to permanent status, and gave every employee a substantial pay increase.

Next came the tedious task of sifting through box after box of paperwork to find out what we had bought. FillTech Incorporated had never been computerized, so the task was truly monumental. What we found—as if we hadn't anticipated it—was that things are not always what they first appear to be. When the dust settled, we realized that FillTech did not have the customers we were led to believe. In fact, the company had only one purchase order left to fulfill. As a result, we would almost be starting from scratch. So at that point we met with the staff and explained the situation. In order to give us time to regroup and contract new business, we sent everyone home for a seven-week vacation with pay; and for the next seven weeks, Cookie, Scott, and I went to work rebuilding FillTech USA into a viable operation.

Over the first nine months, we watched in amazement as the company began to grow, from virtually nothing to a bona fide player in the cosmetics manufacturing industry. With the addition of six new national accounts and six regional accounts in just nine months, the company exceeded the revenue and production projections we had made for the first full year of operation. And while we were very thankful for everything that had transpired up to that point, our vision for FillTech USA was far from being realized.

~

There was a big sign on the front of the building that hadn't been lit for at least ten years. We had that sign restored, and now I have my own little billboard facing the highway where everyone can see it. The first week I put up a message that said, "May God richly bless the town of Rockwell." Every two weeks we change the sign, saying something uplifting to encourage the community—just to let them know that God loves them and they're not alone, especially in this difficult economy.

While we were cleaning and organizing the place, Cookie went in and gutted the little house next door and restored it, turning it into an office and conference room. With that, she revitalized the whole environment. We also bought additional equipment, and then we went out and started negotiating with retailers to purchase our products. Coming out of the cosmetics world, we had ideas about aesthetics and wrinkle reduction that others who make similar products hadn't considered. We developed all of our own formulas and products, so we started incorporating higher concentrations of Vitamin E, grape seed oil, and other ingredients that help to moisturize the lips and reduce fine lines and wrinkles.

When we started offering these new products under our private label, we were able to regain several of the accounts the previous owners had lost, and now we're expanding the line. FillTech is now manufacturing hand sanitizers along with lip balm and other private label products for some of the largest retail stores and pharmacies in the country. To keep up with the new production demands, we've hired more than twenty new employees.

And perhaps best of all, we're getting involved in the community of Rockwell. As we were leaving on one of our early visits, I noticed an African-American gentleman pulling up in his car and going into the church next door. I thought he might be the pastor of that church, so I walked over, knocked on the door, and introduced myself. I told him we were thinking about buying the plant next door. He was courteous, but he said he was preparing for a sermon that night, so I said, "Well, while we're here, I just wanted to say hello, and I wanted to speak a blessing on your life today."

Clearly, he hadn't expected that, so he said, "Why don't you come on in?" We went inside the church office, and while we were sitting there getting acquainted, I felt the Lord speaking to me. So I asked him, "Brother, do you believe in the gift of prophecy?"

He said, "Yes, I do."

So I said, "Well, the Holy Spirit has given me a message for you." This often happens when I'm counseling with someone. The Holy Spirit will show me dates, places, events, and sometimes even what's happening in a man's heart. God showed me that this man of God was at a crossroads in his life. The Lord gave me a clear word that addressed those issues and offered him direction and words of encouragement. When I told him what the Lord was saying to me, he broke down in tears. The presence of the Lord was so strong that when I finished sharing with him, we both knew there was nothing else to say, so I stood up, walked around his desk, gave him a hug, and I said, "I'm going to leave now. The Lord wants to talk to you."

He said, "I know."

I walked out, went back to the car, and Cookie and I drove on home. I didn't see that pastor for another three weeks, but when we came back to work on the plant we met again and have been good friends ever since. It's exciting now to see God doing a work in that little church; and I even have the privilege of ministering in the church on occasions whenever we're in town.

I also went over to the sheriff's office across the street, and one of the officers said, "You know the folks around here love your signs." I said I was glad they liked them, and that Cookie and I hoped they might be a blessing to the people of Rockwell. Then he said, "Mr. Jones, a lot of towns around here have their own chaplain. We sure would like to have someone we could call on from time to time when we need them. Would you be interested in being our chaplain?" Of course I said I'd be delighted. I said I would enjoy going over and speaking to the officers whenever I could.

So today we have our Creative Technologies business that we're working hard to expand, waiting for the Lord to open new doors. We have patents and trademarks that we're negotiating with various companies, and we're looking for God to open doors to bless our wonderful staff. And of course we're continuing to build in Rockwell, not only for our business but also for the whole community.

Our philosophy is simple and direct. I don't believe God has called Christian businessmen and women to just build businesses. I believe He has called us to be involved in building people's lives. People who build businesses are in a position to change communities, and ultimately change the world. That has been our philosophy for a long time now. We believe that God has given us an opportunity to help build the lives of people who in turn will help build communities, our country, and ultimately the kingdom of God.

All my life I've been creating things and pioneering new businesses. I was the first barber doing hairstyling in the state of Virginia. We opened the first unisex hair salon in the United States, in Miami Beach. When I came back to Virginia, I opened the first hairstyling studio in the state. I developed hair care products for hair loss. We were the first ones to put a commercial on national television featuring products for hair loss. Then we came up with the video imaging system.

We were also the first ones to put a revenue-sharing program together in the field of medical hair-transplantation. We were the first to develop a franchise model that provided laser hair-removal and other Med Spa procedures on a revenue-sharing basis, with businessmen and doctors all across the country. We are the only ones to have developed and patented a product for treating white, gray, and blonde hair with a laser.

I've been engaged in creating and building things my whole life, and in the past the fun part was always conceiving, creating, and building something new. Once it was built, the challenge was much less stimulating. That is, until now. Today, with our commitment to FillTech USA, the balance has shifted, and I truly enjoy being a part of the whole process, from concept to fulfill-ment. It's not just about creating a business or a product; it's about building lives and seeing how a motivated group of people can build a businesses and a community that will, in turn, help to bring prosperity and growth to an entire region.

We started with twelve employees at FillTech and within the first seven months we were up to thirty. In the beginning, we were only filling lip balm canisters, but today we're not only filling products for some of the most suc-cessful chain stores in America, but we're creating, manufacturing, and mar-keting our own health and beauty products under private label and our own trademarked names. We've found that many of the major corporations have begun cutting back or downsizing their manufacturing. They've decided it's not cost-effective for them, which opens up a lot of opportunities for FillTech to do everything from filling and co-packaging to turn-key manufacturing.

At the same time, we're finding that the opportunity for generic and pri-vate label products is tremendous. If folks were shopping for a product such as vitamins or antacid tablets five years ago, they might not have wanted to buy the generic brands because they were afraid those products were inferior or cheaply made. But because of the recession, many people are more willing to purchase these private label brands today. And when they discover that our products are almost identical to the more expensive brands, and work just as well, they're much more likely to become regular customers.

When we bought the company, we wanted to emphasize that it's an American company, which is why we changed the name from FillTech Incorporated to FillTech USA. That was an important step for us because more and more people are wary of cosmetics and other personal care products manufactured overseas. When the buyers discover that all our products are made right here in the USA, they wanted to become our customer.

Chapter Eleven

A TIMELY WARNING

GOING THROUGH SUDDEN and unexpected changes is always disconcerting. The Sona experience was frustrating and even heartbreaking at times, but then finding that the Lord had already prepared the way for us to undertake a new challenge was truly exciting. Cookie and I were eager to get back to business, but we were just as eager to renew our focus on the missions work and ministry we feel called to do. I'm convinced we're on the verge of a new awakening in the church in America, and a new understanding of accountability before the Lord. So once we had our new businesses up and running, this was an area where I felt the Lord wanted me to focus my thinking.

Before there can be a fresh outpouring of God's Spirit on any nation, the men and women who call themselves Christians will have to think long and hard about who they are and what they really believe. Not least of all, they have to consider how the faith they claim to believe ought to influence the way they live their lives. A genuine faith ought to determine not only how we live and work, but how we think, and, yes, even how we vote. There's no area of life where our Christian beliefs are irrelevant.

This was one of the things that prompted my friend Ben Kinchlow to publish his book, *Black Yellowdogs*, in 2008. In that book he speaks about the overwhelming numbers of people who vote for certain candidates simply because of their race, seemingly without regard to the anti-Christian beliefs and behaviors of those politicians. The subtitle of Ben's book reads, *The Most Dangerous Citizen Is Not Armed, but Uninformed*, and that's a serious problem.

The people we honor and the things we vote for ought to be important concerns for every believer, because such things reflect the condition of our hearts. Too many people in our churches, both black and white, aren't paying attention to the times we're living in. For two or three weeks we were once again a Christian nation, but, as often happens, once the fear subsided and the world didn't end, the people drifted back into their old lifestyles, and they forgot all about God.

Here again, the Bible shows us what's going on. In Mark 4:15–20, Jesus explains the meaning of the parable of the sower to his disciples, and He gives them an analogy of how various people receive the gospel. When a farmer spreads the seeds for a new crop, some of the seeds will fall on the hard soil along the path. Jesus says, "These are the ones by the wayside where the word is sown. When they hear, Satan comes immediately and takes away the word that was sown in their hearts."

Some of the seeds fall on stony ground. These are men and women who need the gospel desperately. They hear the Word and they "immediately receive it with gladness," but since the soil of their souls is so shallow, they forget what they claimed to believe, and when trouble comes they quickly fall away. Then Jesus says that some of the seeds fall among thorns, where what He calls "the cares of this world, the deceitfulness of riches, and the desires for other things" chokes out the gospel until it becomes useless. This, I believe, is the greatest risk for the church in America today.

Over and over in the scriptures, Jesus says, "Do not be deceived." (See, for example: 1 Corinthians 6:9; 15:33; Galatians 6:7; and James 1:16.) Deception really is the issue, and this is what the church is facing. Many in the church have been led to believe a lie, and the desire for riches and other things has superseded their devotion to the things of God. Jesus said, "seek first the kingdom of God and His righteousness, and all these things shall be added to you" (Matt. 6:33). But we're not content with that. We're not seeking God and letting Him work in our lives; we just want the things. Our focus on gathering riches and piling up things has blinded us to what this life is really about.

Fortunately, Jesus goes on to say that some of the seeds of the gospel do fall on fertile soil, and for some of those who hear the Word, their eyes are opened to the truth and they come to God with all their hearts and bear good fruit. God is not against wealth, and He is not against our having things. God blessed the patriarchs in the Old Testament, and most of them were wealthy. It takes money to take care of your family, build churches, to feed the hungry, to clothe the naked and extend the kingdom of God around the world. We should be trying to gather whatever we can to use it as God directs. In the process we know that God has promised, in Malachi 3:10 and elsewhere, to bless us and let us enjoy the fruits of our labor. He is not against money, per se, but Jesus tells us to "seek first" His kingdom and His righteousness. And I'm afraid that far too often we're not doing that.

In Revelation 18, the apostle John writes that he saw an angel coming down from heaven with great power, and the entire earth was illuminated with his glory. This is a powerful angel, and he began to cry out because of all the evil that was happening in the world—in what the scripture refers to as Babylon. In this context, the name Babylon refers to the economic and social order of the world.

Exactly the same things are happening in John's visions that were happening when God destroyed the earth by a flood in the time of Noah. But then we read, "I heard another voice from heaven saying, 'Come out of her, my people, lest you share in her sins, and lest you receive of her plagues. For her sins have reached to heaven, and God has remembered her iniquities'" (vv. 4–5).

Clearly, God is calling His people to come out from the world and to separate themselves from the sins of the world. But who are God's people? They are Christians, they're the ones who've been redeemed by the blood of the Lamb; the true followers of Jesus Christ. God is calling Christians to turn away from the habits and customs of this world, but He wouldn't be calling His people to come out if they were not already living in the world and living by the values and rules and bad habits of the secular society.

I believe God is calling for His people in these last days to come out from the world's way of doing business, and the world's way of running the churches, our lives, our marriages, and our finances. He's saying, "Come out from among them!" Why? God is saying, I don't want you to participate in their sins, and I don't want you to participate in the plagues that are about to come upon this world. Because, if we are in the world and living just like everyone who is of this world, then we will have to share in the plagues and the economic and social disasters that are coming upon this world.

When Paul said, "Come out from among them and be separate" (2 Cor. 6:17), that was a call for Christian purity. He was instructing believers to live separate and pure lives. But the words of Revelation 18 are a warning straight from God Himself. At this point of John's prophecy, God has already spoken about the judgment to fall upon the nations—Persia, Russia, the kings of the East, and the other kings of the earth. He has already gathered the nations for destruction, but He is calling His people to come out so they won't have to partake of the judgments upon the secular kingdom of this world.

The apostle James says, "God cannot be tempted by evil, nor does He Himself tempt anyone. But each one is tempted when he is drawn away by his own desires and enticed" (James 1:13–14). Or as the King James Version says it, "by his own lusts." It is our own desires and lusts that allow us to be drawn away, and we're carried away from God by our desire for other things.

We can be close to God one day, and the next day we're running in the opposite direction. But what changed? We allowed the desire for other things to pull us away.

If we run our lives, our homes, our finances, our businesses, and our churches by the rules of the world, so long as the world prospers we'll prosper. But if we're no different from the world, when the world falls we'll fall right along with them. Earlier I spoke about the dangers of debt. I don't believe debt is a sin. In the business world, a reasonable amount of debt is sometimes essential as long as it's under control. But the question is not whether or not you're in debt, but who's your master?

If you're in debt and the economy is going along just fine, chances are you'll be OK. But look at what happened in 2009 and 2010 with the implosion of the lending markets. Millions who had what has traditionally been known as the most secure investment of all, real estate, have lost their homes and their livelihoods. Entire regions of the country, and even entire states, have gone into default. They can't pay their bills. Everything they believed in has failed, and they're becoming destitute.

This was what happened in the dot-com boom-and-bust of the late nineties. Millions of people got rich virtually overnight. Some few of them played it safe and salted a portion of their earnings away in safe places. But most did not. Those who put their faith in riches soared to the top with the rising fortunes of the Internet. Then one day, it all came crashing down, and trillions of dollars in equity simply disappeared overnight. Some of the biggest investors lost not only their retirement plans but also their personal fortunes, their homes, their automobiles, and everything else. When you do things the world's way, you prosper when the world prospers and you fail when the world fails.

And that's not the end of it. Since that time, we've seen the real estate boom-and-bust, and the stock market boom-and-bust, and once again we're facing a meltdown in the economy. Only this time on a much, much bigger scale. We all have the freedom within reasonable limits to live our lives as we please. But in the Book of Deuteronomy, God says, "you shall remember the

Lord your God, for it is He who gives you power to get wealth" But then He also says, "if you by any means forget the Lord your God, I testify against you this day that you shall surely perish" (Deut. 8:18–19).

A lot of people in recent months have lost money in the stock market, and some have made money. I suspect most have lost more than they've made, but I believe that God would like to ask us, "Why are you taking the money you've earned and putting it into the hands of people in the world?" Most of them are people you don't even know; yet you trust them with your finances.

The reason we do it is because we're betting on something going up or down—and, quite frankly, it's not much different than going to Las Vegas and betting on the numbers. We believed we could count on the markets to go up and down, and that our investments would always come out all right in the end. We believed things would always repeat themselves, but I don't think that's going to be the case anymore. Things are not going to repeat themselves. We're living in a very different world.

The events of 9/11 were a wake-up call for America, and the conditions of our lives have been changed forever. The breakdown in the world economy has changed the world forever, and the fallout from the 2008 election will change the world even more. It will never go back to what it was. If Christians think they just want to go on the same way they've always done, living in the world and playing by the world's rules, then they will have to accept the fate of the world.

My wife and I have asked the Lord to teach us how to take steps to separate ourselves from the world's way of living and doing business. We look to God to provide for our needs, and in the process, He is taking us through circumstances that will allow us to know Him in a more intimate way. It's important for us to understand that the way we deal with the circumstances of life will determine where God takes us next. If we respond to circumstances the right way, it opens doors of opportunity and He will bless us. But if we respond in the wrong way, it may well destroy us.

I began to learn this lesson through an unusual experience. The Lord had been taking me in a certain direction for a long time, and He was saying,

"Son, the way you respond to these circumstances will determine where I take you and what happens to you next. If you respond the way I want you to, it will be good for you; but if you don't, things will not work out as well in your life."

No one wants to suffer, but we will all experience pain. As a matter of fact, there can't be real growth, maturity, or integrity without it. It's often only through pain, when we come face-to-face with our deepest and most heart-felt emotions, that God is able to reach us. Unfortunately, most people have a difficult time identifying where that pain comes from, and if we don't know the source of the pain, we won't know how to deal with it.

About twenty years ago, a friend shared with me the idea that the pain we experience comes from three different sources. The first source of pain, he said, comes from chastisement. The Bible says that those whom God loves He chastises. Every son and every daughter of God will be chastised and corrected as He seeks to cleanse our hearts and draw us closer to Himself. Our heavenly Father teaches us through the trials and the adversity we endure, and He corrects us when we need it because He loves us. That kind of correction gives us insight and wisdom, and it teaches us the ways of God, which is a good thing.

The second source of pain is tribulation, which comes directly from the devil. The dictionary defines tribulation as distress or suffering resulting from oppression or persecution. That's a direct attack from the enemy. And the third source of pain is the consequence of our own actions. The amazing thing is that we blame God when we're tempted by the devil; we blame the devil when God is trying to teach us and correct our behavior; and we never stop to think that maybe the reason we're suffering all this pain is because of our own bad decisions and behaviors.

I would estimate that less than 10 percent of the suffering we experience is the result of God's chastisement, and less than 20 percent comes from tribulation. But I have to admit that most of the suffering I've experienced in my life has been the consequence of my own actions, behaviors, and choices. A lot of Christians will say, "Well, God forgives sin, doesn't He?" Yes He does, if we confess our sins. But we can all learn from the story of King David. He loved God, and the Bible refers to him as a man after God's own heart. But David fell from favor because of the lust he acted upon with another man's wife. He not only committed adultery, but when he discovered that Bathsheba was pregnant with his child, he sent her husband, Uriah, into battle, to the very hottest part of the battle, to make sure he was killed. So David's sin of adultery was multiplied immeasurably by murder.

When the prophet Nathan came to David and accused him of that crime, saying, "You are the man!" David didn't try to deny it; he realized what he had done and cried out, "I have sinned against the Lord" (2 Sam. 12:7–14). And because He did not try to hide his guilt but confessed it before the Lord, Nathan assured David that God had forgiven his sin and would allow him to live. But here's the lesson. Even though David was forgiven, that did not keep him from reaping the consequences of his actions and paying a terrible price, beginning with the death of the child that was born to Bathsheba.

Later David's wife humiliated him by committing fornication with his son, Absalom. After which, David was driven from the city and spent years hiding from his son and his enemies in caves. Then David's sons were killed in battle. And, perhaps most humiliating of all, David was not allowed to build the temple in Jerusalem because of his sins. Instead, that privilege was given to his son, Solomon. Had God forgiven David for his sin? Yes. But there were consequences of that sin that could not be avoided.

We live at a time when people don't want to be accountable for their own behavior, but that's not a choice. We're all accountable for our actions, and we will all suffer for the consequences of our actions and decisions. But it's important for us to understand where our suffering comes from so we can, at the very least, know how to pray about it and deal with it wisely.

The Lord had been speaking to me about all these things over a period of several months, shortly before I agreed to take part in a conference for pastors in Africa. Then, while I was there, the Lord impressed on my heart how important it is to respond in every circumstance the way He wants us to respond. I understood on a personal level that the way we respond to our circumstances will determine where God takes us next, but I realized this was a lesson I was being led to share.

It seemed like a fairly small thing at the time, but I had been noticing the way some of my Christian friends treated the waiters and waitresses in restaurants on Sundays after church. This really bothered my wife and me because restaurants have always been one of our favorite places of ministry. Some folks would go out right after church, and they were so demanding, snapping their fingers at servers and treating them disrespectfully. If they thought someone had slipped in front of them in line, they would yell out, "Hey, I was here first!" That kind of behavior will never find favor with God, so I spoke about that to the businessmen and pastors at the conference, and they heard the message loud and clear.

It wasn't long after returning home from Africa, while these things were still being impressed on my heart, that my wife and I began making arrangements for an important business trip to Japan. A large firm had hired me to consult with them on a new project, based on a new invention: a video microscope. But Japan is a long distance away, so before going to the airport I asked my secretary, Patricia, to check with the airline to see what it would cost to have our tickets upgraded to first class. I thought that having the more comfortable seats would make a big difference. Especially when my wife is traveling with me, I always try to make the trip as comfortable as possible. So I said I would call and talk to someone at the gate to find out which were the two best seats on the plane.

When I spoke with one of the attendants, she told me that Row 3, Seats D and F, were the best two seats on the plane. However, when my secretary got off the phone, she said, "Mr. Jones, you're not going to be happy. It'll cost you seventeen thousand dollars to upgrade your tickets to first class." That was shocking and totally out of the question. So I said, "OK, forget about it, Patricia. I'm not going to spend that much for an upgrade."

At that point Cookie and I drove to the airport for the connecting flight from Norfolk to Chicago. As soon as we got to the plane, I looked at our tickets and realized that our seats had been changed and we wouldn't be sitting together on the flight from Chicago to Tokyo. I would be on one side of the plane and Cookie would be on the other side toward the back. When I told Cookie about it, she said, "Dennis, I don't want to sit back there. What if I fall asleep and lean over on somebody? I want to be with you."

So I said, "OK. The Lord has been teaching us that the way we respond to the circumstances of life will determine what He does next. Let's pray." I took Cookie's hand and I prayed, "Father, we acknowledge your sovereignty over our lives. And we just commit these circumstances into your hand. We ask you to help us to respond in the way we should. We purpose to be content, however you work it out, and we thank you for it." As soon as we got to Chicago, I went up to the check-in counter and there were at least a dozen people ganged up around the counter trying to get the attention of the flight attendants. Some were pushing and shoving. Others were upset about one thing or another, and they were all talking as loud and fast as they could. By this time the young lady at the desk was visibly irritated.

When I finally got up to the front of the line, she said, "Yes? What can I do for you?"

I said, "My wife and I are on our way to Tokyo. It's our first trip, and I noticed that our seats got a little messed up. She's on one side of the plane and I'm on the other. My wife and I really love each other. Is there any way you can find us two seats together?" Then I gave her a big smile and said, "After all, this is the friendly skies of United, isn't it?"

I guess my approach must have caught her off guard. She paused, smiled at me, then leaned forward and said, "Mr. Jones, I'm going to put you and your wife in first class." That was a real surprise and I was delighted. She made the changes in the computer and handed me the tickets, and I said, "Thank you very much. God bless you," and left the counter. Then, when I looked down at the tickets, I saw that we would be seated in Row 3, Seats D and F. I hadn't asked for those seats, but the Lord took care of it for us. At that point tears filled my eyes as I thought, "How amazing, how powerful God is, and how good He is to us."

Only God can do something like that. If I had gone up to the counter, pounding my fist and demanding that the airline correct their mistake and give us two seats together, you can just imagine what would have happened. Either they would have made no changes at all, or they would have put us side-by-side in the worst seats on the plane. But, thank God, that didn't happen, and that's when God really began to teach me this lesson. If we want to see the hand of God move in our lives—and there's nothing more exciting than that—we need to learn to respond to the circumstances of our life the way He wants us to. And the only reason we don't is because, in the final analysis, we don't really trust Him.

And by the way, not only did that young lady give us first class tickets all the way to Tokyo, but she bumped us up to first class on the return flight as well—Row 3, Seats D and F. Some might call it a coincidence, but we understood what was really at work there. Once again, it was God's way of remaining anonymous. We knew we were very fortunate, but we also knew it was the favor of God.

We are faced with thousands of decisions every day. Decisions as simple as what time to get up, what to wear, or what to eat. But we also decide how we will respond to family members and the others we meet in the course of the day. We decide whether we will tell the truth or tell a lie. Am I going to forgive that person who offended me, or am I going to allow a root of bitterness to take control of my life? Am I going to be faithful to my wife, my boss, my friends, and my God? We're faced with a multitude of decisions, and the decisions we make will determine our success, fulfillment, prosperity, peace, joy, contentment, happiness, love, blessings of God, and all the other things we desire.

If we make the wrong decisions based on selfish motives and without regard to the well being of others, it will generally result in failure, lack, and want. Disrespect and self-centeredness lead to a life of emptiness and discontentment, filled with sadness, anger, loneliness, and bitterness. Unless we respond to life's challenges with genuine integrity, we will envy those who have achieved more or who have more of what we want. We fail because we're not willing to pay the price, to maintain our integrity, or to take responsibility for our own decisions.

Integrity simply means to be whole, complete, one. In other words, we're not living two lives. Are we who we say we are? Those who understand this principle will strive consciously to live with integrity in all areas of life, not just when we're with others, but also when no one is looking. Many times in life we're faced with the reality that if we make the right decisions and do what's right, it's going to cause us some pain. It might cost us financially, or even the loss of a precious friendship. But if you're willing to endure the pain, experience the loss, and go through the suffering regardless of the cost, you will reap the reward. Once you are through it, you will have not only gained wisdom and understanding but you will treasure the depth of the lessons you've learned through that experience.

Not long ago I was faced with that very thing. After building and selling a very successful business, which I described in a previous chapter, I made an arrangement with a new partner and we started a new venture together. We had all the business and marketing experience, knowledge, and capital we needed to succeed, but no matter how hard we worked, no matter how diligent we were, it just didn't happen. We continued to reinvent our strategies and marketing plans, and we tried everything we knew how to do, but to no avail.

I had been successful in every business I'd started since the age of seventeen. Some of those businesses were more successful than others, but I had never been in a place where I was going to have to close the doors, let all my employees go, and accept defeat. I couldn't understand it; it didn't make sense. We were the experts in the field. We thought the timing was right, and I even thought that I was being led by the Lord. But suddenly my wife and I were faced with the reality that the company was going to fail. We had lost hundreds of thousands of dollars, and yet we had no choice but to shut it down.

I found myself faced with some really hard decisions that, like it or not, I would have to make. One thing I've learned is that making the decision is always the hardest part. After you've made it, you can see it through. It doesn't help to wait when you have a hard choice to make; you just have to do it.

Think of the test Jesus faced when He had to make the hardest decision of His life. It was very hard to do, but He did it. There He was in the garden of Gethsemane. He knew who He was; He knew what He came to do. He knew that in a matter of hours the soldiers would take Him away, and He knew what they were going to do to Him. He knew why He was there: this was the very reason He had come, to give Himself as a sacrifice for our sins. And He knew it would cost Him His life. When it came time to go through it, He didn't want to do it. When He prayed, He sweated great drops of blood. He said, "Father, if it is Your will, take this cup away from Me" (Luke 22:42). He even prayed, "if there is any way possible, take this cup from me," but then He added, "nevertheless not My will, but Yours, be done."

He knew they were going to beat Him, hang Him on a cross, and drive spikes through His hands and feet. But in the end He was willing to endure unimaginable suffering for our sake, and He did not turn away. Once He had made the decision, He was able to endure the pain of the whipping post and the cross, and He did what He had come to do. Making the decision to do what is right is always the hardest part.

When we find ourselves in what I call these Gethsemane experiences, we're looking for answers. But the answers don't always come when we're in the midst of them. When Jesus cried out to the Father, the Father didn't answer Him. When He was at the whipping post, the Father still didn't answer Him. And even when He was on the cross and cried out, "My God, my God, why have you forsaken me?" (Matt. 27:46), the Father still didn't answer Him.

There are times in life when we may feel the utter loneliness and sorrow and cry out to God for answers. When we lose a loved one, especially if it's a spouse or a child, we want to know, "Why, God? Why this? Why now?"

But what I've learned is that "Why?" is God's question. Our question ought to be "What?" What do you want me to do, Lord, and how do you want me to do it? We will never know why God does what He does. He says, "For as the heavens are higher than the earth, so are My ways higher than your ways, and My thoughts than your thoughts" (Isa. 55:9). But we know that He is always just, and in time we may come to a better understanding of why certain things happened as they did.

God almost never answers in the way we would like. When Jesus cried out to the Father, there was no answer, but three days later all the questions were answered. In time everyone understood why He had to go through that terrible ordeal. Sometimes we just have to trust God and lean on Him, waiting for God to answer our questions in His own time and His own way. Hopefully that gives comfort for some who are looking for answers and wondering why.

When it came to closing my business, I was faced with some of the hardest decisions I've ever had to make. But we packed things up, moved everything out, repaired and painted the walls, cleaned up the building, and closed the doors, not knowing what was going to happen next. The irony is that just a few years earlier I had helped build a $14 million business in less than eighteen months. Before that I had built the largest medical hair-transplant network in the country. And in this new venture we were opening a business that was very similar to the one I had sold; yet, nothing was working.

We were offering services to physicians, and with the downturn in the economy we knew that medical doctors were looking for other sources of income, so we put together a revenue-sharing program in which the laser manufacturer would place lasers at their own expense in the doctor's offices. That way, they could offer laser hair removal and Botox treatments to their patients, and we would cover all the up-front costs. In addition, we provided advertising, marketing, and media, along with technical services for the equipment and access to our nationwide network. But this time it simply didn't work.

Three months out we had spent hundreds of thousands of dollars with no return on investment. It was like we were pouring cash down a black hole. After a while, I was asking, "Lord, what are You trying to say to me?" I saw what was happening, but I agreed to put even more of my own money into the business for another ninety days. If things didn't improve after that, we would pull out and close the business, and that's what happened. The Lord did not prosper our efforts.

Compared to the suffering that Jesus endured, my decision was easy. But I knew if I did the right thing in the right way, it was going to be painful, humiliating, and costly. One of the hardest things was calling in our employees and telling them that we had to close the business, and they would all have to find new jobs. Those men and women were like family to us, and it really hurt to see the disappointment and fear in their faces.

I'm grateful that we were able to help by contacting friends in business and finding jobs for several of them. Others volunteered to stay with us at half salary until we were able to start something new, so that was a blessing. But then, even harder, I had to go to the landlord and tell him we were leaving, even though we still had four years left on our lease. We were in a brand new office that had been built out just for us, and the landlord had spent hundreds of thousands of dollars getting everything ready. We had only been in business for a year, and we never got off the ground.

My partner and I met with the landlord and explained that the business wasn't going to make it, and we had to move out and close things down. Some of my colleagues suggested we should try to manipulate the situation and come up with a way not to pay him what we'd agreed to pay in the lease agreement, but I refused. The landlord hadn't done anything wrong, and that would have been unethical. Instead, I said I would make a good faith effort to honor our commitment and make a substantial payment toward the unused portion of the lease.

Unfortunately, my offer was rejected, and the landlord ending up suing us, causing all of us a tremendous amount of pain. And even though many of those who were involved in the process will never know what it cost us to maintain our integrity before God, the landlord was paid every penny. Doing the right thing is not always easy, and sometimes it can be very painful. But when you get to the other side of the ordeal, you will not only be equipped with a new level of wisdom, understanding, and knowledge, but you'll have the confidence of knowing that your actions were pleasing to God.

Chapter Twelve

THE DECEPTION OF COMPROMISE

M OST OF US are so afraid of experiencing anything unpleasant, especially anything that causes pain. We fear it so much that we will do almost anything to avoid it. We spend our working years trying to gain wealth—or at least enough to retire on—then we spend the rest of our lives in fear of losing it. Solomon said that a rich man's wealth is like a high wall in his imagination. We think that if we make enough money we can isolate ourselves and protect ourselves from the pains of life. If we can just get a little bit more, we think, then we'll be happy. But it doesn't always work out that way.

There's nothing wrong with having money, but the more prosperous we become, the greater the temptation to compromise our integrity and our beliefs. The greatest danger of losing your honor and integrity is not when you're just starting out. It's not usually a major problem while you're still growing. The real danger comes when you're becoming successful. For many years I wondered what happens to so many people to cause them to fall at the highest point of success in their life. What was it that caused them to shipwreck their lives and self destruct just at the point when they were becoming successful? I've seen this phenomenon happen so often to men and women in every walk of life.

Sometimes they're business people, politicians, or community leaders who started out with nothing, but they managed by hard work and self-discipline to build a large and successful organization. Sometimes it's a pastor or church leader who has built a dynamic ministry, but for some reason everything changes and they lose it all. For years I wondered and prayed about that: what brought so many of these people to the brink of corporate and personal ruin? In fact, one of the most influential men in my early life, a leader in business and the church, and someone I really looked up to, ended up shooting himself. That was devastating, not only for me, but for our entire community.

I asked the Lord why so many people fall, and then one day while my wife and I were relaxing, playing a game of golf, the Holy Spirit spoke these words to me: "The deception of compromise." That's all He said. But the message was so strong that I knew I needed to pray about it. So when I got home, I went upstairs to my office by myself and I asked the Lord to speak to me about "the deception of compromise." What came to my mind was that deception is a silent killer—a danger that always threatens people who are experiencing success in any area of life. Understand, if people realized they were being deceived, they would stop whatever they're doing and they wouldn't be deceived. If they could see what was coming at them, they would turn away, and I believe most people would do the right thing. But too often, they don't see what's happening until its too late.

God showed me that in every business and every ministry there will come a time when your integrity will be challenged. You may start off well, doing everything honestly in the right way, but then as the business or ministry or other activity you're engaged in begins to grow and it becomes apparent that God is blessing you, there will come a time when you're challenged to compromise what you know is right. For ministers and church leaders, it's often a challenge to compromise what the Word of God says in regard to ethical, moral, or financial issues.

Because of all the pushback from the secular society, some of our leaders are reluctant to deal with the hard issues facing them. The temptation to compromise always comes as a "Yeah, but..." proposition. I can't count the number of times I've been sitting at the table with a group of business and church leaders when we knew we had to take firm corrective action that would cause some pain, and someone would say, "Yeah, but....," and then they would go on to explain why it would be OK to bend the rules or compromise the Word of God. Whenever I would speak up and say, "But the Word of God says...," someone would object and insist that we needed to compromise. Not always, but in most cases, it was about money.

That's the deception of compromise. When you know that God's Word says to do things in a certain way and you choose, for convenience, to do something else, at that point you're no longer building the kingdom of God; you're building your own kingdom. The Bible says that if we insist on believing the lie, God will allow a deceiving spirit to come upon us that will perpetuate the lie, which will only entangle us, even further in the deception of compromise.

I eventually realized that most of the time this is because of either lust, greed, or the abuse of power. Most of the people who succumb to deception don't start off wrong. As a matter of fact, in most cases they start off with good intentions. They believe they're pursuing noble causes. In most cases they're good people with good values and good intentions, trying to play by the rules, to make an honest living, and to lead lives of integrity. But then they come to a place of major pressure, where they think they have to bend the rules.

We may feel that in order to take our business, our ministry, or our personal lives to the next level of success we just need to bend the rules a little. Unfortunately, it never stops there. There's always time to stop. We can say no. With every temptation, Paul tells us, there will also be a way of escape. (See 1 Corinthians 10:13.) But if we give in and make the wrong choice, we will have chosen the deception of comprise. And that choice always ends in disaster.

If there are areas in your life—whether its lust or greed or envy or any other issues you've never taken the time to deal with properly—believe me, you're asking for trouble. Trying to keep it a secret or cover it up will only make it worse. Too often, people will try to ignore these weaknesses, to hide them in the recesses of their heart and pretend they're not really a problem. But sooner or later all those things will come to the surface, and there's nothing that will bring them to the surface faster and more destructively than power, money, and success.

This truth has been made real to me. God is very patient with all of us, but the devil is patient as well, and he will wait until you're right at the pinnacle of success in your life to launch his attack. And if there are unresolved areas in your life—especially if you've been living a secret or double life—he will make sure those things come to the surface. The spirit of darkness will push you along, right up to the end, and then, when you least expect it, he will destroy you.

If you take the time to figure out where you went wrong, most of the time you can trace it back to the time when you compromised what you knew was right. Some people will try to convince themselves that "the ends justify the means." They'll say things like, "I'm just trying to meet the needs of the people," or "I did it in order to grow the ministry." But any time you make the decision to compromise what you know to be right; you've put your foot on the slippery slope. This is what happens with the deception of compromise, and it always leads to a painful and humiliating fall from grace.

A couple of years ago I got a call from one of the individuals who was part of a new company that had put together a DNA-matching service that would allow individuals to find out about potential health risks and related issues online. From a simple cotton swab they would be able to see if they were prone to diabetes, heart disease, Alzheimer's, or certain other serious illnesses. And with that information, they would be able to take steps to minimize the risks of conditions they might have to deal with later in life. That's where the latest DNA research has taken us.

When we got together, they told me that another online company similar to their new venture had already lost millions of dollars; but they said they had a new concept that they wanted to discuss with me. Up to that time people were primarily using DNA testing to determine the paternity of a child, and offering this service online hadn't really caught on. They decided that one way to bring the new technology to the marketplace was to develop brick and mortar DNA centers around the country, and some of the people I had worked with in setting up franchises for our hair-removal centers had suggested they come down to Virginia Beach and meet with me, to help them put their franchise plans together.

The pharmaceutical industry had been looking at this concept for years. Rather than just selling one-size-fits-all types of medication, they thought it would be a lot more profitable to manufacture individualized medications to meet the patient's needs. So the idea was for people to come in to these centers and have their DNA tested. In a week or two, when the results were available, they would come back for a private consultation, and based on what they learned, the patients could make an appointment with a physician who would then prescribe whatever treatment or medications might be called for. This would work for individuals as well as for expectant mothers who wanted to check on the potential health risks of their unborn children.

Based on those initial conversations, I did a lot of reading and studying on the advances in DNA research, and I took it very seriously for a time. Eventually, however, even though they offered me a great deal of money, I realized there were aspects of the program I couldn't support. I felt that once it was determined that someone possessed a genetic makeup that predisposed them to certain life threatening illnesses, you couldn't just send them out the door and tell them to deal with it. There needed to be a support system and follow-up programs to help those individuals address the issues identified by the tests.

So I told them I didn't want to be involved, but through that experience I came to realize just how many of our physical, emotional, and spiritual traits are passed down through the bloodline, and how an understanding of DNA can open doors to some important spiritual principles. All through the Old Testament, God required blood sacrifices to absolve the people of their sins. In Hebrews we read that, "According to the law almost all things are purified with blood, and without shedding of blood there is no remission [of sins]" (Heb. 9:22). God is Spirit, but the life of man is in the blood, and without blood there is no life. God requires blood for the atonement of sins.

This is, of course, the essential Christian doctrine: Jesus Christ was the ultimate sacrifice for mankind's sin. He shed His perfect blood for us so that all who believe in Him could have eternal life and be freed of their sin. Christ's sacrifice meant that the traditional blood sacrifices offered under the Old Covenant would no longer be required. No mere animal sacrifice could ever approach the significance of the death and resurrection of God's own Son.

But here's the point. We know the Bible doctrine of "original sin," which says that the sin of Adam has been transmitted generationally to every man, woman, and child. And when we understand that life is in the blood and that our entire genetic makeup is transmitted through our DNA, we ought to realize also that just as sure as the color of our eyes and hair are passed through the blood, so is sin passed through the blood. The Bible makes it clear that God's wrath still abides on "the sons of disobedience" and on all those who refuse the sacrifice of His Son. Jesus said, "He who does not believe the Son shall not see life, but the wrath of God abides on him" (John 3:36). This means, quite simply, that if you're not a Christian and have not chosen to come under the atoning blood of Jesus, you are still under the Old Testament law and will ultimately be judged as such.

I believe we can see the impact of this truth today throughout the world, our society, and especially in the explosion of illegitimacy worldwide and in our own inner-cities. According to Scripture, a child born out of wedlock cannot receive the blessings of God unless they come to salvation through faith in Jesus Christ and repent of generational sin. Moses writes, "One of illegitimate birth shall not enter the assembly of the Lord; even to the tenth generation none of his descendants shall enter the assembly of the Lord"

(Deut. 22:2). This means that any child born out of wedlock is born with the curse of sin on their life, which I believe that curse includes poverty, for up to ten generations. This was God's Law in the time of Moses, and I believe that for the unbeliever this principle is no less true today than it was 3,400 years ago when the Mosaic Law was written, because God never changes.

The only way we can make the right decisions regarding the circumstances of our lives is by having the wisdom, understanding, and knowledge necessary to make the right decisions. Some people will say that they can't be successful, or they can't attain their dreams, because of the environment they were raised in. It's their parents' fault, or their lack of education. After all, isn't that what all the experts have been telling us? Your environment, your genetics, or your education will determine your destiny. I've met a lot of people who bought into that theory, but there's just one problem. It's not true. From the beginning of creation, history refutes that idea.

In the Genesis account of Creation, we learn that God created Adam and Eve and brought them together as husband and wife. Then we see the first two human beings born into this world, Cain and Abel. Both of them were raised in the same environment, with the same upbringing, and there has never been a purer genetic makeup or bloodline than that which existed in those two boys. And yet one of them was a worshiper of God and the other turned out to be a murderer.

Now, I'm sure Jesse Jackson, Al Sharpton, and others will not like what I'm about to say, but a lot of ministries are trying to work in the inner-city to help the poor and provide them with opportunities for growth and improvement, and I believe that's a good thing. The Bible tells us that those who give to the poor are giving to the Lord, and the Lord will repay. I believe we should always help the poor. Unfortunately, the programs that the government and the state are implementing—and I would have to say also the church in many instances—are only dealing with the symptoms of poverty, and they never get down to the real problems.

We can expect that from the government, but we should expect more from the church. We're called to bring people out of poverty and destitution, and lead them into a place of real freedom so they can enjoy the rights given to them by God. With genuine freedom they will have opportunities to make something of their own lives—to be whatever they want to be.

Before I go any further, let me clarify my perspective by saying that I know what I'm talking about. I experienced all these things as a child. I grew up in difficult circumstances. My family struggled financially. I never got more than a seventh-grade education, and I got caught up in a lot of bad things as a boy. I was in jail when I was fourteen years of age, sentenced to nine years in prison, and spent almost eighteen months behind bars. The sociologists love to say that kids from backgrounds like mine are victims of their environment, but I'm not buying that. The problem in sin and rebellion. That's the real cause of society's problems, and until we deal with that we'll never be able to help these people.

I was talking about some of these things with a dear friend, who is an African-American pastor not long ago. He was working with people in the inner-city, and I asked him, "Brother, do you really want to make a difference?" He said, "Yes, I do." So I began to share with him what the Lord had shown me. There are only two people from the beginning of time until now that were born with pure sinless blood, and that was Adam and Jesus. They are the only two that God directly infused with pure sinless blood. So, I said, when God created man, He created him with a pure sinless bloodline, and He breathed His own breath into him.

God created man and woman for each other, ordained the family as the first and most important institution of human society, and He made them one flesh. The Bible shows us three examples of this oneness. The first is the Father, Son, and Holy Spirit: They are three in one. The second is Christ and His church, and they are one. And the third is man and woman united in holy matrimony, by which the two become as one. That's all. There are no other states of oneness ordained and commended by God in His word.

But when God created Adam, He created him whole and complete in every way. Adam had it all. He didn't lack anything, except a helpmate. God saw that it wasn't good for man to be alone, so He created for him a wife and companion who would share in the blessings and responsibilities of the family. Prior to that, all the qualities of the male and female gender had been present in Adam alone. The genders were not separate and they were not fighting with each other, as they are today. Adam was whole and complete in every way except for one thing: he lacked a companion. So God lays Adam down, takes a part of him, created Eve as a wife and companion, and the two were united as one flesh. Why? Because I believe they were one from the beginning. But what happened? When sin entered the world through rebellion and defiance of God's Law, it was transferred from generation to generation through the DNA of that first family.

When God blesses you, you are truly blessed; but as we see in the scriptures, when He curses you, you are truly cursed. So what does it mean when we're told by Scripture that illegitimacy can be part of a curse upon the family unto the tenth generation? The Bible teaches that all humanity is under the curse of the law and needs the redeeming work of the cross. However, some individuals are born inheriting generational curses that must be addressed in a spiritual fashion. According to the Christian faith, if you have not received Christ you're still under the law of the Old Covenant. And if you or your child is born out-of-wedlock, the curse of the law, which I believe includes poverty, rests upon you to the tenth generation, and even with a very generous estimate of just twenty years per generation, that's a minimum of two hundred years.

It is estimated that in 2008, 52 percent of all children born in the United States were born out-of-wedlock, and almost 70 percent of African-American children were born out-of-wedlock.[1] God has declared illegitimacy to be a sin, and it must be assumed that many of those who bear children out of wedlock, as well as the illegitimate children they bear, are not followers of Jesus Christ, and if they are, they are either not aware or just don't understand the yoke and burden they are placing on their children's lives. That means that perhaps as many as two-thirds of Americans are born under a curse that will succeed them to the tenth generation, and this curse brings not only broken-ness, unhappiness, and alienation, but poverty and strife.

That's an issue that has to be dealt with in America, and nowhere is this of greater importance than in the inner-city. Unfortunately, it's an issue the state is not going to deal with. Government is doing its best to condone and nor-malize this behavior, and the church has been dangerously silent about it. But I told my friend, that God was ready to lift up any man who would confront this issue and speak God's truth in love to men and women in the inner-city.

I thank God for all the programs that feed the hungry, clothe the naked, and teach the skills needed in order to be successful in society. But for the church to go into these neighborhoods and do all those wonderful things but then fail to warn the people about the consequences of illegitimacy and the wrath of God to come is a terrible mistake. The only thing that will bring renewal and break the curse of poverty in the inner-city is for there to be a fresh outpouring of grace and a true revival of faith in Jesus Christ.

Jesus became a curse for us by taking our sins upon Himself, and He paid the full price on the cross. The Bible says, "Christ has redeemed us from the curse of the law, having become a curse for us (for it is written, 'Cursed is everyone who hangs on a tree')" (Gal. 3:13). How tragic to think that for many young people today it's considered cool and modern to have an out-of-wedlock child. But as soon as that child is born, there's a ten-generation curse upon the family; and the only thing that can break it is the shed blood of Christ.

Wherever you see illegitimacy, you'll see poverty—this is as true in America as it is anywhere in the world. It wasn't until illegitimacy began to rise in America that we were faced with widespread poverty. I've spent many years working with missions and with Christian businesses in Africa, and I have many wonderful friends in Ghana and Nigeria. But you'll see much the same thing in Africa, where illegitimacy has wreaked havoc. I've been told that by the age of twenty-one, the typical young man in Nigeria has already had more than fifteen sexual partners, and this is a pattern throughout the culture. That's also why the AIDS epidemic is so widespread in that part of the world.

Illegitimacy breeds poverty, and vice versa. Where there is a high rate of poverty, you will almost always find a high rate of illegitimacy. Most of the pastors I've talked to about the problems in the inner-city just want to talk about "social justice." When they say that, I tell them, "Social justice is an issue that needs to be worked out between one man and another. But the moral breakdown taking place in the inner-city is an issue between man and God, and that ought to be an issue of much greater concern and importance."

Jesus spoke against poverty, but He also said, "The poor you have with you always" (John 12:8). Was He against social justice? No. He was against prejudice and partiality in any form. But social justice tends to be the main focus in many communities rather than the most deep-seated issues that separate people from one another and from God. When I see what is taking place today in America, I believe in many cases social justice is just a new term for socialism. It is being used by those only concerned with promoting their agenda, using the term *social justice* and causing racial unrest in order to redistribute the wealth of this country and take the nation in a direction the Founding Fathers never intended.

The Bible is clear that God and the church are, and should be, for equality. But we are also admonished to give, not grudgingly or of necessity, but out of a free will and a cheerful heart. How does that fit in with the way social justice is portrayed today? Many pastors know this, but very few are willing to admit it. No one wants to deal with it, but coming to grips with this one issue can do more to change the situation in the inner-city—and the rest of America, for that matter—than anything else.

In the presidential election of 2008, race became a huge factor. African-Americans overwhelmingly voted for Barack Obama because, understandably, they were thrilled at the prospect of seeing someone of their own race in the White House. The vote of the black community, combined with those of young voters who were equally excited about the possibility of a black president, was enough to secure victory for Mr. Obama. Many exit polls showed that upward of 95 percent of blacks voted for him, according to CNN, CBS, NBC, Fox, and *The New York Times* on election night and thereafter.[2]

The Bible is very clear when it says, "If anyone is in Christ, he is a new creation; old things have passed away; behold, all things have become new" (2 Cor. 5:17). The apostle Paul said, "I have been crucified with Christ; it is no longer I who live, but Christ lives in me; and the life which I now live in the flesh I live by faith in the Son of God, who loved me and gave Himself for me" (Gal. 2:20). How can we be "new creations in Christ" professing that all the old things have passed away and still leave the altar holding our brother in bondage to the sins of the past? If we truly believe that we are new creations in Christ, shouldn't our priorities line up with God's priorities? But what we saw in 2008 was that millions of voters decided that race and gender were more important than the social and moral issues in that election. During the primaries, millions of women voted for Hillary Clinton mainly because she's a woman, and million of men and women in the African-American community voted for Mr. Obama mainly because he's black.

That made me think of the Israelites under the Old Covenant. God led the Hebrew people through the judges, but one day they said, "Give us a king to judge us" (1 Sam. 8:6). God had warned them that kings would bring shame upon the house of Israel, and the prophet Samuel became angry with the people. But God said, "Heed the voice of the people in all that they say to you; for they have not rejected you, but they have rejected Me, that I should not reign over them" (v. 7). In the end, of course, great evil fell upon the land through the kings. God had warned them what would happen, but they chose to disobey Him.

When you consider the things that the Obama administration has championed since entering the White House, we can see the dangers we now face. Not simply economic crisis, the humiliation of America in the eyes of the world, foreign policy that punishes Israel and praises nations that fund Islamic terrorism, while withdrawing support for our military and giving suicide bombers constitutional rights, but also the unwavering support of the president and his entire administration for unrestricted abortion, gay marriage, embryonic stem-cell research, and so much more that is anathema in the eyes of a holy God. The principal goal of the health-care legislation that has created such turmoil is the push for unrestricted government funding for abortions. How can anyone believe that is a just and good cause?

And for this disastrous situation, I believe, we can credit the Christian vote. After all, it is estimated that as many as 82 percent of Americans profess that they are Christian.[3] Many of those men and women who are praising the Lord on Sunday mornings, reading the Word of God, and singing in the choir, went down to the polls and voted for abortion, gay marriage, and all these things. No, that's not what it said on the ballot. But beyond the rhetoric, the glamour, and all the wildly exaggerated promises was an agenda that is now taking this country down a very different path toward heartbreak, brokenness, and the judgment of God—all dressed up under the masquerade of "hope-and-change."

If we are truly followers of Jesus Christ, shouldn't our priorities be the same as God's priorities? I believe most Christians would say yes to that. And if that's the case, what is God's number-one priority? Many people would say "love." Others might say "peace" or "happiness." Those are all important, but they're not God's number-one priority. His number-one priority is "life." Without life there is no love. Without life there is no peace or happiness or anything else. Without life there is no existence. Jesus said, "I have come that they may have life, and that they may have it more abundantly" (John 10:10).

OK then, what is God's number-two priority? The answer is marriage. Why? Because human life can only be created through the union of man and woman. God created Adam and Eve to bring forth life. Remember that God was building a kingdom for Himself, and this was how He chose to do it. The sexual union of two men or two women will never create life. This is also why the covenant of marriage, as the first and most important institution of creation, is a sacred union in the eyes of God.

Life and marriage are God's number-one and number-two priorities. So my question to the church is, if these are God's priorities, shouldn't they be ours as well? Yet we had whites going to the polls voting for certain candidates because they were white, blacks voting for others because they were black, and women voting for other women primarily because of their gender. So what we saw in the church was that race and gender trumped our relationship with Christ. This is one of the main reasons America is in such desperate trouble today; and unless some of the leaders of our churches wake up and begin dealing with these issues, the church will continue to lose favor.

When I was incarcerated as a boy of fourteen, I was a minority in the jail, but I got to know many of my fellow inmates and we became friends. Over the years, I've been privileged to have many African-American friends and business partners, and I've come to care deeply for the things they care about. This is one of the reasons that I've spent so much time mentoring businessmen and ministry leaders in Africa. I love my black brothers and sisters, but my hope and prayer is that all of us will come to grips with this issue which is such a threat to the success and happiness of their people. This is what's facing America today, and it's becoming a major challenge to the church.

Chapter Thirteen

A MESSAGE TO THE CHURCH:

Are We Becoming More Politically Correct than Biblically Correct?

At this point I want to drill down a little further on these issues, but let me be quick to say that my message isn't to the politician, it's to the church. Because the battle we are facing today in America cannot be won politically, but only spiritually. So when I talk about political things, I'm not talking to the world. If the reader is not a professing Christian or concerned about the things of God, then what I'm about to share in the next couple of chapters is not for them. This message is only for those who calls Jesus their Lord and Savior. The message is a challenge and a warning to the church about where we're headed. And the underlying theme of my concern is that the church at this time in history is becoming more politically correct than biblically correct.

I remember a dear friend who heads a large and highly visible Christian ministry telling me several years ago when we were out on the golf course that political correctness ("P. C.") would be the downfall of this country. I believe he was right about that, but today I would have to say that it may well be the downfall of the church as well. The problem is that too many Christians are afraid to speak out about the drift toward secularism in the church; so I think it's important that we see how the Word of God deals with this issue. I don't want to be overly pious in what I'm about to say, but we need to understand that the scriptures are still relevant to the times we live in. We need to know what God is saying to the churches.

Everybody talks about freedom. We all want to be free, but freedom is not measured by the circumstances of life. It's measured by our relationship with God. We can have financial freedom and still be in bondage. On the other hand, we can even be in slavery and have freedom, because men cannot determine our freedom—only God can do that. There are men like Chuck Colson who work with men and women who are incarcerated in prisons and jails around the world, and their message is that once you come to know Jesus Christ, freedom resides in your heart and soul. The Bible says that, "Where the Spirit of the Lord is, there is liberty" (2 Cor. 3:17). And, "If the Son makes you free, you shall be free indeed" (John 8:36).

Every day it seems we see new reports of wars, disasters, floods, fires, hurricanes, earthquakes, and every kind of tragedy known to man. The world is being shaken as never before, creating tremendous fear in the hearts of people everywhere. We have acts of terrorism almost every day somewhere in the world, and this is now one of the greatest threats to our nation. Within a short period of times the United States has fallen into trillions of dollars of debt. Banks, mortgage companies, investment firms, airlines, and corporations of every kind are on the brink of bankruptcy, and millions of people are facing financial ruin.

I serve on the board of directors of a bank in our area, and when I hear that more than a 130 banks have closed in the last few months, with the possibility that another 300 failing in the coming year, I know we have reasons to be concerned. As I write these words, more than seventeen million Americans are out of work, and the published unemployment rate is well over 9.5 percent—even though in reality the unemployment rate in many areas of our country is closer to 20 percent. And on top of this, we still have nuclear threats from Iran, North Korea, and other rogue states that would like nothing better than to destroy this country.

The world we live in is not a safe place, and all of these things are genuine threats. But I believe God is speaking to us through these things, and what I believe He is saying is that we must return to the first things. If we allow our hearts to turn away from the things of God, He cannot and will not bless this nation. And if the church turns from its "first love," God will not withhold judgment from us much longer.

All these things were prophesied centuries ago, and the words of Scripture are being fulfilled before our eyes. We can read about them in Luke 21 and Matthew 24 where Jesus speaks of the "signs of the time" and the "end of the age." He said there would be wars, earthquakes, and famines in the earth, and these things would come as advance warning of His imminent return. But He warned us not to be deceived by people who want to lead us off into things that are contrary to the Word of God.

Jesus tells us not to lose hope, but He warns us of two signs that are especially critical for the church in the End Times. First, He says that when we see Jerusalem surrounded by armies seeking to destroy her, then we will know that the abomination of desolation is at hand. Then He goes on to say that before the end of the generation that witnesses these things, "the sign of the Son of Man will appear in heaven, and then all the tribes of the earth will mourn, and they will see the Son of Man coming on the clouds of heaven with power and great glory" (Matt. 24:30).

Right now we see Jerusalem surrounded by hostile armies. The president of Iran has said he wants to drive the Jews into the sea and wipe Israel off the map. Even our own president, a large proportion of the United States Congress, the U.S. State Department, and the United Nations are doing their best to divide Jerusalem down the middle and strip the land of Israel from the Jewish people who, as the prophets foretold hundreds of years earlier, have turned the desert into a fragrant garden.

I don't know when the Lord is coming back. Jesus said, "Of that day and hour no one knows, not even the angels of heaven, but My Father only" (Matt. 24:36). But God's people need to be ready to face the things that will be coming in this country and around the world, certainly economically, and be prepared for that. We need to have contingency plans in place because, quite frankly, many people are heading toward bankruptcy and unemployment who think they're secure and free from danger.

This will be the situation from this point on, for the foreseeable future, and the church needs to be dealing with these things with messages that are timely and relevant. The pastors need to encourage God's people, but too often many of our pastors and teachers are preaching a feel-good gospel that has little to do with the realities of our disintegrating culture and the breakdown of the moral order.

Iran has made a pledge to destroy Israel, and the Jews have hinted strongly that they will make a preemptive strike against Iran if they feel the threat is imminent. Frankly, I believe that is going to happen. I believe Israel will carry out the threat in their own self-defense, but the enemies of Israel around the world will be outraged that the Jews would dare to think about defending themselves. As believers, we need to understand that it all started in Jerusalem and it will end there.

Jerusalem is referred to in Scripture as "the holy hill of Zion" (Ps. 2:6), and the focus of God's love for His chosen people. But in our time this city has become the focus of what the enemies of God want to take and destroy. Even though we may believe we're safe from the coming cataclysm in the Middle East because we're half a world away, this ought to be something that concerns every believer in Jesus.

It's very clear from the prophetic words of Scripture that the countries that align themselves with Iran will be wiped off the face of the earth. Which countries would that be? First of all, it will be Iran and the other Muslim countries in the Middle East that have sworn to destroy the Jews and the nation of Israel. Then, according to Old Testament prophecy, God will rain down his wrath upon Russia, China, and other socialist and totalitarian nations such as North Korea, Cuba, and Venezuela, that have taken sides with the Muslim world against the Jews. All these countries are already in league with one another, and I believe we will see them continue to form new alliances with each other. But the danger for America is that, for the first time in history, we have an administration and national leaders who agree with Israel's enemies and are trying to divide the ancient city of Jerusalem.

Will America stand with Israel? It's still not clear, but we have to believe that, for His own reasons, God has given us leaders in this country who are not standing with Israel, and who do not believe in the sanctity of that place. So these are very serious times for the world, for America, and particularly for the church.

Unfortunately, I fear that the administration in Washington will not side with the Jews in the event of conflict in the Middle East, and many God-fearing men and women in our churches are complicit in that fact. In 2008, the American people elected the first president in our 230-plus year history who does not and will not support Israel and the Holy Land. And now we see all these things happening around the world. The prophetic word is being fulfilled every day in the headlines, over the broadcast media, and on the Internet. These are indeed perilous times, and we need to be ready at all times, for the Lord could come at any time. But what will He say when He appears?

In 1 Chronicles 12, we see an important illustration of what the Lord expects of us. It says that the sons of Issachar prospered because they understood the days in which they lived, and they were careful to prepare for the changes taking place around them. The question for us is, does God want to bless His church in the midst of a bad economy? The answer is yes. He can do that, and I believe He will. But what if He doesn't? What if our economy collapses and we suddenly find ourselves scrambling to make a living? Are we going to turn our backs on God? Are we going to join the Socialist Party? Are we going to turn to the government instead of God to solve our problems?

I believe with every fiber of my being that the Holy Spirit has drawn an invisible line in the sand. Without even knowing it or saying it, but by their actions, Christian men and women are making up their minds, whether they're going to follow Christ or follow the world. That's what it's really all about. And all too often it comes down to the love of money. Many of the people who voted in the 2008 election had never voted before, and when interviewers for the exit polls asked why they had come out, many voters said, "I'm here to get some of that Obama money."[1] But when reporters asked where that money comes from, either the voters didn't know or they just said it was "government money." Many of them had never paid taxes, and the idea that all that money was coming from the pockets of their fellow citizens apparently never crossed their minds. But it's also possible, of course, that they didn't care where it came from, just so long as they got their share. It was all about the money.

As we prepare for what's to come, the church must ask this question: are we serving the Lord? Are we really committed to Christ, or are we more concerned about our own well-being? There has never been such division as we see today in the church. Blacks and whites are more divided than I've ever seen in my lifetime, and everybody is aware of it, but it is not "politically correct" to talk about it. Jesus said we can discern the seasons, but we can't discern the signs of the times in which we live. That's tragic. Terrible things are happening all around us, and we can see that; yet, a lot of Christians act as if it's just business as usual. But here's the message: it's time for every believer to wake up, stand up, and come back to our first love.

In October 2009, the president signed a hate-crimes bill that had been tucked into the Defense Appropriations Bill. If anyone voted against the bill because it promoted homosexual rights such as gay marriage, they would also be voting against funding the military. As a result, behaviors that have been outlawed by civilized societies since the beginning of time are now not only legal but protected by the United States government. And if anyone claims that homosexuality or any of the new protected rights are an abomination in the eyes of God, they can be charged or even found guilty in a court of law and either fined or imprisoned for speaking out.

So what we now have is laws that punish moral judgment and give freedom and license to perversion. The day is coming that if someone inadvertently overhears your conversation in which you say that homosexuality is a sin and an abomination to God, they can have you arrested and jailed. We've already seen how these laws have played out in Europe, where pastors have been snatched out of the pulpit and jailed for preaching the Word of God. But if this sort of thing is happening in America today, how long will it be before the preaching of the gospel is outlawed?

The same people who have pushed for hate-crime laws are the ones who will say that the Bible is hate speech. They will say that accusing people of being sinners is hate speech, and how dare you claim that your religion is true and that every other religion is false! If your pastor dares to speak the whole truth and call sin by its name, anyone sitting in the pews can bring charges against him and have him tried for hate crimes in a court of law. That's where we are heading today. And mark my words: if something doesn't happen very soon, it won't be long before they start taking the 501(c)(3) tax exemptions away from churches. And what will that do?

The question is where does this sort of policy eventually lead? If you look at Russia, Romania, Poland, Hungary, and any of the Eastern European nations that had been free nations before they fell under the yoke of Communism, the first thing that had to be done in order to enslave the people was to create pain, break the economy, remove the Bible, and shut down all gospel preaching in the churches. If you think it can't happen here, you need to understand that it has happened many times around the world. As I mentioned in a previous chapter, I remember going to Russia in the early 1990s. It was amazing. I had heard about revivals and I had read about revivals, but for the first time in my life I found myself in the middle of one. Thousands upon thousands of Russian men, women, and children were coming to God, weeping when they heard the gospel preached for the first time.

For seventy years under communist rule, they were told there was no God.

Three generations were born and raised believing there is no God, and if there is no God there is no morality. During all that time, the Russian Orthodox Church still existed under the government's watch and control. The people could go to church if they wanted to, but the priests were not allowed to teach the virgin birth of Jesus, the resurrection from the dead, or the second coming of Christ. The people could come and hear Bible stories, but the gospel had been gutted. Predictably, the church dried up and faded into insignificance, no longer relevant to people's lives. And I fear that same process is already happening in many American churches.

Political correctness is one of the greatest dangers to the United States of America, and unless it is brought under control, it will lead to the downfall and eventual destruction of our country. I think most reasonable people would agree that this country has become more politically correct than common sense would dictate. But my real concern is that many churches are becoming more politically correct than biblically correct, and that's a far more serious issue.

Political correctness is becoming one of the most divisive forces in our nation. Advocates of P.C. are setting the rules and standards that dictate what is good, bad, and even what is funny. They want to tell us what is honest and dishonest, what we can eat and drink, what we drive, and how we heat and light our homes. Political correctness—which first appeared in one form, as I understand, during the Red Chinese takeover in China under Mao Tsedong—is a pernicious and potentially deadly doctrine. Yet, today it is dividing our country, dividing the churches, and dictating the morality of the day. It's forcing many pastors to compromise their beliefs and even to compromise the Word of God, just to keep from offending a few misguided individuals in the pews.

The secular society is always pushing us to make dangerous and unwise choices—choices that always seem to wage war on our Christian values—forcing us to make a choice between Republican or Democrat, Right or Left, black or white, conservative or liberal, Jew or Gentile, and even Christian or Muslim. As Christians—and this is especially true for ministers of the gospel—we don't have the luxury of making such choices. As followers of Christ, our standard must always be the Word of God. Rather than accepting without question whatever the secular society demands from us, shouldn't we be taking a stand with God on all these issues and following what the Bible teaches? Yes, we should. And rather than getting caught up in some philosophy, cause, or political agenda, shouldn't we be looking to His Word for guidance?

What we're seeing in many churches all across America is a spirit of compromise. In many cases pastors avoiding the relevant issues of the day in order to keep from "stepping on toes." They're ignoring the issues that are changing and reforming our country, which are the issues their congregants are having to deal with and make decisions about every day. Men and women in the pews are looking for direction. They're asking for leadership from their spiritual leaders, but in far too many cases they're not getting it.

When the Founding Fathers were laying the foundations of this great nation, pastors and men of a profound Christian faith played a major role in drafting the language and content of our great founding documents, including the Declaration of Independence and the Constitution. Pastors in those days took strong stands and led their flocks not only into the marketplace but into battle when it was called for. Sadly, many of today's spiritual leaders have chosen to teach their congregations how to avoid pain and suffering. Rather than preaching a gospel that is truly relevant to the times we're living in, some prefer to deliver a feel-good doctrine of peace, prosperity, and self-esteem.

Don't get me wrong. There's a place for practical teaching, for Bible stories, and for simple messages of encouragement in the church today; but if that's all there is, it's not enough. A storm is coming and any pastor who fails to prepare his people for the tidal wave that is going to sweep this nation and the church in the very near future is failing the flock. A rising tide of antagonism and bigotry is already threatening the church, and threatening our religious liberties. The freedoms we've enjoyed for more than two hundred years are at risk. Not only are there powerful forces that want to strip away our liberties, but there are false teachers undermining the truths of scripture, attempting to replace the Word of God with notions that are, as the apostle Paul warned, "contrary to sound doctrine."

We may not be there yet in this country, but the handwriting is on the wall. If the churches in America fail to stand up and speak out about the assault on religious liberty, there is every reason to believe we could end up going the way of Europe, where Christianity is essentially dead. And once we lose our freedom of religion and freedom of speech, we can be sure that freedom of the press, freedom of assembly, and the right to petition the government for the redress of grievances—which are the rights and privileges guaranteed to every American by the Bill of Rights—will be lost as well. At that point a reign of tyranny will have begun.

Thanks to political correctness, it is already against the law to speak the truth in public. How much longer will it be before it's against the law to preach the Word of God in our churches, or even in our homes? It's just a matter of time. At that point the secular humanists and government elites will be asking, "Where does all the hate come from?" And their answer will be, "Why, it comes from that book, that Bible." What is really at stake in America is the truth of God's Word, and I believe the ultimate agenda of the humanists is to remove the Bible from the people and to deny the authority and truth of the Word of God.

Over the past four decades we've seen the Ten Commandments removed from public buildings and classrooms. We've seen nativity scenes and Christian monuments removed from both public and private property. We're seeing more and more attacks on our churches and religious institutions all across the country. But I believe that, ultimately, the goal is to silence the Word of God. All of which leads me to ask: at what point do we wake up and stand up against the loss of our freedoms, our faith, and our entire civilization?

Do we wait until our freedoms are gone and then try to get them back? Or do we rise up now to defend and preserve the rights and privileges our forefathers died for? King George III of England never went as far as our own government has gone over the past few years. Yet the colonists rose up in fury and defeated the armies and navies of the British Empire to claim the liberty that comes not from government but from the hand of God.

One of my favorite scenes in the movie *The Patriot* is when the pastor is standing outside of a small church in South Carolina, and he says, "There's a time for ministering to the flock, and there is a time to defend the flock from the wolves." Then, as he peels back his clerical robes to reveal the military uniform he's wearing underneath, he says, "Who's with me?" That's the way it was then, and the people responded to the challenge.

Christian pastors led their flocks: they weren't afraid to stand up and speak, and many battles were won by pastors leading the men and boys of their congregations into war. In New England, there were so many pastors leading the troops they became known as the "black regiments," because of their black clerical robes.

Pastors like Jonathan Mayhew, of the famous Old West Church in Boston, were among those who lit the fire of revolt in the hearts of the people. In one of his most impassioned sermons, called "Discourse Concerning Unlimited Submission and Non-Resistance to the Higher Power," Rev. Mayhew warned that, "Civil tyranny is usually small in its beginning, like 'the drop of a bucket,' till at length, like a mighty torrent, or the raging waves of the sea, it bears down on all before it, and deluges whole countries and empires."[2] Many students of history have suggested that this sermon was the first volley of the American Revolution. But we have to wonder how many of our pastors today still have that kind of passion.

I fear that if something dramatic doesn't happen soon, we're going to see churches all across America closing their doors. This will happen for two reasons. First, as of this writing the laws are being changed so that anyone who earns more than a certain income can no longer deduct charitable contributions. In the beginning, this may have only a small impact, but there's no question that in time it could reduce and even eliminate giving to religious and charitable organizations.

The apostle Paul said that some people preach the gospel out of a pure heart and others for personal gain or selfish ambition. But whatever the motivation, he said, "Whether in pretense or in truth, Christ is preached; and in this I rejoice" (Phil. 1:18). If Paul were here today, I believe this is what he would say: many are giving to the Lord out of a pure heart. Others are giving only for the tax deduction. But whatever the motivation, I rejoice because the gospel is being preached.

If government can take away the tax deduction and the incentive for people to give to the church, we will still have the "widow's mite." The faithful will continue to give; but many of those whose motivation has been the ability to reduce taxes through charitable giving will find other ways to protect their money. And I have to believe this is the primary reason that the administration in Washington has taken this disastrous step—to cripple and limit the influence of the Christian church in American society.

The church will no longer be able to depend upon the tithe. A lot of good, hard-working people who have been faithfully giving their tithe will not be able to keep it up. Thanks to the sad state of the economy, giving to the churches is already down and it's going to continue to fall. Those who were giving primarily to get the deduction were the biggest givers. This is not only going to impact the churches, but every ministry, every good work, every missionary program, and virtually every charity, whether religious or not. Remove the sources of support and you're going to see an incredible shrinkage of philanthropy. Many churches won't be able to pay their staffs, and all the important programs, from missionary support to feeding the hungry to turning on the lights on Sunday morning, are going to be hurt.

That's the first thing. The second thing is that many of the churches are already so deeply in debt that it's just a matter of time until the banks and lending institutions start calling in their notes, and many churches are going to have to close their doors. This means that these pastors will have two choices. Either they can stand up with integrity and preach the whole truth of the Word of God, knowing that there may be a price to pay, or they can stick to the safe and comfortable kind of shallowness and equivocation that will avoid controversy and keep them out of trouble.

Of course, many of them have already compromised. I don't see anything in God's Word that calls on pastors and church leaders to burden the members of the church with millions (and in many cases tens of millions) of dollars in debt. In Deuteronomy it says, "You shall lend to many nations, but you shall not borrow" (Deut. 15:6). We ought to be helping people, but not going into debt to do it, when we do not have the resources to protect God's work. You can't tell me that if a pastor knows he has to make a fifty thousand-dollar payment to the bank on Monday morning, and doesn't have it in the account, that's not going to influence what he preaches on Sunday.

Solomon warned that "The borrower is servant to the lender" (Prov. 22:7). But let the church get three or four months behind in payments to the creditors and you'll find out who really owns that property. Does the bank own it, or does Jesus own it? By taking on large amounts of debt, many of our churches have sold themselves into bondage. Jesus said, "No one can serve two masters; for either he will hate the one and love the other, or else he will be loyal to the one and despise the other. You cannot serve God and mammon" (Matt. 6:24). We need to ask ourselves, are we building God's kingdom or are we building our own?

The issue is not simply whether or not to borrow. The issue is who is the master? Jesus said we cannot serve two masters, but in many cases, I have seen church leaders let the bank become the master of the church, and don't even know it. As we begin tightening the purse strings in America, we're going to see the finances of the churches begin to shrink. And when that happens, we're going to see the doors of some of our biggest churches closing. There's no question that there is a premeditated attack under way against the churches, but the churches have also put themselves into a precarious position by compromising many of the principles of God's Word they know to be true.

Chapter Fourteen

A MESSAGE TO THE NATION

HOW MANY TIMES have we seen it? A religious leader is being interviewed on television and the host says, trying to discredit him, "Are you telling me that only Christians are going to heaven?" And then he dodges as quickly as he can, and says, "Well, God loves everybody." The host, pressing the issue, then says, "But are you saying that Hindu's and Muslim's will not go to heaven?" Feeling that he's boxed in, the minister finds some way that ends up compromising what he knows to be true in order not to "discriminate" against non-believers. After all, he doesn't want be accused of indulging in what the media now call "intolerance" or, worse, "hate speech." As a result, he compromises his beliefs and denies the Word of God.

Jesus said, "He who does not believe is condemned already, because he has not believed in the name of the only begotten Son of God" (John 3:18). There's no wiggle room in that. But some of our Christian leaders have lost their courage, and as a result, if they don't begin standing up, will end up losing the church in America. Pastors and spiritual leaders who have the courage to stand up and speak the truth will be persecuted and ridiculed, but they will be blessed. God will have mercy on them, even in times of stress. But those who compromise the gospel will not only lose their churches, they will go down in shame.

God is calling men and women of God to stand up for what's right, and this pertains to white churches, black churches, multi-racial churches, and all the others, and to every other congregation committed to the truth of the Word. And as I shared previously, those who feel a calling to the inner-city, any minister who goes into the inner-city and preaches the truth of the gospel will discover that miracles can still happen. If men and women who are bound by the sins of their fathers and the deceptions they've been subjected to by their environment receive this message and repent, they will be released from the poverty and brokenness that has kept them in shackles. Too many people believe that going into the churches on Sunday morning, singing the hymns, praising the Lord, and listening to the sermons is all it takes to be a Christian and to inherit the promise of eternal life. But Jesus gives us a powerful warning: "Many will say to Me in that day, 'Lord, Lord, have we not prophesied in Your name, cast out demons in Your name, and done many wonders in Your name?' And then I will declare to them, 'I never knew you; depart from Me, you who practice lawlessness!'" (Matt. 7:22–23).

Some will cry in the last day, "Lord, we went into the inner-city and taught them how to read. We set up food pantries and gave them clothes and money and food to eat. We were your hands and feet." And while all of this is good and worthy of praise, it's not enough. Unless the whole gospel is given and people come to God so that their lives can be transformed from the inside out, they will remain in poverty and bondage from generation to generation. You may have done many good deeds, but how many believers ignored the priorities for which Jesus died when they went to the polls and voted for men and women who support the killing of innocent babies in the womb?

How many "Christians" ignore the sins of homosexuality, gay marriage, illegitimacy, and the destruction of living embryos in the laboratory? Is the church in America becoming completely tolerant of those who indulge in adultery and cohabitation and other sexual sins? How many Christians who disagree with these things and personally refrain from engaging in them themselves nevertheless went to the polls and voted for men and women who support them all? Has race and gender trumped Christ in His church today? Have they not helped to perpetuate the very sins that the apostles condemned and that Jesus gave His life to set them free from?

I fear that Jesus will say to them,

> You have taken sides with the workers of iniquity and yet you dare to say that you know Me and you love Me? When it came to My priorities, you wanted nothing to do with Me, and you voted your race and gender over what you knew to be right. Depart from Me, you workers of iniquity. I never knew you.

I know that's a harsh indictment. But who can argue with it? We claim to be new creations in Christ, but if we show so little regard for the sanctity of life and the sanctity of marriage, which are two of God's primary concerns, how can we claim to be following Him? If we know what God says and you do something totally opposite, how can we claim to be on the same side with Him?

In Matthew 24 and Luke 21, Jesus answers the disciples' questions about the last days. They say, "What will be the sign of your coming?" And in both passages, He begins by saying, "Don't be deceived." Four times in Matthew 24 He says the same words, "Don't be deceived." Clearly, this is one of the most important issues in our day that men and women who claim to be followers of Christ are being deceived by the world.

As I mentioned earlier, I believe The Lord has drawn an invisible line in the sand. The sheep and the goats are being separated at this moment. But God is not separating one from the other. We are deciding which side we're on. I don't believe God is a Republican or a Democrat, but the Bible is clear on where God stands on certain issues. If we claim to be followers of Jesus Christ, shouldn't our priorities be the same as His?

Jesus said that He came that we might have life. He is the way, the truth, and the life. God created life and declared the taking of innocent life to be a sin. He established the family as the first and most important institution of society, and Jesus said that a man shall leave his father and mother and cling to his wife, and the two of them shall become one flesh. How much more do we need to know? God cares about the sanctity of life, and He cares about the sanctity of marriage.

But these are the two things that are under the greatest threat in America today. Yet, born-again Christians in churches all across America are choosing political correctness over biblical correctness. Without realizing it, they've fallen into the very things Jesus warned us about, saying it would be just like the days of Sodom and Gomorrah, when even the elect would be deceived. Choosing death over the life of the unborn and same-sex marriage over the kind of marriage that God ordained.

Some would say today that the issue of social justice is more important to society than either abortion or same-sex marriage. I know God cares about social justice. He cares about the unjust things that men have done to other men. But God is not unjust, and one day we will each have to face God and answer to what we believe concerning the things He cares about. And what can those who have trivialized the gospel of Jesus Christ possibly say in their own defense?

I was at a conference in Toronto, Canada, in August 2007, where I was asked to speak on Christian leadership. I was doing three two-hour sessions each day, which is a format I actually enjoy. Whenever I'm in Africa I'm generally expected to speak for about the same amount of time. If a minister can't speak for at least an hour over there, it's doubtful they will be invited back. But this pace can be exhausting after a few days. So while I was there I went up to my room between sessions for a quick nap.

On this occasion I was resting—I wasn't awake, but I wasn't really asleep. I was in one of those in-between stages when I suddenly felt the presence of the Lord. The Holy Spirit spoke to me and said, "Get up and write this down."

So I grabbed my pocket recorder and starting speaking what the Holy Spirit was saying to me.

At that point, He gave me a message concerning His shepherd's in His church, especially in America. He began by showing me the present condition of the church today, why so many believers are leaving the churches, and why so many are transferring from church to church. There's very little first-time salvation happening in America today compared to what the churches are experiencing in other parts of the world. Most of the so-called "church growth" we're seeing is transfer growth, and church groups are paying hundreds of thousands of dollars to the so-called experts to come in and tell them why this is happening. But God began to show me why that afternoon.

Many of God's people are leaving the church because they feel their needs are not being met. They blame it on everything. They will say they don't like the music or the preaching or the way the service is run, but the problem is actually deeper than that. Today in the church of the Lord Jesus Christ, we have a lot of pastors who are preaching from the pulpit, but no where as many who are truly shepherds to those God has entrusted to them.

So the Spirit of God said to me, "I have an indictment against many of My shepherds." And He referred me back to Ezekiel where the prophet speaks about God's call upon the shepherds. Today, the Holy Spirit is establishing and positioning the five-fold ministries in the body of Christ around the world. Each of these offices—apostle, prophet, evangelist, pastor, and teacher—has a different calling and a different function in the church. But there is one specific office that the Lord holds accountable to watch over the souls of His people, and that is the pastors who are the shepherds of the flock.

The Bible says, "Obey those who rule over you, and be submissive, for they watch out for your souls, as those who must give account" (Heb. 13:17). Even though we should honor and show our respect for all in authority, the Bible is clear that we are to submit ourselves to the pastor of the church. And I believe that's why the pastors are under such incredible attack today, because they're the ones who are accountable to God for the souls of His people.

Serving as the pastor of a church and shepherding the flock of God is not just a profession, it's a calling, and it's one of the hardest callings anyone can have. It demands genuine love and compassion for God's people, and the ability to encourage and lift up those who are wounded. It also requires a willingness to speak the truth and confront sin, but I'm sorry to say that some pastors are more concerned with their own ambition and building their ministries than with the well-being of the flock.

I felt the Sprit of God say to me, "I've seen what's happening in many of the churches all across this land and I have seen the way some of my shepherds' hearts and minds have shifted away from their flocks. Some of them no longer look at their flocks as those who have been redeemed of the Lord, or as those who have been bought with the price of My own Son, but they look at My people as a resource to fund their own dreams and visions. Rather than seeing them as My beloved children, many see the members of their congregations as a means of fulfilling their own ambitions and desires." He told me, "Many of My churches are being run like a worldly corporation, and the passion that many of My shepherd's had for My people in days gone by have been replaced with their own desire to grow bigger and more powerful, and to become well known.

"Some of My shepherds have grown weary of shepherding the flock and they no longer see My people as children of God but as a burden, a responsibility, a problem, as trouble and headaches that are too much to bear. Caring for them as individuals, they think, is too much responsibility. They look for ways to find fault and say that their flocks are not faithful because they don't give as much as they would like. In many cases, it's not that the flock is unwilling to give, but that the shepherd is not shepherding the flock with the tender care I intend for them to demonstrate."

It was a harsh indictment, but I knew it to be true. This is certainly not true of all pastors, but some shepherds are simply looking to the flock for the funding and manpower to empower their own vision, and that can change from month to month. Every time these pastor comes up with some new scheme or new program they wants to launch, they go back to the flock and expect them to supply all the money they need to meet some personal goal.

If the things they desire were truly motivated of God, they would be looking to the Lord Jesus Christ, who, Scripture tells us, "Shall supply all your need according to His riches in glory" (Phil. 4:19). But, rather than looking to God for provision, they will go outside the walls of the church, outside the wisdom and knowledge that God desires to impart. They go to the world, looking to the world for ways to raise money and build their programs, using all kinds of fundraising tricks and entertainments to build an earthly kingdom that in many cases will be void of God.

Rather than calling the elders and the congregation together to seek God's counsel for wisdom and direction, we see too many pastors today calling in the fundraisers and "professionals," at great expense to the church, to teach the pastors and deacons how to fund their programs. They pay outside consultants to tell them how to conduct fundraising campaigns, as if God could not take an anointed vessel—a man who has been called and anointed—and give him instructions on how to begin a new work. If it's truly of God, the Lord will provide everything needed for the work to be successful. But it will be for God's glory, not man's.

Have we forgotten how to seek God's counsel for the wisdom, understanding, knowledge, and insight we will need to build the church and fulfill the work and the call of God on our lives? Have we lost the ability to pray, and the faith to wait upon the Lord until He answers? Scripture tells us, "The Lord is not slack concerning His promise, as some count slackness, but is longsuffering toward us" (2 Pet. 3:9).

Today in many leadership meetings, you will hear pastors and elders using terms such as "giving units," referring to the families in their churches. These "giving units" are the people Christ died for, but suddenly they're merely "units" whose value to some shepherds is how much they contribute to the vision of the elders and church leaders. They will say privately that the typical "unit" is worth a certain amount of revenue per year. If you have a hundred units giving one thousand dollars each, the church can expect one hundred thousand dollars a year in tithes. If they have a thousand units, they can expect a million dollars a year. Rather than looking at the members of their churches as children of God with gifts and talents to be used by God, some of our shepherds see them only as "resources" to accomplish their own dreams and visions.

These things are repugnant, a stench in the nostrils of a holy God, and a reproach before Him. Have some of our pastors lost their love and passion for their flocks? Surely not all of them, but they know who they are. I believe that once you begin to change the name of the saints of God to "giving units," not only in name but in spirit, you've lost contact with the humanity of the souls Christ died for. At that point you've begun to look at the men, women, and children in your church simply as vehicles to fund your dream.

Those who do not have a true shepherd's heart, a heart for God almighty, and a pure heart for the flock that God has entrusted to them will soon lose the calling that God has given them. He warned the church at Ephesus in the Book of Revelation, "Remember therefore from where you have fallen; repent and do the first works, or else I will come to you quickly and remove your lamp stand from its place; unless you repent" (Rev. 2:5).

As I've already said, most of the growth taking place in our churches today is merely transfer growth. These are not new souls who've been saved through the preaching of the word: they're Christians who've been attending other churches—some for many years—but they end up leaving those churches to join another church. Why? One reason, I believe, is the feeling that the pastor is not shepherding the flock. When a pastor doesn't have the passion in his soul and the love of Christ in his heart, the flock knows that. When they begin to feel they've been deserted, they soon lose their sense of belonging.

They no longer feel the sort of concern for them and their families they once felt. Even though they may hear the words of a good sermon from time to time, it's the unspoken words from the pastor's heart they're responding to. I believe that most Christians are looking for dedicated and surrendered men and women to lead them, to watch over them, to pray for them, to love them, and to care for them. But there are not enough pastors in the churches today who are truly committed to shepherding God's people. Those who have been faithful to their calling will reap the blessings and anointing of God in their lives and ministry; but those who have compromised for the sake of worldly success will fail.

What God laid on my heart in Toronto was a message for the church, which says: "Woe to you shepherds who have misused the flock and have taken the fat of the land for yourself and have left your flocks destitute and in need." It is a warning to some pastors that the Spirit of God is coming into your churches. His eyes are seeking those pastors and church leaders who do not have a pure heart toward the flock. He is watching those who see God's people merely as "giving units." The Lord is saying He will pluck His people out of those churches, and He will place them in other churches, to be cared for by pastors who truly have a shepherd's heart. He will lead them to churches that will care for them, provide instruction from the Word of God, and minister to them.

When the Spirit of God leaves the church, that church will die. The word *Ichabod* will be inscribed over the doorframe, meaning, "the glory is departed" (1 Sam. 4:21–22). But where the Word of God is preached in its fullness, and when the people of God are being challenged to walk in the Word, the Spirit will abide, and He will draw all men to Himself. Wherever that happens, the church will thrive. Word will spread that something is happening there. The Word of God is being preached, people are coming to repentance, and there is a spirit of hope and a passion for truth. You won't need programs and fundraising campaigns: the Spirit of God will move the people to share in the building of the church, and there will be an explosion of excitement and new growth.

Most of the churches that drifted away from God's way of doing things never realized what was happening to them. They didn't start out wrong, but they lost focus on the mission and began looking at the church with the eyes of the world. The problem was the growth. Their idea of success had changed. One thing we know about the church: if it's of God, it's alive: and if it's alive, it's going to grow.

Another thing that's being taught in many places today in this country is called "marketplace ministry." They've given it a name, and it's beginning to spread around the world. Unfortunately, as soon as any new ministry concept gets a name, some people will try to merchandise it. What they're teaching ministries is how to work with business leaders—although often with very questionable motives—to get them to give money for their own work. It's not true marketplace ministry: it's simply fundraising by another name. There are some who may be well-intentioned and sincere who will say that God has called them to raise money to build the kingdom of God. But that's not marketplace ministry either. It may be a good work, but it's not ministry.

Marketplace ministry is not going to church and praising God on Sunday and then going back to the world on Monday and living like everybody else. And it's not doing whatever you want to do and just asking God to bless it. It's by allowing Jesus Christ to live in you and through you in everyday life, in every business affair, every strategy session, and every aspect of your life. In so many of our church "meetings," the men and women who serve as church leaders spend more time talking about money and fundraising than about fulfilling the ministry and vision of the kingdom.

God has called us to go into the marketplace as His hands and feet, His eyes and ears, and His heart and compassion, and all that He is in our everyday life and circumstances. That's what true marketplace ministry should be. And He has given every business man and woman the same opportunity to serve if we will seek Him with all our hearts. If we will not compromise our integrity, if we're willing to accept the circumstances of our life and respond to them in the way God wants us to respond, He will use everything in our lives, including even our pain and suffering, to bring us into a place of intimacy with Him. Then He will begin to live His life in us and through us, everywhere we go, and in everything we do.

What's lacking in many of our churches is a willingness to bring the whole gospel to bear on the issues their people are dealing with every day. When half the congregation is out of work, when many have already lost their homes, and others are in danger of losing theirs; when their retirement is in danger and everything else in their world is in jeopardy; haranguing them for more money is not the way to go. It should never be about the money. It should be about whether or not the gospel is being preached, and whether people are growing in their relationship with God.

The shepherd is there to offer healing, consolation, and restoration. He is there to teach the principles of faithful living, not to fall back on some worn-out sermon with three points, all beginning with the letter *P*, which has little or no bearing on the issues his people are facing. Too many in leadership don't want to come down to the place where the people are actually living. They don't want to counsel them; they don't want to get their hands dirty. If there's any one-on-one ministry taking place, in most cases it's being done by lay ministers and volunteers. But that's not how we are supposed to take care of the flock.

As I suggested in chapter 6, I believe God is trying to restore the five-fold ministry of the church. The sad thing is that every time the Lord begins to manifest one of the five offices of ministry, many in the church find a way to merchandise it and turn it into a fundraising opportunity. I've seen this for nearly forty years now, ever since I've been a Christian. In the fifties, it was the office of the evangelist. In the seventies, it was the office of the teacher. In the nineties, it was the prophet, and since 2000 it has been the office of the apostle. And every time the Spirit begins to move, you find the fundraisers launching a new campaign.

The Bible tells us that as the time for the Lord's return gets closer, the foundations of the churches will be built upon the ministry of the apostles and prophets. This is very important. But while the Lord is trying to establish the ministry of apostolic and prophetic gifts, some of our church leaders are off doing their own thing, building what amounts to an earthly kingdom. I get so many letters and e-mails from some of these apostolic networks that it has become a joke around our office. When the letters come, my secretaries will tell me, "Mr. Jones, you got another letter wanting to recognize you as an apostle to the body of Christ, and they want you to join their network."

It's sad, but I just laugh and say, "Yeah? How much will this one cost me? What's the price for being an apostle with this network?" Of course, we throw all that mail in the trash. It's repugnant to me to take the ministry that God is trying to establish and merchandise it that way. But I've noticed that many of the same people who were involved in the "shepherding movement" of the seventies are the ones involved in the "apostolic movement" in the church today. Some of them have repented for what they did at that time. Many more were part of the "prosperity movement" of the eighties, and some of those folks have repented. But, despite all of that, they're preaching and teaching today in the same spirit, in what I perceive as a spirit of exploitation and control. The only difference is that they're wearing a different cloak.

God's priorities for this nation are the same ones He has for the church: defending the sanctity of human life and protecting the sanctity of traditional marriage. God put such a high premium on the institution of marriage that He compares the marriage of man and woman to the relationship of Christ and the church. He says to men, "Husbands, love your wives, just as Christ also loved the church and gave Himself for her" (Eph. 5:25). God wants husbands to have the same care and concern for their wives that He has for us. Most of us don't really get that, but it's a priority with God.

The priority of the enemy, on the other hand, is to destroy the Word of God in this country and take the Bible out of our society. Marriage is as much a part of God's creation as the sun, moon, and stars. The atheists would like to convince us there is no God, because if they can make enough of us believe there is no God, then there will be no moral restraints. They believe that everything the mind of man can conceive will be possible if they can only eradicate the fear of God from our hearts. This is, of course, a pernicious lie of the devil. The Bible says the devil is a liar, and the father of lies. But this is what the atheists have in mind.

What the world believes, then, is based on a lie. Scripture tells us that God ordained marriage, but if there is no God, why be married? There's no penalty to be paid for sexual sin if there is no sin. And if marriage is not God's creation, but merely a repressive social convention, then who's to say that marriage has to be between a man and a woman?

So the ultimate goal in all these things is to take the Word of God out of our lives, out of our churches, and crush our dependence upon Him. The only way that can be done is by destroying two of the things that God cares most about: the sanctity of human life and the sanctity of marriage. At this hour, Satan is waging war with the people of God, trying to eradicate the true religion and erect his own earthly kingdom. It's a war that will determine, one way or another, the future of everything we hold to be sacred and true. If we lose this battle, we will lose the church. If we lose this battle, we will lose our country. And if we lose this battle, we will not only lose the war, we will lose our freedom and everything else we hold dear.

Chapter Fifteen

SIGNS OF THE TIMES

Most of the things that are going on in America today could never have happened even ten years ago. A decade ago no one would have dreamed we would be voting whether or not to legalize gay marriage. But everything seems to be upside down and it's moving so fast, which is exactly what Scripture says will happen in the last days. Who would have believed that such a large portion of the American people would condone the slaughter of millions of innocent unborn babies? But this is the reality of how the world thinks.

If a major corporation today announces that they're going to be laying off ten thousand more employees in order to cut expenses, in the current economy, that will likely mean that those men and women will be losing their livelihoods. Some of them will no doubt lose their homes, college funds for their children, retirement funds, and everything else for which they've labored. But, despite the suffering of all those individuals, there will be a great roar of applause on Wall Street because their stock will go up a few more points.

That's the way the world goes, and far too often the church is willing to go right along with it. Many of our churches are indistinguishable from the world. We've been taught in our universities to leverage everything. Put down as little as you can and finance it for as long as you can. That's the savvy way of doing business, using other people's money. As long as the economy is strong and everyone is thriving, you may be fine with that approach. But as soon as the economy turns south, all that clever strategy goes right out the window. But by that time, history has proven it's already too late.

The Bible talks about birth pangs. The closer you get to the birth of a child the faster the birth pangs come. We've already experienced several unprecedented shocks over the past ten to fifteen years, and look what has happened in just the last couple of years with all the "hope and change" in Washington. The labor pains are coming closer and closer together now, and I believe all these things are pointing to exactly what God is trying to tell the church: "Come out from the world's way of doing things, so you won't be caught up in the sin of the world." God is calling us to come out from among them so we won't have to suffer the plagues that will come upon the secular society in the full outpouring of His wrath.

As long as we're invested the same way as the world, we will profit when the world profits. But if the world suffers, we're going to suffer right along with it. Revelation 18:8–13 speaks about the kings of the earth mourning over the city of Babylon, the great city where the merchants of the world came to buy and sell their goods. The chapter goes through a litany of items—gold, silver, precious gems, and then goats, horses, cattle, and finally the souls of men.

In this passage, the Lord is speaking to the church about the world's way of doing things versus His way of doing things, and we quickly discover that in God's kingdom it's almost the reverse of the world's way. Notice that gold and "the love of money" are at the very top of the list for those living by the world's standards, while the souls of men are at the bottom, after goats, cattle, and sheep. We're living in a time when what's right is considered wrong, and vice versa, which the apostle Paul warned about. The chronicle of sins identified by Paul in the first chapter of Romans is as timely today as it was in the first century, at the height of the corruption and excess of the Roman Empire.

Whenever God says something repeatedly in one chapter, it's usually a good idea to pay attention. In this chapter, three times the apostle says, "In one hour ..." describing the destruction of the great city of Babylon. Merchants and kings around the world looked on in astonishment at the smoke of her burning. John writes:

> The kings of the earth who committed fornication and lived luxuri-ously with her will weep and lament for her, when they see the smoke of her burning, standing at a distance for fear of her torment, saying, "Alas, alas, that great city Babylon, that mighty city! For in one hour your judgment has come." And the merchants of the earth will weep and mourn over her, for no one buys their merchandise anymore.
> —Revelation 18:9–11

I suspect it's no coincidence that, from the moment the first plane hit the first building of the World Trade Center in New York City, on September 11, 2001, in one hour those buildings were down. Not fifty-nine minutes, but precisely one hour. Exactly sixty minutes. Up to that moment anyone would have said such a thing was impossible. Ever since that day conspiracy theories have been rampant, with people trying to figure out how in the world such a thing could happen. How could those two massive towers have collapsed and burned so quickly? And the smoke of her burning continued to rise for weeks, and the merchants and kings of the world were awe stricken by what had happened in that great city.

I cannot say with certainty that the biblical passage is referring specifi-cally to New York City or the Twin Towers, but it is certainly something to consider. We know that the Book of Revelation often has more than one meaning. I believe the name Babylon has a dual meaning. The first meaning is literal. It refers to a city such as New York that is grand, on a scale com-parable to the city of Babylon in Mesopotamia, which dominated the ancient world with its power and wealth. But the second meaning is of a world eco-nomic order that is diabolically opposed to the Word of God. Babylon in this sense is a world system that is opposed to the traditional Judeo-Christian moral order.

The real danger is that some of the pastors and teachers in our churches have been seduced by a false system of belief. When it comes to orthodox Christian beliefs, they believe they can go a little to the right or a little to the left in their teaching, so long as they maintain contact with the essential doctrines and sacraments of the church. Unfortunately, the acceptable limits of change keep shifting further and further from the core doctrines of Scripture with each generation. Any time you hear a church boasting about how open-minded, welcoming, and affirming they are, in most cases you can be pretty sure the things they're affirming aren't the ones taught by Christ and the apostles. In the midst of all this open-minded theology, the authentic teachings of Scripture are being watered down, faster today than ever before.

If the drift away from Christian orthodoxy continues at this pace, what's happening to the churches will mirror what's happening to our country. It's like the old story of the frog in the kettle. If you try to put a frog in a pot of hot water, he'll hop out of there immediately. But if you put him in a pot of cold water and warm it gradually to a boil, he'll just sit there enjoying his warm bath until it's too late. Before you know it, he'll be cooked.

I'm afraid that what's happening to many of our churches today. It's a slow boil that's allowing the churches to be lulled into apathy, and this is happening in large part because of one central issue: the love of money. When our church leaders are spending more of their time worrying about how to fund the vision instead of seeking God's counsel on how to fulfill their calling, they have fallen into error. That's where a lot of churches are today, and it's one of the greatest dangers for believers.

⁓

The Bible tells us that salvation is a free gift of God, but if we want to live our lives with integrity and without compromising what we believe, it's going to cost us something. God wants every man, woman, and child to come to Him through faith in His Son; but He is not satisfied with us just coming to the altar. He wants us to be in fellowship with Him on a daily, hourly, and moment-by-moment basis. He created us for that purpose. If we want our ways to be in keeping with His ways, we will have to be willing to stop what we're doing at any point in time when He shows us it's wrong.

I recently heard a young woman attempting to justify her marriage, even though she knew her fiancé was not a believer. She knew he was the wrong man for her. She knew it would likely end badly. But she said she had already told all her friends, the invitations had been sent, and it was too late to back out. I told her I had counseled a young woman in a similar situation a few years ago. She came to me the day before the wedding, and when she explained her situation, I told her I would stand behind her in her decision, but she needed to speak to her parents and tell them why she didn't want to go ahead with the wedding.

If you know the person to whom you're engaged is not the right person, and not someone who will honor your own beliefs, then God does not want you to be bound to them in marriage. We must not forget that marriage is a sacred bond. When you make your wedding vows, you're not just pledging your commitment to that person, you're making a vow to God. Some people who come to that point are willing to make the hard choices. Others are not. But it's never too late to do the right thing. Once you've crossed that threshold and become unequally yoked with an unbeliever, the choices you make from that moment on will be much, much harder.

I've been involved in businesses, invested a lot of money, hired attorneys, and gone to the wire, right up to the time of signing the contract, and realized, "This isn't a person that I want to be in business with!" Someone might have said, "Yeah, but we've invested all this money, and we've got to pull the trigger." But I believe it's never too late to do the right thing. This is just as true for pastors and teachers as it is for everyone else. Sometimes we just have to bite the bullet. It may be painful to stop and turn around before making a dreadful mistake, but we have to be willing to do that. God assures us that not only will He see us through those difficult decisions, but He will bless us on the other side if we're faithful and obedient.

True success cannot be measured over the short run, and not even over a few short years. True success can only be measured over the course of a lifetime. If you take a stand for what you know to be right, not yielding to money or fear—or the fear of losing money—there will be times when even your closest friends will desert you, because they don't understand the journey you're on. But I've learned that if we will forgive those that hurt us along the way and keep an open door, even though it may take many years to happen, they will come back through that door and be reconciled.

We have two choices in life concerning this matter. We can close ourselves off, harden our hearts, and never get hurt. Or we can open ourselves up to others, knowing we may get hurt, but the few friends we do acquire over a lifetime are worth far more than the pain we experience from others. Even Jesus, though He loved all He came in contact with, had only twelve close friends, and one of them betrayed Him. But through all the circumstances of life, whenever we will allow God's will to be done in our lives, He removes the pressures of our circumstances. When we deliberately choose to obey Him regardless of the cost, He will reach out to us and give us the strength to follow through, demonstrating His almighty power.

The reason God is trying to restore the offices of the apostles and prophets is because the true church is built on that foundation. The need for the wisdom of these servants has never been greater than now. Unfortunately, we have some people in the churches today who think they can buy their apostolic ministry. Ministries that can only come through spiritual anointing from God Himself are being offered for a price. And this is preventing the power of God from accomplishing what He wants to happen within the body of believers.

I fear that the only way the church will ever be cleansed of sin and self-indulgence will be by going through a time of suffering. When I think about the great revivals that have taken place in this country, I think about the outpouring of the Holy Spirit on whole regions of the nation, with men and women falling on their faces before God, repenting of their sins and rejoicing in the manifestation of signs and wonders. We haven't seen that kind of revival for a long time, and we haven't experienced the blessings God wants to bring to America. We're long overdue for a new awakening.

The last true revival in this country was the Azusa Street Revival that lasted from 1906 to 1915 in Los Angeles. That was a true revival. The conviction of the Holy Spirit flowed into the living rooms and dining rooms of millions of Americans, and there was a dramatic change in the way people lived. Sadly, I don't believe we're ready for that kind of anointing at this moment. We're not going to be seeing anything like that until we go through a period of suffering. But I believe the Lord is going to allow that to happen very soon.

Now that hate-crimes legislation has become law, there will be more and more assaults on the churches. Pastors will be faced with the decision whether to remain true to the Scripture or to water down the gospel to avoid prosecution. Eventually contributions to the churches will fall off because of the way the tax laws have been rewritten. The groundwork for a major shift in the way people think about religious liberty has already been laid. When God wants to get the attention of the churches, He knows that the best way to do it is to tighten the purse strings, and that's already happening.

The church needs to understand that success is not measured by how much money they have in their bank account. It's measured by how well the lives of men, women, and children are being transformed and renewed by the Word of God. Many of our church leaders tend to believe that as long as there's plenty of money in the bank, that's a sign of God's approval on what they're doing. But that's dangerous. There are apostate ministries today that appear to be thriving and growing, just as there are anointed and Spirit-led ministries that are struggling to pay the bills.Contrary to what many of the prosperity preachers have been saying, lack of money is not necessarily a sign of God's disapproval. And that's equally true in your life, your business, and your ministry. At the same time, an abundance of money is not necessarily a sign of God's approval, because it can be removed as quickly as it was given. The Bible says, "The rich man's wealth is his strong city, and like a high wall in his own esteem" (Prov. 18:11). He thinks he's ten feet tall and invisible. But wealth is not necessarily a sign of God's favor.

When a man becomes wealthy, he thinks he can buy his way out of anything. There are no problems he can't solve, no crisis he can't overcome, and no obstacle he can't avoid if he has the cash. Up to a point, he may be right about that. Money can be a powerful insulator. But sooner or later he will come to a moment of truth that no amount of money can avoid. I think especially of the scandals that have rocked the sports world over the past few years. Some of the richest, most popular, and most successful athletes in the world have been stopped in their tracks and dishonored in the eyes of the world for their personal failings. But it's not just athletes. Churches are subject to the same conceits. Some think they can do whatever they want behind the scenes and nobody will notice. But God will never allow His true church to be contaminated by deceit and apostasy.

Ultimately, all these things come back to the issues of integrity and wholeness, being one person and not two. You can't live two lives and expect the world to ignore what you're doing. Whether it's a famous golfer, the preacher in one of the country's largest mega-churches, or the head of some national association of evangelical Christians, eventually you will be found out and justice will be served. The Bible says, "be sure your sin will find you out" (Num. 32:23). Whatever is hidden in the dark will be revealed, and every sin will be exposed to the light of day.

It's tragic when we see that some man or woman we admired has fallen from grace. How sad to learn that what they've been doing was wrong and untrue. Politicians seem to be falling by the wayside every day. We find that some who claimed to be Christians, who claimed to be against gay marriage, were having homosexual affairs while leading huge ministries. And others who claimed to hate pornography and prostitution were, in fact, up to their necks in it.

It's shocking how many of these men and women actually believed they could hide what they were doing by preaching against their own sins. It's as if they were trying to exorcise their own demons when, in fact, they had never surrendered their hearts and minds to Christ. But God knew all along what they were doing, and God will not be mocked. (See Galatians 6:7.)

I believe revival will come to America, but it will only come when the people of this country fall on their faces before a holy God and repent of their sins. It wasn't that long ago that Jesus was "in." Jesus was "cool." In the early seventies, we had the "Jesus Movement," when tens of thousands of mostly young people became enthralled by the love of God and the love of their fellow man. Even though the movement eventually faded away and left many of the faithful dispirited and unfulfilled, it nevertheless helped to spark an era of spiritual growth and renewal, and some of today's most gifted pastors and teachers came to faith at that time.

Two thousand years ago, when Jesus came into Jerusalem riding on the colt of a donkey, all the people were singing, "Hosanna, hosanna, hosanna!" They were loudly praising God and casting palm branches on the path before him, proclaiming that Jesus was the Messiah. Six days later the same people were screaming, "Crucify him! Crucify him!" But that's human nature. That's the world we're living in today. First Jesus was in; next thing we know, He's not in. And it's the very same people.

Some of the pastors standing in the pulpits are timid. They don't have the backbone to stand against the drift of the culture and preach the full gospel. A lot of the teaching in the church is on how to feel good about yourself, about how much God loves you, and how much grace there is for sinners. And even though the message of grace is true and important in the church, those messages alone will not see people through the hard times.

Some of our church leaders, especially in the megachurches, don't really feel the stresses and the pain that people are going through today. Recently we learned that one of every six Americans is unemployed. That's devastating news; yet, in many cases leaders in the churches are isolated from the pain of their members by the salaries they get, the lavish homes they live in, and the entourage that surrounds and protects them. They are so isolated that they are no longer able to feel the suffering their congregations are going through. They've lost touch with reality.

But that will change. I believe the Lord is getting ready to shake the churches. He is shaking everything that can be shaken. We've been hearing that the earth is being shaken for the last forty years, but it has never been shaken to the extent that it is now. The whole world is being shaken. Every nation is being shaken economically. Every church, every home, and every individual life is being shaken, and God is asking us, "Whom are you going to serve?" Are you going to follow the world and adopt their ways, or are you going to stand up for righteousness as followers of Christ? If we believe in the truth of the Word of God, then we must confess that what Jesus says is right is indeed right, and what He says is wrong is still wrong.

The Bible says, "The time has come for judgment to begin at the house of God; and if it begins with us first, what will be the end of those who do not obey the gospel of God?" (1 Pet. 4:17). I believe the apostle's warning is directed to the church of our day. The shaking of the church is going to take place from the top down, from the most well known church leaders down to the least. And those whose hearts are not right before God will be exposed. This will happen more and more as God brings his flock to many no-name pastors who really love God. And those are the ones who will prosper.

I believe we will see an escalation of war in the Middle East very soon, as Israel responds to the threats and provocations from Iran and the Arab world. I also believe that America is facing another terrorist attack within a short period of time—like a 9/11, only worse. After 9/11, America was once again a Judeo-Christian nation. For one week the nation was united. For one week we were a Judeo-Christian nation again. People were flooding into the churches. They were scared, and when people are afraid they come back to God. In times of suffering they come to the churches; but as soon as the fear dissipates, they forget God and return to their old ways.

So long as there is peace, prosperity, and freedom from fear and want, the people say by the way they live, "We don't need God. We will accept the abortions. We will accept gay marriage and all the other abominations the world demands." But when God begins to shake America to its foundations, the only thing that can bring the people back to God will be a level of devastation like nothing we have ever experienced or even imagined in this land.

It is one thing to turn your heart from God because of your money, but when it comes down to a matter of life and death, fear for your own life, and fear for the lives of your family members, that's when we'll find out who we really are. Even the loudest and most doctrinaire atheists suddenly change their tune when it gets to that level. And that, I believe, is our only hope of true revival. In His mercy, God will allow something to take place in this country that will turn His people back to Him.

What scares me most, however, is that for the first time in American history our nation is not standing with the nation of Israel. The Bible says that those who bless the people of Israel will be blessed and those who curse the nation of Israel will be cursed (Gen. 12:3). America has remained strong in part because we have been such a staunch ally of the nation of Israel. But not long ago our own government declared that if Israel attempts to send its fighters over any territory in the Middle East where American fighters are stationed, such as Iraq, they might be shot down. How is that possible?

From the earliest foundations of this country, we were a God-fearing people. The Pilgrims and Puritans came to this country seeking the freedom to worship Jesus Christ, as they wanted to, in the purity of the scriptures. Our Lord, Jesus Christ, was a Jew, born in Israel. For more than sixty years this nation has been committed to the well being of that nation. Yet we have now, for the first time in our history, an administration that is trying to divide the land of Israel, to partition the city of Jerusalem, and to steal the birthright of the Jewish people.

And worse, many of America's churches and mainline denominations teach a type of "replacement theology" that is hostile to the Jewish people and their ancient homeland. They want to say that the New Covenant God made with the church has replaced the Old Covenant, but that is false theology. God told the Jewish people He would never revoke His Covenant with them. Both the Old and New Covenants are still very much alive, and those who are teaching that the nation of Israel is no longer precious to God will feel the wrath of God, and very soon, if they don't correct this falsehood. (See, for example: Psalm 105:10; Isaiah 55:5; Jeremiah 32:40; and Ezekiel 37:26.)

Jesus said, "Do not think that I came to destroy the Law or the Prophets. I did not come to destroy but to fulfill." He added that, "till heaven and earth pass away, one jot or one tittle will by no means pass from the law till all is fulfilled" (Matt. 5:17–18). We need to understand that the Word of God is not up for grabs. It says what it means and means what it says, and every Word is as true today as the day it was written.

Loren Cunningham, the founder of Youth with a Mission, spoke at my church in Virginia Beach in 2009, and he gave a sermon in which he went through all sixty-six books of the Bible, showing how every one of those books reveals that Jesus is the Creator. He recited at least one passage from every single book that demonstrated the divinity of Christ. When we look at all of the laws that were given to us by God, and all the ceremonies and observances ordained by God, we find that there isn't one where we don't see the person and the ministry of Jesus Christ.

Every law we live under today was established there. For the church to come to the place where we say the Old Testament no longer applies is to lose our way. If all the passages in the Word of God concerning God's love for the nation of Israel no longer apply, then neither do the laws derived from the Ten Commandments.

Over and over again we see Christ's warning, "Do not be deceived." Unfortunately, many of the church fathers were deceived about this. They honestly thought they were helping God out when they decided that the church was the new Israel. Little did they realize that centuries later—on May 14, 1948—the physical nation of Israel would be reborn in Palestine. But the "replacement theology" they created is still alive, creating enmity within the body, and preventing believers who hold to those beliefs from understanding the depths of the miracle that God is working among His "chosen people."

Chapter Sixteen

FINISHING WELL

THERE'S ONE THING we all can be certain of in this life, and that's change. Change is inevitable, and when we feel that a change is coming, it's important that we transition through it in the right way. If we fail to do that, the results can be disastrous. We're living at a time when most people are restless, concerned not only about their jobs but also about their future. Unemployment is at an all-time high, and the government is making changes so fast we can't keep up with them. We are all looking for ways to protect what we have and provide for our families, and the stress we feel can rob us of our peace and joy.

But if you believe that change is coming in your life, and that God is speaking to you about some sort of transition that's about to happen, it's important that you let Him bring it about in His own way and in His own good time. Otherwise you're going to break something. If you race ahead to do things on your own without His guidance, you can cause yourself a lot of grief, waste a lot of time, and end up doing more harm than good.

So let's be honest. Back in the 1920's, it was President Calvin Coolidge who famously said, "The business of America is business," and, to a large extent, that was true. A big part of our freedom as citizens today is a direct result of the free enterprise system that has developed in this country ever since the founding era. If you're in business today, you're in business to make money. Unfortunately, some Christians in the business world aren't completely honest about that.

When I first met the Lord, while I was sitting there on top of that mountain, He told me that the silver and the gold were all His. He reminded me of the scripture that says He owns the cattle on a thousand hills. He still reminds me of that from time to time. But many Christians are prone to separate their business life from their relationship with God, or they may try to make things happen on their own without seeking His counsel and guidance. I know. I struggled for years trying to decide which part of my life was ministry and which was business until I reached a point of total confusion and frustration. Then, in 1985, the Lord settled that issue for me once and for all.

I had been struggling with the issue of what is spiritual and what is natural, and while I was standing in my office one day the answer came to me in a flash. The Holy Spirit said, "Don't ever try to be spiritual again. There should not be a competition between the spiritual and the natural, because the things of the Spirit are carried out in the natural world." Why hadn't I thought of that before? I mean, what does it mean to be spiritual anyway? What do we learn from the Ten Commandments? Worship the Lord God, make no idols, avoid profanity, and keep the Sabbath day holy. After that, honor your father and mother, don't murder, or commit adultery. Don't lie, steal, or envy your neighbor's goods. All those things are just as practical in everyday life as they are on Sunday morning. God gave us those laws for our good.

So how does this apply to those of us in business? It means don't cheat on your taxes, pay a fair day's wage for a fair day's work, and give a fair day's work for the wages you earn. After all, the most spiritual things in life are the natural things carried out in a spirit of honesty and integrity. All the commandments of the Old Testament have one basic goal: to protect us from the kinds of behavior that will destroy us.

I don't think there's anything more spiritual than speaking the truth in love in your everyday business life and in your everyday circumstances. Unfortunately, we're very good at compartmentalizing. How many of us act one way on Sunday and another way on Monday? But God wants something better for us, and that's why He has given us His Word, where we read, "Thus says the Lord, your Redeemer, the Holy One of Israel: 'I am the Lord your God, Who teaches you to profit, Who leads you by the way you should go'" (Isa. 48:17). When we obey God's laws and live by His precepts, we will prosper spiritually and in every other way.

Many businessmen and women have come to me for counsel, and it quickly becomes apparent that they are struggling with this in their business and personal life. They can't understand why they don't succeed, and even when they appear to be successful financially, they are still not happy. There is no peace in their hearts. More often than not I find that it is because they have been compromising their integrity in their business, especially when they are under stress. They bend all the rules, and then they wonder why God is not blessing their life. They never stop to think what they have actually been doing, playing by the world's rules, taking advantage of people, skimming here and there, and expecting God to prosper them. And they wonder why their life is not working out.

The problem is that they have allowed a spirit of deception to enter their life, and this is affecting their business and their family life. If we believe God is doing a work in our lives, we really need to be aware of it, because every work of God is going to be tested. Psalm 119 says, "The word of the Lord tested me until He delivered me."

It works like this: you may feel like God has given you a vision to start a business, a ministry, or maybe it's a move or a new relationship, but you know in your heart that change is coming. At that point you can be certain that God is going to allow the circumstances of life to test your vision or dream, and the way you respond to that test will determine the level of success you will enjoy. During the time of testing, you really need to know that God is leading you, because if you don't know for sure that He is there, guiding your footsteps, you will be tempted to give up. The Bible describes it as a refining process, and this is when most people begin to doubt their vision or dream and give up.

It is very important to continue in prayer and fellowship with the Lord whenever you are going through a time of transition. When you feel a big change is coming, you also need to be careful and observant, because the rules can change. The risks are higher, the stakes are higher, and the cost of failure can be much higher at this point. If it turns out you are not prepared in your personal life for the growth or promotion you aspire to, in most cases you will fail.

If your bank account is growing faster than your soul is growing in the Lord, your life is out of balance, and sooner or later it will catch up with you. This is why honesty and integrity are so important. If you try to go to the next level and you have not dealt with the hidden areas of your life where you keep certain secrets you do not want anyone to know about, there is no way God is going to promote you. If you have not conquered the enemies of your soul where you are today, then you are not ready for a transition to a higher level.

That is one reason so few men finish well. Before God can bless any man or woman, He must know beyond a doubt that He can trust them. He must know that they will walk with integrity, that they will be honest and above board with their neighbors, friends, and customers if they are in the business world. God expects you to overcome the demons in your life, and to have self-control and composure. Before He will make any major transitions in your life—whether it's landing a new job, starting a new business, or expanding your ministry—He wants to know that you're prepared to deal with the challenges and temptations you will have to face.

The Bible tells us, "we do not wrestle against flesh and blood, but against principalities, against powers, against the rulers of the darkness of this age, against spiritual hosts of wickedness in the heavenly places" (Eph. 6:12). If you're getting ready to go to the next level in your life, believe me, there are demons there that will wage war against you, and they will defeat you if they can. They already know your weaknesses, and they will come after every area that you have kept in darkness. If there are any areas in your life that you have left in the closet, and even though you have closed the closet door you have allowed it to remain there, it will eventually come out. They will tempt you in ways you have never known, with one goal in mind: to destroy you.

Before you make that final commitment and make your move, whatever the goal may be, take time to examine your heart and your life to make sure you're living each day with integrity. Make sure you're prepared, that you understand the challenges ahead, then go out and conquer that giant in your life, and you will experience the joy and fulfillment of living a truly successful life.

It is important to understand that when you're going through a time of transition you should try very hard not to complicate things more than you have to. There will be more than enough to deal with, so focus on the things that really matter and do your best to keep it simple. When you're going through a transition, it's always best to let God do things His way and in His own good time. The Bible gives us a clear pattern for starting a business, a ministry, or any other new endeavor. It is a pattern Cookie and I have followed for more than twenty-five years, based on the principles in the Book of Nehemiah that I described in chapter 5. It's a pattern that's just as reliable for building a business as it is for building a church.

There's just one caveat, and it's a big one: unless you have the faith to walk by these principles, don't try it, because they will test you to the core of your being. Your faith and trust in God will be tested, and many times you may be tempted to give up. But if you're willing to believe that God not only loves you but also desires to bless you, He will bless you. If you're content to do things God's way, He will reveal Himself to you in ways that will see you through, from success to success and victory to victory.

As you make this journey, make sure you know what you're called to do, and don't let yourself be tempted to take on a role that is not the one God gave you. There have been a lot of people over the past thirty years who have tried to talk me into pastoring a church, but I have to tell them I haven't been called to be a pastor. I'm called to be a businessman and to exercise my gifts and talents in the marketplace. As a businessman, I'm not confined to the pulpit. I've been given the privilege of enjoying success in business, as well as the joy of sharing many of the principles in this book before some of the largest congregations in the world. So in that sense the world is my pulpit.

It's important that we look into our hearts and be honest with ourselves about who we really are as men and women of God. We need to have a realistic understanding of what we want to do with our lives and then let God lead the way. Every life and every gift we possess has a certain flow to it. By that I mean there's a natural fit for our talents and abilities that God can use to build our lives, and we need to seek His guidance for how we identify and use those gifts. Find your flow. Find what makes you happy. Seek Him and His will for your life, and He will show you the way. No verse of scripture says it better than this: "Trust in the Lord with all your heart, and lean not on your own understanding; In all your ways acknowledge Him, and He shall direct your paths" (Prov. 3:5–6).

I used to wonder how I ever got from being a barber with an eighth-grade education to building one of the largest medical spa franchise companies in the world. I had medical doctors and highly skilled surgeons working for me in transplant centers all over the country. But when I thought about that, I realized what it means when the Bible says a man's gift makes room for him (Prov. 18:16). Life has a flow and rhythm to it. God put me into the hair business. I've done many other things in my life and I've traveled all over the world in missions work. But I know what God has gifted me to do, and forty-seven years later I'm still doing it.

My suggestion to every Christian is this: don't fight the giftings in your life. Take what God has given you and use it for His glory. If you walk with integrity, and remain faithful and diligent in all your affairs, the natural flow of life will take you from a stream to a river and from a river to an ocean. I think most of us know instinctively where we belong. We also know when we're in danger of wandering outside the natural flow and rhythm of our gift-ings. It's important that we know how to wait upon the Lord and allow Him to make a way where there is no way.

The Bible says that many are called but few are chosen. What this means, I believe, is that the difference between being "called" and "chosen" often comes down to whether or not we're willing to wait upon the Lord for His blessing. Most of those whom God would like to bless are not willing to wait upon His leadership and guidance. Why are we always in such a hurry, and so afraid that we're going to miss out on something? By not waiting upon the Lord, we make so many mistakes. We get off to false starts and cause ourselves more pain than is necessary.

Sometimes I counsel with people who are consumed with fear. It's like they gave their life to God and got saved, but then they act as if Jesus said, "OK, you're saved now, so you're on your own. I'll see you at the resurrection." But that's not how it works. Jesus made it clear that He would never leave us nor forsake us. His final words recorded in the Book of Matthew are, "I am with you always, even to the end of the age" (Matt. 28:20). What we have to understand, however, is that God is more concerned with building the man or woman than He is with building the business, the church, or the ministry. He wants to be involved in every area of your life, and He wants you to trust Him. Once you come to that point in your walk with Christ, you're on your way to the next level.

No one who knew anything about the way my life started out would have expected me to have done all the things I have had the privilege of doing. To say that my life has been a roller coaster ride would be an understatement. I promised Cookie when we got married that our life together would be an adventure, and it has been all of that and more. It's a miracle I didn't end up dead or incarcerated for life at an early age, but clearly God had another plan. My parents were simple people, and I'm sure there were times when they believed I was headed for a bad end. But when I consider all these things and the remarkable journey I've been on, I realize just how special they were. They're two of the best examples I can think of for finishing well.

If my journey was tough, theirs was tougher, and I couldn't end this book without a final tribute to the life they lived. As I mentioned briefly at the beginning of this story, my father was raised in a Baptist home in rural Virginia, but he never went to church as a boy. His image of Christians wasn't a good one, and he wanted nothing to do with religion of any kind. It was people who claimed to be religious who had abused him when he was a kid. My mother was a Catholic, raised in an Italian family that spoke almost no English, and she had some small experience of faith. But she had never really participated in religious services until one day when she and my father had an argument, and she left the house and took a long walk by herself.

On that Sunday morning she passed by a small inter-denominational church on Harpersville Road in Newport News, Virginia, and she heard the sound of music and beautiful singing coming from the church. She went inside and found a seat, and she heard the gospel for the first time in her life. When the pastor gave the altar call at the end of the service, my mother walked down the aisle to the front of the church and gave her life to Jesus.

When she came home that day, my mother was a changed woman. From that day forward her whole life was about Jesus. From that time, as long as my brothers and I were still living at home, she sat us down at the breakfast table and made us read one chapter from the Bible every morning. We had to take turns reading. I was probably eight or nine years old when that started, and I hated it. But she made us do it, and I'm so glad she did.

My mother loved God all her life, but she suffered for many years from various illnesses, including a rare disease her doctors described as tuberculosis of the brain. There were very few known cases of that illness anywhere in the world, and the doctors didn't know how to treat it. They operated on her the year after my father retired, but there was really nothing they could do. The most amazing thing was that, after all the struggles he had caused her over the years, my father had a chance to serve my mother for the last nine months of her life while she was bed-ridden.

Dad took that responsibility without the slightest hesitation. I believe he knew this was a kind of redemption, a way to make up for all he had put my mother through. He would not let anyone bathe her but him. He took care of her and did everything for her. He had always been so hard and insensitive to other people, but there were times when he would weep over the opportunities he had missed. "All the years I wasted," he would say with tears in his eyes. "Not knowing God, and not giving myself to your mother. What a wonderful woman God has given me, and I waited so long to show her how much I love her."

When they took my mother to the hospital, she went into a coma, but my father would not let the nurses bathe her. He changed her hospital gown and did everything except give her the medication she needed during those final days. He took care of everything and rarely left her side. During that long week her condition never changed, but I would go in to see them every day. Then, after she had been there seven days, the Lord told me, "Your father is holding her back." So I took my dad out into the hallway, and I said, "Daddy, you have to let her go. Mama is so close to God and she's ready to go. God is calling her home, but you're holding her too close, and she won't go until you let her go."

He had tears in his eyes, but he knew that what I was saying was true. He protested at first, and said, "Dennis, I can't let her go."

I said, "Dad, you have to let her go. You can't leave her like this."

When we went back into the room, Dad walked over to my mother's bed, took her hand, and with tears rolling down his cheeks, he said, "Honey, it's OK. I give you to the Lord. I let you go now." At that moment, after seven days in a coma, she opened her eyes, looked at him, smiled, and whispered, "I love you." With that she went home to be with the Lord, and that's the way I will always remember my mother.

As I said in previous chapters, my father worked from 4:00 p.m. until midnight for almost forty-seven years in the shipyard at Newport News. When he left the house at two o'clock in the afternoon to go to work, my mother stayed home. She didn't go anywhere. Her life was just caught up with the Lord, and she was so happy. She became so intimate with the Lord. She had a ministry of cards, but my father would even complain about that. He said she was wasting money on cards and stamps, but she told him this was something the Lord wanted her to do, and he grudgingly let her continue.

I believe now that my mother prayed me into the kingdom. I'm convinced of that. Even when I was as far from God as a man could be, she never gave up on me. When I was into all sorts of New Age cults and false beliefs, she never wavered. She assured me that Jesus is the way, and when I eventually came home and told her that the Lord had revealed Himself to me, she was thrilled. Her prodigal son had come home at last. My father was a different story, however. We never did get along. He was jealous of my relationship with my mother. And when I told him what had happened, and how the Lord had spoken to me, he said, "Dennis, you've been involved in some crazy things in your life, but this is the craziest."

Whenever I would go home to visit my mom and dad after that, I would try to talk to him about the Lord. I was all fired up, filled with the Holy Spirit, and just bursting with enthusiasm. But every time I would try to say something he would reject me even more. Then one night as I was leaving the house, I prayed, "Lord, why won't my father ever listen to me?" And the Lord said, "Don't ever go home again as a prophet. Instead, go home as a servant."

From that day forward, whenever I went to his house I would go as a servant. I would say, "Let me take the trash out, Dad." He would try to stop me, but I would insist, and take it out. I did anything I could to be of service around the house, but I never spoke to him about Jesus. I tried to let my life reflect the Lord as much as I could without speaking about it, and this went on for many years.

My mother could get my dad to drive her to church sometimes, but he would never go in. Then, at age sixty-five, after all those years of backbreaking labor, my father finally retired. He had never been in the hospital a day in his life. But less than a year after he retired he came down with a serious illness and found himself in the hospital for the very first time. He had been an alcoholic for years, and he had smoked ever since he was a teenager. When the doctors examined him they found that he had intestinal problems and related issues, and after they had performed an exploratory operation, they sent him home. Ten days later we had to rush him back to the hospital, and this time the doctors said it was serious and they would have to operate the next day.

Whenever I visit people in the hospital, I like to go after eleven o'clock at night, when it's quieter and the patients are alone and thinking about their situation. So I walked into Dad's room about 11:30 that night before his scheduled surgery, and I could just feel the fear and uncertainty he was dealing with. So I walked up to the bed and said, "Daddy, why are you so afraid?" and he broke down crying. It was the first time I ever saw my father cry. He was a tough man.

He said, "I know that if they operate on me tomorrow I'm going to die."

I said, "Dad, Jesus wants to take care of you. You've resisted Him and rejected Him all your life. Would you like for me to pray with you and give your life to the Lord? Do you want to do that?"

He said, "Yes."

I never thought I'd hear him say that. But I prayed with him and he received Jesus into his heart as his Lord and Savior. And as soon as we said Amen, I said, "Dad, I think the Lord wants to heal you. Can I pray for you?" Again, he said yes. So I prayed a simple prayer and asked God to touch my father, and whatever needed to be corrected in his body, to heal him. And I asked the Lord to manifest it so that Dad would know the reality of how much God loved him, and that it was He who did it.

As soon as I finished praying my dad's whole countenance changed. He said, "I've been healed! I know I've been healed!" All the pain was gone.

I said, "Dad, tomorrow morning when they come to take you down to the operating room, you tell the nurse that Jesus has healed you. And tell her that you're not going to let them operate on you until the doctors reexamine you."

He said, "I will."

The next morning the nurses came in to insert the I.V. in his arm, preparing him for the operation, and Dad said, "My son was here last night. He prayed for me, and Jesus healed me. Before you operate on me, I want the doctor to reexamine me."

The nurse said, "Well, that's fine, Mr. Jones. But they have the O.R. all set up, and we need to go ahead and get you started on the I.V. ..."

But Dad said, "Didn't you hear what I said? Jesus healed me last night, and I'm not going to let you touch me until they reexamine me!"

Well, the nurse could see he wasn't going to cooperate, so she went down and spoke to the doctor, and he ordered an MRI. When they got the results they said there was no sign of any problems, and they released him to go home. Dad had been healed, and at 12:15 that afternoon we left the hospital, went home, and he was never in the hospital again until the end of his life, eighteen years later.

From that day, when he was sixty-five, until he went to be with the Lord at almost eighty-three, he would always remind me of that day, and he would say, "I'll never forget the time you put your hand on my hand, and for the first time in my life I knew that Jesus was real."

For the rest of his life, my father and I were best friends. Like me, he didn't have much formal education. He only went through the fifth grade, so from that time on he always looked to me for advice on bills, taxes, legal matters, or anything like that. He wouldn't make a move without my input, and for the rest of his life on earth we were the best of friends. My mother only lived for three years after Dad came to the Lord, but she had that time with him, and they were the three best years of their entire forty-eight years of marriage.

I remember fondly the time I took my dad on a trip down to Florida. Cookie and I had a condo in Fort Lauderdale at the time, so I took him down there for a golfing vacation, just the two of us, and I took him to places he had only seen on TV. We played a round at the Doral Country Club, and two weeks later he watched the PGA tournament at the Doral. Every year after that, he would watch that event and tell everybody, "You know, I played there."

I took him to Ruth's Chris Steak House for a great meal. He was totally surprised when the valet came up and took our car. He didn't know they really did that. He always thought valet service was only in the movies. We would have long talks every night, and Dad told me so many things about his life that I had never known.

On Christmas Day, 2004, my father came over to our house for Christmas, and we went out for Christmas dinner at the Founder's Inn in Virginia Beach, as we did every year. Dad, my brother Marvin, and Cookie and I had played golf the week before, but two days after Christmas, Dad said he wasn't feeling well. The doctors had been treating him for emphysema, and for gout in his knees, but when we took him to the hospital to see what was causing his discomfort, they found cancer in his lungs, and it had spread throughout his system, even into his bones.

They wanted to start treatments right away so they scheduled his first session for the following day and kept him in the hospital overnight. When I came to see him that evening, he said, "Dennis, they put me on this gurney and left me in the hall for four hours, and then they brought me in and put me in this tube. I didn't like that. Do I have to do this?"

I said, "Daddy, you know the situation. The doctor said you would probably live from nine to twelve months with the condition you're in, unless the Lord heals you. If they do the chemotherapy, you might live six months longer. You don't have to do anything you don't want to, but the choice is yours."

He said, "I don't want any more treatments," and I said, "That's fine." So we prayed together.

That was the second day in the hospital, and when I came back on the third day with Cookie and Marvin, Dad said, "Every time I close my eyes I see your mother."

I said, "Really, Dad?"

He said, "Yes. And when I went to sleep last night I saw Mama, and I saw Jesus."

When he said that, I asked him, "Are you ready to go home to be with the Lord?"

He looked up at me with the most peaceful expression and said, "Yes, I am. I'm ready."

I spent the rest of that day with my father, and it was one of the best experiences I have ever had. Dad had always been very closed about his life. I realized later that what had kept him from coming to the Lord all those years was that he couldn't believe God would really forgive him for all he had done. But, lying there in the hospital, he shared with me about his early life, how he was abused and mistreated and forced to live in barns.

He shared with me about his experiences in the Korean War, the men he had killed, and how that had tormented him his whole life. During all that time he believed that God could never forgive him. But the Lord allowed me to be with him, to walk him through his entire life, and to remove all doubts that God had not only forgiven him but He loved him. And I have never seen my father with such peace in his heart.

When Cookie, my brother Marvin, and I got to the hospital the next morning, Dad was resting peacefully. He greeted us when we came in and told us again, "Every time I close my eyes I see your mama, and I see Jesus." He closed his eyes for a few minutes to take a rest, and less than two minutes later he was gone. It was such a merciful passing. All his life he was scared he would be a burden. He didn't want to go to a nursing home or be in a situation where he couldn't take care of himself. But, rather than the nine to twelve months the doctors had said he would have, God in His mercy took him home that day.

We all have seen the stories of men and women throughout history who defied the odds and rose from obscurity to fame and fortune—people who went from nothing to greatness, securing their place in history. Many of them were men and women of integrity who made the right choices. They started out as ordinary people who had a dream or a vision, and because they stood up to adversity and refused to compromise, they succeeded in their quest. They discovered that they could play by the rules and win, and they learned that true success can only be measured over the course of a lifetime. But there are many people who are making the same choices today, and these are the ones who will finish well.

True success cannot be measured by your bank account. When you come to the end of your life, are you really going to be concerned about how much money you have in the bank? Or will it be more important to you to know that you have the love and respect of your loved ones and friends? Will you wish you had socked a little more away in the safe-deposit box, or will you wish you had spent a little more time with your family? And most of all, will you wish you had spent more time following the latest fads and fashions, or will you wish you had spent more time getting to know Jesus in a more intimate way?

We all have the same opportunity to make the right choices, but we can only make the right choices if we have the wisdom, understanding, and knowledge to do so. And we can only get that by coming to know God in a more personal and intimate way. Every one of us has the same opportunity to do that. God says, "you will seek Me and find Me, when you search for Me with all your heart" (Jer. 29:13).

This is something I have seen in Africa, China, Russia, and many other places around the world. It does not matter where you are; everyone has the same opportunity to gain wisdom, understanding, and knowledge for life, because we all have the same opportunity to seek God's favor. True wisdom only comes from Him. When we see what is really in the hearts of the men and women we look up to and admire, we will often find that most of them have a relationship with God. And in most cases, the grace and wisdom we admire in them comes from Him.

Solomon, whom many consider to be the wisest man who ever lived, said it this way, "The fear of the Lord is the beginning of wisdom, and the knowledge of the Holy One is understanding" (Prov. 9:10). Solomon believed that wisdom is the principal thing. But without the knowledge of God, there is no wisdom. We need wisdom to make the right choices, but true wisdom does not come from the world's way of doing things. It comes from the knowledge of God. But if true wisdom comes only from God, doesn't it make sense that we should ask Him for it?

This is something I've learned to do every day, asking God to give me the wisdom, understanding, and knowledge I will need for that day. I ask Him for His favor every day of my life. And we have the assurance that if we ask Him, He will hear us. And if He hears us, He will do it.

Everyone at some point in his or her life will experience adversity, whether it is a troubled relationship, a wayward child, an ailing parent, the loss of a job, or even being wrongfully accused. The list goes on and on. But we do not have to be defeated by our circumstances. There is a lot of truth in the old saying, "When life gives you lemons, make lemonade." It is not always easy to see the bright side in the midst of a storm. But the next time you find yourself in a place of adversity, I encourage you to consider this: instead of relying on the work of your own hands and spending hours, days, or weeks making gallons and gallons of lemonade—try asking the One who created the lemon for His help and direction. There is no one more capable, more understanding, or more willing than He is. If there is one lesson I have learned in my life, it's this: climbing out of adversity can be tough, it can be grueling, and it can be overwhelming—until you reach out and grab hold of the one strong and solid rock that can pull you to safety. And that rock really is Jesus.

NOTES

CHAPTER 12

1. U.S. Department of Health and Human Services, National Vital Statistics Report: Vo. 59, No. 1, Final Data for 2008. Published Dec. 2010. p. 15. "(Table C). The birth rate for unmarried women, which relates nonmarital births to unmarried women in the childbearing ages, rose slightly between 2007 and 2008, from 52.3 to 52.5 births per 1,000 unmarried women aged 15-44 years ... the rate for black women (72.5) was essentially unchanged," from website: <http://www.cdc.gov/nchs/data/nvsr/nvsr59/nvsr59_01.pdf> (accessed January 25, 2011).

2. Exit poll data from website: http://elections.nytimes.com/2008/results/president/exit-polls.html (accessed January 28, 2011).

3. Gallup poll data, taken from website: http://www.gallup.com/poll/103459/questions-answers-about-americans-religion.aspx (accessed January 28, 2011).

CHAPTER 13

1. Taken from website: http://www.examiner.com/pop-culture-in-cleveland/obama-money-detroit-videos-getting-national-attention-due-to-rush-limbaugh-riling-up-folks (accessed January 28, 2011).

2. Taken from website: Jonathan Mayhew, "Discourse Concerning Unlimited Submission and Non-Resistance to the Higher Power," 1750. Available online at Digital Commons at the University of Nebraska, Lincoln. <http://digitalcommons.unl.edu/etas/44/> (accessed June 12, 2010).

ABOUT THE AUTHOR

Dennis R. Jones was once quoted as saying; "There are those who read about the experiences of others, and then there are those who experience what others only read about."

From a very young age, Dennis acknowledged that his life would never be normal, that one day he might be sleeping in a hut in Africa, and the next in a beautiful mansion. But one thing he knew deep within his heart was that his life would always be filled with exciting experiences.

Born in Newport News, Virginia, Dennis was the son of a hard-working father, who was "farmed out" as a child, and a loving mother who was raised in a Catholic orphanage. Many would assume that the odds were stacked against him, but God had amazing plans for his life. Through astonishing twist and turns, Dennis realized that plan.

Over the past forty years, Dennis has exercised his entrepreneurial gifts through the creation, start up, and full operations of successful corporations, to the formulation, development, and manufacture of specialty products for the aesthetic industry, including patented, niché products. Dennis also has extensive experience as a national seminar instructor, minister, and public speaker, and has provided financial management, contract negotiations, corporate development, and counsel to businesses and churches around the world.

Presently, Dennis is the Chairman/CEO of FillTech USA, an FDA product development and manufacturing facility, Founder/President of the

Franchise Visionary Group, and the Founder/CEO of Creative Technologies, Inc., a product marketing and distribution company.

In addition to his business involvement, Dennis is an ordained minister and serves the church at large by ministering and counseling pastors and church leaders. Dennis also works with established and start-up churches, providing consulting and implementation in the areas of development, strategic planning, and church growth.

Dennis serves as an apostolic leader and is involved in world missions. He has traveled to Russia, Africa, China, and Jamaica where he has helped pioneer and plant churches in these countries. Through Global Harvest International, which Dennis founded and currently serves as President, he trains Christian leaders and businessmen and women around the world how to apply biblical principles in their daily lives, ministries, and businesses, and live these principles out. He also serves as Chairman Emeritus and is on the executive board of Accelerating International Mission Strategies (AIMS).

Dennis is married to Cookie Jones, the love of his life.

CONTACT THE AUTHOR

Website:

www.DennisRJones.com

E-mail:

Info@DennisRJones.com

Or:

Dennis R. Jones

PO Box 2141

Chesapeake, VA 23327